AF540844

RISK MANAGEMENT

Editor's

K. RAMAKRISHNA REDDY
P. MURALI KRISHNA
Sri Krishna Devarya University,
Anantapur (A.P.)

First Published-2000
Reprinted-2011

ISBN 81-7141-546-6

DISCOVERY PUBLISHING HOUSE
4831/24, Ansari Road, Prahlad Street,
Darya Ganj, New Delhi-110002 (India)
Phone: 3279245 · Fax: 91-11-3253475
E-mail:dph@indiatimes.com

Printed at:
Sachin Printers
Delhi

-Dedicated To-

The Sacred Lotus Feet of

SHIRDI SAI BABA

FOREWORD

There is an element of risk in any development strategy for; all forecasts or anticipations are based on certain hypothetical factors of measures and results. Thus preparedness in risk management would help to mould different unforeseen consequences into a perspective to minimise risks. Totally risk free planning is a myth for, good business means ability and preparedness to take risks.

In this context deliberating on risk management as welfare measure in India is a very timely exercise. In any forward looking country, where citizens life and care in areas like health, means of livelihood, child care, care of the senior citizens and so on which are all risk oriented in one way or the other, requiring aggressive governmental intervention, are all well planned and appropriate legal and operational measures taken. In fact it is the effectiveness of these measures and their reach to the citizens, which is considered as an indicator of the level of development in a given country. While discussing Risk Management as a welfare measure in India, a very critical contemporary area of gender perspective would have given fullness to the content of the seminar. Nevertheless, the scholarly presentations covered in this book are a very valuable contribution to the literature on the subject and I congratulate Sri Krishnadevaraya Institute of Management as well as the editors Dr. K. Ramakrishna Reddy and Dr. P. Murali Krishna for bringing out this book.

I am sure that the faculty and students will be benefited much.

Y. SARASWATHY RAO

Vice-Chancellor
Sri Krishnadevaraya University

PREFACE

Man has always been a risk bearing person. One may even go to the extent of saying that human history would have been monotonous and dull had there been no risk element at all. As long as we live in the flow of time, we are confronted with an unknown tomorrow. What it brings and what it fails to bring has challenged man to reach a higher and higher potential of his being. Man is in eternal quest of the unknown. The cost of this journey may be regarded as one of risk bearing and uncertainty.

This cost, predetermined or otherwise has always been a legitimate item of our accounting. Whosoever was successful in identifying before hand this cost - its nature and dimension, its occurrence and its recurrence, and the flow of its consequence - stole a march over others not only in earning profits but also in adding to the fund of our knowledge, theoretical as well as technical, encouraging a whole stream of new entrepreneurs into this formerly unforeseen area of activity and events.

Man is not only a risk bearer but also a risk promoter and a cause of risk. It looks as though as traditional and historical risks either vanish into insurable costs and hedging operations, or become normally manageable, new ones seem to raise their head assuming all the properties of a so called risk. As our social consciousness becomes ever awake we tend to discover newer and more varied types of risk involved in our day to day activity.

The droughts, the flood, the so-called risks due to natural forces, remain today as a private concern of the individual incumbent or group. The advancement in technology in issuing forewarnings seen to be unmatched with our willingness to profit by that information. The usual complaints relate to one of 'poor will' than of poverty of resources.

We have also a new kind of risk blowing across not only our country but also the entire world. We refer to the risk of unevaluated adoption of technology and ways of living generated in different cultures. A prominent illustration is in the field of environment. In view of this above frame work different authors tried to present their papers under three main themes namely 'Risk in Industrial Sector', 'Agricultural' and 'Financial Sector' in India. Moreover insurance policy as a tool of risk management is also covered in this volume.

We are also grateful to the University Grants Commission, New Delhi and Sri Krishnadevaraya University for their liberal grant in conducting the Two-day National Seminar on "Risk Management as a Modern Welfare Measure in India". The selected ones out of the papers presented in the seminar are classified into different group and are edited to form a basis to publish this book. We are grateful to our beloved Vice-Chancellor **Prof. Y. Saraswathy Rao** for writing foreword to this book. We thank Prof. L. Venugopal Reddy, Head, Sri Krishnadevaraya Institute of Management for his generous support in successful conduct of the seminar. We are thankful to late Sri. Siva Kumar, Divisional Manager, United India Insurance Company Ltd., who initiated interest for the subject in us.

We thank all the authors of different papers that appear in this volume. We also thank Mr. Tilak Wasan of Discovery Publishing House, New Delhi for publishing this volume with personal care. We thank every one who helped us directly and indirectly both in conducting the seminar and in the preparation of this volume.

Place: Anantapur.

K. Ramakrishna Reddy
P. Murali Krishna

CONTENTS

SECTION – II INDUSTRIAL & FINANCIAL RISK MANAGEMENT

SECTION III— INSURANCE RISK MANAGEMENT

1

AGRICULTURAL INSURANCE IN DRYLAND REGIONS: SOME POLICY INTERVENTIONS

R. P. Singh,

Director, Centre for Sustainable Economic Development,
National Institute of Rural Development, Rajendranagar, Hyderabad 50030, A.P.

INTRODUCTION

Agriculture is one of the major sectors of Indian economy which supports more than 70 per cent of rural population. Agricultural production is greatly influenced by climatic factors and level of infrastructure, especially irrigation, and use of improved inputs such as seeds, fertilisers and pesticides, etc.. In India, crop cultivation in 91 million hectares of total 142.1 million hectare of arable land is mainly dependent on rain. These rainfed/dryland areas suffer from many constraints, which can broadly be grouped under four major categories, such as geographical, socio-economic, technological and institutional. Besides, the dryland farmers face various types of risks such as weather related, pests and diseases, input and market related risks, market risk, resource risk, production risk, health risk, asset risk, and other types of risk, etc. (Hazell 1991). The most commonly risk faced by the dryland farmers are yield risk and climatic risk which are highly correlated. However, there are some non-covariate risks such as loss of earning members, death of bullocks, etc. that also influence level and stability of household income.

Dryland regions are not homogenous and vary to a large extent in terms of soil type, rainfall pattern, cropping system, resource base and development of infrastructure. Instability in agricultural production in these regions mainly due to climatic variability is one of the main problems that need special attention of both the scientists and policy makers alike. Scientists need to focus their efforts in developing technologies that not only increase the production but also minimise the risks. As has been mentioned that these dryland regions are not a homogenous region, therefore there is a need to develop various technological options that suit the local conditions and can minimise the risk in agricultural production. Besides, these regions need strong political will and special policy interventions to ensure the farmers against various types of risks.

How to Define Risk

Defining risk in a real sense is quite difficult. The definition of risk varies according to the perception of people. In a day to day working an individual makes a number of decisions. Some of these decisions have effect for a short period while others may have long terms effects. Individuals' decisions are based on certain expectation but quite often they do not match because of uncertainty. Uncertainty is a state of mind in which the individual perceive alternative outcomes to a particular action while risk has to do with the degree of uncertainty in a given situation. It may be caused by exogenous, stochastic forces (e.g. weather), ignorance, indeterminacy or by combination of these factors (Anderson 1979).

Economists and statistician measure risk either as a measure of dispersion or the probability of expected returns to a given decision that fall below some critical "disaster" level. Definition of risk has been deduced from the definition of risk aversion (Rothschild and Stiglitz 1970), which is characterised by diminishing marginal utility of income, while risk is what risk averters will pay to avoid that. For example, if there are two frequency distributions with the same mean, the one with the greater "weight in the tails" is one with greater risk. But if two distributions have different means, one cannot, in general, deduce which is the more risky one without knowing the exact form of the utility function. Hence to avoid this ambiguity one can use the word "risk aversion" rather than risk per se (Roumasset 1979).

In general, variance or coefficient of variation in two distributions are compared for estimating the degree of risk but this does not really provide clear idea of risk unless the mean is also considered. However, to test the significant differences in the variance is easy but testing significance of differences between two coefficient of variations is difficult. Any conclusion drawn merely on the basis of differences in coefficient of variation may not be meaningful. It is always useful to plot the cumulative distributions of whole series to get a better idea of variability and first or second stages of stochastic dominance of different distributions.

There seems to be no consensus about the meanings of risk and risk aversion. Hence, researchers while reporting their results should specify which definitions they have used. However, in general, the researcher's definition of risk should evolve out of his answers to some of the questions. What additional information about each distribution (what number) would be most useful in making a choice among alternative distributions when the means of alternative frequency distributions are known? What particular parameter would help to predict an individual's preferences over frequency distributions? For example, would it be more helpful to know the variance of each distribution or the probability for each distribution that returns would be lower than critical level (Anderson 1979)?

Measuring Risk

Basically there are two methods by which risk can be measured. (1) Interview method eliciting certainty equivalents and (ii) experimental gambling approach with real pay-off. Interview method is subject to interview bias and its results are totally inconsistent with the experimental measures of risk aversion (Binswanger 1980; 1981; and 1983). While the experimental game is really costly affair and is beyond the capacity of many individuals and organisations with limited funds. However, without going into the intricacies of definition of risk and its measurement the focus of the paper is more on type and extent of risks faced by the farmers and some policy interventions for minimising risk in dryland areas.

Objectives

This paper focuses mainly on the risk management strategies in rainfed/dryland regions of India and suggest some policy interventions that can help in stabilising the income variability of farmers.

Risk in Dryland Regions

Farmers in rainfed/dryland regions often face drought like situation leading to crop failure[1] and due to this risky nature they are reluctant to invest in farming. This low level of investment adversely affect the overall agricultural production in these regions and in turn makes these regions vulnerable. The agricultural production in these regions are greatly affected by unreliable and low rainfall. The area falling in the low rainfall zone with droughts being a frequent occurrence. In the medium and high rainfall zones, even though severe droughts do not occur as frequently as in the low rainfall zone. Rainfall uncertainty, especially at the time of planting causes great variability in cropped area from year to year, and affect cropping patterns (Walker and Ryan 1990). Hence, even though the precipitation may be adequate in terms of its quantum, onset of monsoon and uneven distribution of rainfall during the cropping season may result in poor agricultural production (Sharma and Singh 1993).

The yield risk in dryland is quite high and leads to instability in agricultural production. Results of a study in three regions of India's Semi-Arid Tropics (SAT) indicate that risk of crop failure varies markedly across the India's Semi-Arid Tropics (Table 1).

Table 2 shows that sowing crops in the rainy season is riskier than in postrainy season on deep black soils in drought-prone areas; risk of planting sole crop is riskier than intercrop in dryland; risk of crop failure is considerably higher in dryland than in irrigated land; risk of crop failure in owned plots is less compared to leased-in and sharecropped-in fields mainly because of differences in management practices (Singh and Walker 1984).

Price which considerably influence the cropping decisions of the farmers is important factors that affect the income variability of the dryland farmers. But analysis of data from 90 districts in the Semi-arid tropics of

India shows that yield risk is greater than the price risk in dryland agriculture (Table 3). Price risk is more important in irrigated areas (based on 88 districts data of Indian SAT).

Table 1
Incidence of crop failure (percentage of plots failed) in three Dryland regions of India.

Definitions	Agroclimatic Regions			
	Mahbubnagar (850)	Sholapur (2100)	Akola (950)	All regions (3900)
1. Complete crop failure				
No main product	6	17	4	12
Nothing	5	13	4	9
2. Partial crop failure				
No main product	9	24	7	17
Nothing	8	19	5	13
Rainfall (mm)	740	660	805	740

Note: Figures in parentheses are number of plots in respective regions.

Table 2
Probability of Crop Failure (% of plot failed) by variable

Variable	Crop failure (% of plots)		Predicted probability	
	Complete	Partial	Complete	Partial
Village				
Shirapur	22	26	0.26	0.35
Kalman	14	23	0.19	0.27
Aurepalle	9	13	0.09	0.14
Kanzara	5	8	0.05	0.06
Dokur	3	5	0.04	0.08
Kinkheda	3	5	0.03	0.04
Season				
Kharif	13	19	0.18	0.20
Rabi	9	14	0.07	0.10
Soil depth				
Deep	9	16	0.09	0.16

Medium	9	15	0.11	01.6
Shallow	12	16	0.14	0.17
Poor	29	33	0.19	0.24
Irrigation				
Unirrigated	14	20	0.15	0.20
Irrigated	6	8	0.07	0.11
Cropping system				
Sole cropping	14	20	0.16	0.14
Intercropping	7	22	0.07	0.24
Tenancy				
Owned	15	24	0.08	0.17
Crop shared	19	17	0.11	0.21
Cash renting	8	16	0.09	0.23

Table 3

Share of Yield and Price Risks in Dryland and Irrigated Agriculture

Areas	Share of risk (Percentage)	
	Price risk	Yield risk
Dryland	38	62
Irrigated	60	40
All	45	55

Besides, it has been found that soil type also affect the variability in crop production. The results based on 900 plots in one of the major sorghum growing areas of Sholapur indicate that growing sorghum in poorer soils provides lower profits and is more risky compared to better soils (Table 4). Similarly, high profits from improved technologies are also associated with high risk (Table 5). Based on 3700 plots in Kanzara-one of the dryland villages in Akola district of Maharshtra, it was found that improved technologies such as improved varieties of sorghum and cotton provide higher profits compared to traditional system but are associated with greater risks (high coefficient of variation).

Table 4
Average profits (in rupees per hectare) and risk (measured in terms of coefficient of variation) from sorghum in different types of soils in Sholapur District.

Soil	Profits (Rs/ha)	CV (%)
Deep black	545	75
Medium black	385	90
Shallow black	285	97
Gravely	200	130

Table 5
Profits (Rs per hectare) and Risk (Coefficient of variation) from Various cropping system in Kanzara village of Akola District of Madhya Pradesh.

Cropping system	Profits (Rs/ha)	Coefficient of variation (%)
Traditional Cotton/Pigeonpea/ Local sorghum intercrop	535	57
Improved Cotton/Pigeonpea intercrop	660	80
Hybrid Cotton sole	750	94

Risk and Technology

Farmers' practices are greatly influenced by the level of risk and their risk bearing ability. It is often assumed that once a farmer can make decision to adjust to technological change, resource allocation in agriculture will be efficient, except for distortions induced by the government policies. Also, it is argued that traditional agriculture tends to be rational and efficient. But, rationality does not necessarily lead to efficiency. For example, if a farmer is rational but poor he will be averse to risk and may not adopt improved technologies even if it is profitable. Farmers' preference for a particular technology is not simply because it provides high income at low variance. In fact, diversification in agriculture often tends to increase mean income as well as reduce variation. It has been also observed that risk aversion causes farmers to plant too much land to a subsistence crop and too little land to a cash crop in relation to risk-neutral or efficient acreage allocation

It is a common belief that risk retards adoption of improved technologies and leads to under-investment if a farmer is risk-averse while risk-neutral farmers try to maximise average or expected net returns regardless of the extent of variability in the returns. A risk-averse farmer may forego some expected returns if this also reduces the extent of variability of his income stream. In general, cash crops provide higher profits but have also high risk or income variability than low-value subsistence crops. This is mainly due to the usually higher price of cash crops. A risk-averse farmer allocates inputs to cash and subsistence crops in such a way that the value of marginal products of any input in a high risk crop is lower than in low risk crop. In practice new technologies increase expected outputs or yields but a few of them may shift in the production curve which may not increase yield risks very much. However, the risk associated with higher profits or net returns largely depend upon levels of the investment in a particular new technology (the smaller the less risky) and shift or change in the shape of the yield distributions. But, if these farmers have sufficient mechanisms at their disposal for self-insurance or risk-diffusion, they may still invest up to the risk-neutral optimum.

It has been found that there is not enough difference in risk attitude among small and large farmers. Hence, there is no sense to advocate for the development of risk-graded technologies in SAT India so that small farmers may adopt the low-yield and low-risk technologies and large farmers adopt the high-yield and high-risk technologies (Binswanger 1981, 1983). Also, since risk attitude does not vary much across farm size classes (in SAT) there is a need to reconsider the point of risk aversion versus credit constraints (Binswanger 1983).

Some of the technologies such as improved seeds or fertilisers shift the probability distributions of yields without necessarily decreasing probability levels at the lower tail of the distributions. While some of the inputs such as pesticides and disease-resistant varieties (not necessarily used for increasing the yield) increase expected yield primarily by reducing probability levels at lower levels at the lower tail of the distribution but do not tend to increase yields under favourable circumstances. Besides, some inputs which have dual role such as investment in irrigation, etc. increase potential yields as well as reduce frequencies at the lower end of the distributions (by avoiding drought, for example). A risk averse farmer may over-invest in pesticides and disease-resistant varieties and irrigation while under-invest in improved seeds and fertiliser. Similarly, high degree of investment required for land reclamation compels the farmers to consider the risk involved as unacceptable. Hence, a subsidy is considered essential to encourage small and marginal farmers to undertake such reclamation programmes (Joshi & Agnihotri 1982).

A better understanding of the role of risk and uncertainty in agricultural production requires clear idea that (1) How risk and uncertainty affect the efficiency of production and investment decisions of individual farmers i.e. what are the growth implications; (2) how risk and uncertainty affect the distribution of income and wealth among households, i.e. equity issue; and (3) how risk and uncertainty affect policy prescriptions and its effectiveness i.e. sustainability issue. These issues can further be broken down into more complex questions or concerns in which the attitude towards risk of the farmers or decision makers involved may potentially have major influence. Besides, it is also useful to address some basic issues that can help in policy formulations. Some of them are given below.

1. How should the decision process of the farmers can be incorporated into growth models?;
2. What are the probability distributions of the outcomes of the alternatives available to the decision makers?
3. How much risk a decision makers can take (whether he is risk averse or not) and which categories of decision makers risk aversion counts?
4. If risk aversion has adverse efficiency or distributive consequences, what can be done in terms of policies to redress these consequences, i.e. what are the policy instruments available?

Household Income

Farmers in dryland regions have many sources of income. They can broadly be grouped under five major categories namely, crop, livestock, wage earnings, trade and handicrafts, and transfer income such as gifts, remittances, etc. Crop is one of the major source of income followed by wage earnings, livestock, and other sources of income. It has been found that crop income variability strongly influence the household income compared to livestock, wage earnings, etc. In this paper income risk has been measured as the coefficient of variation (Singh et al. 1982).

Income Stability

Risk leads to instability in crop production which in turn affects the income stability of the farming households to a large extent. Fluctuation in income of a household can be more precisely measured by standardising for the number of people in the households which fluctuates over time in response to life cycle events. The variation in income (measured as coefficient of variation) of a family is positively and significantly correlated to the variability in family size over time. Though it is always not true in all the environments but in drought prone villages fluctuation in income is closely linked with the changes in family size.

It has been found that large farm households enjoy significantly higher mean per capita income than the other households. However, there is no significant difference in the mean per capita of landless labour households and marginal/small farmers. This raises a policy issues that even if some land is provided to landless labour households it might not help much in improving the income of landless labour households. Hence, one policy option would be distribute the surplus land acquired from ceiling to marginal and small farmers to increase their size of land holding so that they can become economically viable (Walker and Singh 1983).

Table 6 shows that per capita income stability is influenced by a variety of factors. Agroclimatic events are covariate to produce significant inter-temporal differences in per capita income within each agroclimatic environment. In good rainfall years when crop income is high, labour income is also invariably high. However, in some of the villages during bad rainfall years when crop and labour income are low the active government public works programmes could protect households from covariate agricultural risks.

Table 6

Determinants of net crop income stability

Explanatory variable	Region					
	Mahbubnagar		Sholapur		Akola	
	GR	NR	GR	NR	GR	NR
Crop diversification	0.10 (0.35)	0.39 (1.32)	-0.55** (2.61)	-0.52** (2.04)	-0.60 (-1.40)	-0.57** (-2.27)
Plot diversification	-0.04 (-0.19)	-0.65*** (-2.74)	0.18 (0.80)	0.16 (0.58)	0.04 (0.16)	0.34 (0.87)
Gross Cropped Area	-1.80* (-1.77)	-2.11 (-1.94)	0.27 (0.41)	-0.61 (-0.77)	-0.70 (-1.54)	-1.31* (-1.81)
CV Gross Cropped Area	0.10 (0.65)	0.42** (2.48)	0.39*** (3.44)	0.21 (1.55)	0.40*** (2.60)	0.18 (0.74)
Irrigated Area	-0.04 (-0.20)	0.22 (1.04)	-0.11 (-0.55)	0.21 (0.82)	0.90* (1.86)	1.39* (1.79)
CV Irrigated Area	0.05 (1.09)	0.05 (0.97)	0.04 (1.40)	0.06 (1.59)	0.10* (1.80)	0.06 (0.66)
Superior soils	-	- 0.12	0.05	-	-(1.04)	(0.32)
CV Superior Soils	-	0.07 (0.63)	0.21 (1.58)	-	-	-
Land Value	-0.05 (-0.53)	-0.15 (-1.40)	-0.07 (-0.68)	-0.12 (-0.99)	-0.09 (-0.56)	0.07 (02.8)
CV Land Value	-0.08 (-0.90)	-0.33*** (-3.54)	-0.002 (0.02)	-0.03 (-0.27)	0.14 (1.18)	0.33* (1.70)
Village dummy	-5.32 (-0.48)	-4.19 (-1.21)	-4.97 (-0.95)	-7.76 (-1.20)	4.60 (0.96)	4.21 (0.55)
Intercept	57.41	67.20	1.88	20.22	-0.36	-12.73
R2	.16	.55	.48	.38	.48	.39
Number of observations	43			45		46

a. GR and NR designate gross and net returns respectively.

b. t values are reported in parentheses; ***, ** and * denote statistical significance at the .01, .05 and .10 levels, respectively.

The average cropping years effects are positively but not significantly associated with cumulative rainfall probabilities. This suggests that a lottery on total rainfall would have a blunt instrument to stabilise crop income. Besides, average income variability is much higher in marginal production environment than in assured rainfall regions. However, in marginal production environment landless labour households and small farmers enjoy significantly greater income stability than larger cultivator households (Walker et al. 1983).

Shortfall[2] in income might be due to sudden drop in income due to yield risk, fluctuation in cropped area, marriage and sub-division in the family leading to changes in the composition of labour market participants, low labour market participation due to economic forces, life cycle effects, loss of productive assets, and individual specific risks such as accidents, death of earning members. It is rather difficult if not impossible to design any policy focusing on a single market to protect households from incurring shortfalls in income. Examining the relationship between the probability of shortfalls and household characteristics using "Probit Model "suggest that households who heavily rely on labour market as a major source of income are less susceptible to abrupt shortfall in income. However, non-covariate risks require special attention of the policy makers.

Rural households who rely heavily on agricultural income had higher income than those who depend more on labour earnings. However, in some of the drought prone areas the correlation between share of crop income and per capita total income is low. This indicates stagnant technical change in the cropping years. The total income stability of a household very much depend upon the stability in the income sources. Partitioning of variance in total income of households over a period of time indicates that (the second and third interaction effects were ignored to focus on the covariance between per capita income from each source and per household income) labour income had a much higher share in mean than their share in variance (Table 7). This suggests that income from wage earnings was more stable than other sources of income (Walker and Singh 1983).

The question arises what would be the best way to stabilise the total income of the rural people. Since, crop and labour income are the two major sources of income of rural households it was considered appropriate to examine the relative effect of stabilising these two sources of income separately on total household income. However, before examining the perfect stabilisation of these two major sources of income it is necessary to assume that the household does not materially change its behaviour in response to perfect income stabilisation from a particular source. The results suggests that on average perfect stabilisation of crop and labour income reduces the mean variability (coefficient of variation) from 38 per cent to 30 per cent and 32 per cent respectively.

Table 7

The effects of stabilising crop and labour income on household income stability.

Village and farm size class	Variability (CV in %) in		% Reduction in CV in	
	Crop income	Labour income	Crop income	Labour income
Aurepalle				
Landless	36	24	0	34
Small farm	23	26	26	17
Medium Farm	34	44	36	11
Large farm	21	50	58	0
Shirapur				
Landless	32	27	5	20
Small farm	26	23	16	26
Medium Farm	24	23	28	13
Large farm	34	35	20	17
Kanzara				
Landless	24	11	5	55
Small farm	30	19	5	40
Medium Farm	22	26	16	0
Large farm	22	28	23	3

The rich households with higher income, who are mostly large farmers, would gain much more from crop income stabilisation than those households who are poor or have low income. In contrast, stabilisation of labour income is relatively more effective in reducing the fluctuation in income than crop income (Table 7). This raises a policy issue that for stabilising income of rural households it is necessary that more employment opportunities are created and higher wages are provided especially to the weaker sections of the society (Walker, Singh and Asokan 1986).

In dryland areas, emphasis on increasing crop income either through yield-enhancing technologies or through higher output prices is necessary but these alone may not be sufficient to ensure farmers against risk and stabilise their income in such as harsh environment. in dryland Diversification of income sources is one of the strategies that need to be encouraged in dryland areas. Though all the sources of income not necessarily provide same level of income every year and some of them may be more variable than others, the dependability on major source of income will greatly influence the fluctuation in the income of a household and affect his investment and consumption patterns.

In general, households try to compensate for low income from one source by making greater efforts to earn income from another source. There is a strong and compensatory behaviour between different income sources. However, successful compensatory behaviour would depend upon the correlation between various income sources. In some years when people in one season get low income from crops due to low yields or prices they participate more in labour market in the next season. However, if income sources are highly covariate within the village or region the scope for compensation would be less.

The another issue is of insurance which is based on the principle of sharing the risk. All the people in any village or region do not face similar degree of risks from abrupt change in climate or any other eventuality. Hence, insurance mechanism is a effective way to minimise the risk of those who suffer most. In this manner, the other households who do not suffer any risk or suffer to a lesser degree share the risk and compensate the loss incurred by other households.

A group of households with command over a heterogeneous resource base and with access to a wider array of opportunities would be less likely to have covariate incomes than other groups of households with a more homogenous resource base and access to a narrower range of opportunities. The degree to which income is covariate between households determines the scope for effective insurance mechanism to develop within a given ecological environment such as a village. Income is highly correlated between households within the same group of households than between those from different groups or farm size classes (Walker et al. 1983).

The labour market plays an important role in dampening fluctuations in income in rural areas. In those areas where labour market is not developed or active labour market do no exist the rural household are subject to face more fluctuation in income. Hence, it becomes important for policy makers to design policies which can provide higher and assured employment in rural areas. During bad monsoon years and in the event of natural calamities the households who rely mainly on labour market are the worst sufferer than those who depend upon crop production. The labour household with very low saving potential find it difficult to cop with those eventualities while most of the cultivating households can adjust with their good production or food stocks in the good monsoon years.

Policies and investments that increase and enhance the stability of labour demand will be more "progressive" than those that focus directly on crop income stabilisation which will differently benefit large farm households. Although exposed to sharper income fluctuation caused by crop income variability, some of the large farm households are able to cope with greater income variability by using land as collateral to draw on informal sources of consumption credit during abnormally low income years.

It would also be useful to mention that stabilising labour income will be a much more effective way to stabilise income of majority of rural households while emphasising crop income stability for marginal and small farmers especially in dryland areas is a misguided means to an end. The Employment Guarantee Schemes is apparently able to confer stability benefits on many rural families. But it has to be considered that how cost- effective these programmes are in building rural infrastructure. However, in some of the harsh and drought prone areas public work have been effective in stabilising income of rural households. In contrast, there is little empirical evidence available to draw any conclusion that other public interventions, such as crop insurance and price support programmes have been quite effective in minimising income fluctuation of majority of rural households (Walker et al 1986).

Risk Management Strategies

Over generations farmers have developed a number of risk management strategies based on their rich farming experience of ground realities. They exploit vertical, horizontal and temporal dimensions of the natural resource base to reduce production risk. To minimise the risk and facilitate development and adoption of new technologies it is necessary to have sound policies and adequate political support. There may be mainly two types of strategies to deal with risk: Risk reducing and Risk spreading strategies. Risk-reducing strategies are used before damage occur and include crop diversification, inter-seasonal adjustment of sowing times, and cropping patterns, soil and water management techniques, etc. While risk spreading strategies (risk diffusion) or loss management are designed to deal with the consequences of losses and include storage, salvage operation, accumulation of financial assets, reduction of financial commitments in drought years, borrowings, etc. (Jodha 1978).

Any strategy may be either risk-specific or non-risk specific. Risk-specific strategies are those that where it reaches its ultimate efficiency or equity goals primarily via the effect which its risk spreading or risk reducing impact has on farmers' behaviour towards the choice among risky production processes. While non-risk specific strategies are those which main effect on efficiency or equity is not reached primarily as a consequence of risk-spreading or reducing, but in direct way. Some of the traditional risk management strategies adopted by the farmers are as under.

Crop and Plot Diversification

To minimise the weather-induced risk farmers makes a number of critical decisions based on the onset of monsoon. Similarly, he makes various arrangements in the field through splitting of the field in different manner. Sometimes he splits main field into smaller plots vertically and horizontally. Also they keep on changing this arrangement over the years. Spatial diversification of farm plots is one of the informal means of risk adjustments. Access to heterogeneous agroclimates across which production risks are not perfectly correlated, endows farmers with greater flexibility to cope with yield risk. Even within village, there are considerable heterogeneity in yield. In general, for most crops, yields of individual farms are positively correlated with the average village yield. But, it is always not true. For example, in major cotton growing areas spatial diversification is effective in stabilising local cotton yields. For many cotton producers still spatial diversification does not appear to be as strongly associated with instability in net crop income as does crop diversification. There are evidences that in some areas crop diversification is negatively and significantly correlated with the variability in crop income, while greater spatial diversification is not. At the same time in other regions greater spatial diversification is inversely associated with the variation in crop income (Walker et al 1983).

Intercropping is an important features of traditional farming system in dryland areas (Jodha 1978; Singh 1981; and Singh and Walker 1982). Measuring of the extent of intercropping based on area devoted to sole or intercrop does not clearly reflect the diversity offered by intercropping. This can be measured by estimating the relative contribution of dominant crops in total output received from all the crops planted in the intercrop system. Intercropping is primarily determined by agroclimatic and ecological factors. A high degree of certainty of cropping environment reduces the extent of intercropping. Although, intercropping offers low net returns mainly because of poor resource allocation and low value of intercrop but risk (variability) of return is less compared to sole cropping system. It allows greater yield stability because of (1) higher yield in stress conditions, (2) lower incidence of disease and pests, and (3) compensatory yields. Though crop and plot diversification are not strongly correlated with mean level of crop income, they are the single most important farmers' management strategy to combat crop income stability. It has been found that crop and plot diversification are not strongly correlated with mean level of crop income. However, plot diversification does not offer significant protection against instability in gross crop income.

Crop diversification appears to be more sensitive to agroclimatic determinants than plot diversification. Different regional and ecological conditions offer differential opportunities for risk averse farmers to diversify. The effects of risk attitudes on diversification differ across regions. Crop diversification effectively imparts stability to net crop income in dryland areas. Whereas in highly irrigated villages income stability and crop diversification are not significantly associated. Bullock availability significantly determine the level of crop and plot diversification across farm households within a region. This is mainly because bullock hire markets are imperfect in meeting seasonally peak period demand requirements for planting and other timely operations. Larger land holdings are also associated with plot diversification. The impact of irrigation on crop diversification and income stability hinges upon cropping conditions and existing level of irrigation. More profitable production opportunities in turn translate into greater relative variance in net crop returns/incomes and increased crop income instability. The net effect of irrigation on crop diversification and income stability depends on the source of irrigation, ecological location, and level of development of irrigation facilities.

b.Tenancy

Tenancy (crop sharing or cash renting) is another important risk sharing and loss management strategy which also affords to manage loss incurred in previous cropping years. Besides, it also offers enough flexibility to share the risk parties and helps in equalising factor endowments and enable sharing of production risk (Jodha 1978). Crop sharing arrangement seem to be common in areas of relative economic uncertainty where there is less scope for risk in decision making, for example, for production as well as factor substitution, and where the entrepreneurial capability is low (Rao 1971).

Crop Insurance

As has been mentioned earlier that over generations farmers have developed a number of traditional risk reducing and loss management strategies but most of them were developed for the traditional method of livestock farming system. In the changing economic scenario with increased use of modern inputs and growing external economic pressure they are not very effective. Modern technology is undoubtedly more productive and profitable but is associated with greater risks also. Hence, most of the farmers, especially small and marginal farmers need outside interventions from the government to ensure against the risk. This will help farmers in allocating more resources in profit maximising way if they are sure about the financial compensation. These farmers may like to grow more profitable crops even if they are risky and would adopt improved technologies to increase crop production. This is not only in the interest of individual farmers but has far reaching consequences for the society and country as a whole.

Crop insurance is one of the government interventions to minimise the income loss to farmers. But, it is not in practice in many states. There are a few states which have a very well designed Comprehensive Crop Insurance Scheme. Andhra Pradesh is one the main states having such benefits. However, these schemes are simply not effective in reducing income variability of the vast majority of farm households producing the low value crops, most often grown in dryland areas. Even those farmers growing cash crops are also not adequately ensured against risk of crop failure.

Crop is the major source of income and contributes significantly to the income variability of household income. A single or multi-commodity crop insurance does not make much of a dent to the stability of crop income. A large share of area variability in dryland agriculture stems from decisions taken by farmers to cope with agroclimatic risk. Crop insurance can be more effective in the more stable regions where area variability caused by climatic risk is less. Besides, as long as crop insurance is linked to credit, voluntary participation is only way to combat adverse selection to the credit agency. The participation of farmers in Crop Insurance Programme is limited and the one possibility to entice more farmers to participate in crop insurance program would be to increase the subsidy content of the programme. But increased subsidy is hard to justify either on efficiency or equity grounds.

To make these programme more effective output prices should be stable to ensure that price variability does not unduly influence revenue variability directly or indirectly through fluctuation in areas. Crop insurance would be incomplete without an assessment of the alternatives available to farm households. Many cropping strategies and farming practices substitute for crop insurance by stabilising crop revenue. Efficient risk management strategies adopted by the farmers would reduce the risk of loan and enable banks to increase lending to agriculture and improve loan recovery. Even the smaller high risk farmers would become more attractive to commercial banks. However, stabilisation of crop revenue does not necessarily imply stabilisation of consumption. It is necessary not only to know that how well farmer manage risk without crop insurance but also to know how competing policies and crop insurance interacts with traditional risk-management measures. The potential benefits of crop insurance is greater in more risk-prone dryland regions, mainly because yield variability is the predominant source of risk in these regions.

There is a less scope for crop diversification to be an effective self-insurance measure (Walker, Singh and Jodha 1983; Walker et al. 1986).

Effective insurance mechanism very much depend upon how easily likelihood of events can be identified and how quickly the damage can be accurately assessed. However, they should not be affected by the insured behaviour of the farmers (moral hazards). Often public insurance programme fails mainly because they invariably attempt to ensure uninsurable risks and or hazards that occur so frequently that the required premiums are too high for most of the farmers to afford. Besides, administration cost becomes to high to cover large number of marginal and small farmers.

Financial viability of insurance programme is another area of major concern. Evidence from many countries indicates that public crop insurance programme invariably fail to reduce the cost of administration compared to premiums collected from farmers. For financially viable crop insurance programme without government support, it is necessary that an insurer should keep the average value of its annual outgoing - indemnities plus administration costs- below the average value of premiums it collects from farmers (Table 8). Public crop insurance programme invariably fail to meet this condition (Hazell 1991). To be financially solvent, an insurer must satisfy:

$$Z = \frac{A + 1}{P} < 1$$

Where A denotes average administration costs

I denotes average indemnities

P denotes average amount of premiums collected from farmers

Z can be divided into two components such as:

I/P = Loss ratio

A/P = Administration cost as a proportion of the total premium collected from farmers.

Table 8

Financial Performance of Seven Agricultural Insurance Programmes

Country	Period	I/P	A/P	(A+I)/P
Brazil (POAGRO)	1975-80	3.62	0.23	3.58
Costa Rica (INS)	1970-82	4.07	0.28	4.35
Israel (INFRA)	1967-76	1.44	0.09	1.53
Japan (Agriculture)	1947-77	1.48	1.17	2.60
Mexico (ANAGSA)	1963-78 1980-88	1.96 3.23	0.27 0.45	2.23 3.68
Philippines (PCIC)	1981-89	3.55	1.78	5.32
USA (FDIC)	1980-88	2.03	0.51	2.54

Source: reproduced from *Appropriate Function of Agricultural Insurance in Developing Countries*, Peter BR Hazell, Agricultural Insurance in Asia: Planning and Practices, Asian Productivity Organisation, Tokyo, 1991.

Legend: I = Average indemnities
A = Average administration costs
P = Average amount of premium collected from farmers

To improve Crop Insurance Programme, it is necessary that the insuring organisation must know the maximum probable loss (MPL) in any given year and prepare adequate funds to compensate for any such loss. There are mainly to methods of assessment of losses i.e. Plot to Plot Formula and Farm Unit Formula.

In India, Comprehensive Crop Insurance Programme was initiated in 1985 which covered a limited number of traditional crops such as cereals, pulses, and oilseeds only. The performance of these programmes has been highly disappointing in terms of high loss ratios and administration costs. Besides, it has not been able to show any positive impact on farm productivity and income of farmers (Gairola 1991). Some of the major reasons for failure are:

1. severe moral hazard problems associated with many of the insured yield risks
2. insurance of some risks that occur so frequently that they are necessarily expensive to insure.
3. reduced incentive for good insurance practice but increased incentive for cheating once government financially guarantee the insurer.
4. undermining insurers by using them to achieve government's other political objectives
5. use of insurer by guarantee yields at unrealistically high levels which reduces insurance as a mere income transfer mechanism
6. inability of crop insurers to overcome the covariability problem which, in turn, increases their financial dependence on the government, and
7. failure of the program to reach out to the poorest and most vulnerable farm households because insurance is usually tied with credit.

The experience of crop insurance programme in some other countries like Japan indicates that these programmes have been successful mainly due to (1) Well balanced government leadership and spontaneous farmers' participation; (2)Well-organised social infrastructure; and (3) Continued financial support by the national government

Suggestions for improvement

Despite many weaknesses in the crop insurance programme it has been quite helpful in many states and still there is enough scope to further improve it with some modifications and careful implementation and monitoring of the programme. A few of the suggestions are given below.

1. Coverage of non-loanee farmers in addition to loanee farmers
2. Coverage of more crops
3. Reduction in unit areas by State Government to provide benefits commensurate to crop losses
4. Crop insurance should be operated on the basis of both insurance and mutual relief principle especially among countries where small farmers comprise the majority.
5. Make the insurer financially responsible for its own affairs (no automatic access to government funds).
6. Subsidies should be set at some fixed percentage of total premium. No ex-post adjustment of the government's contribution each year to

reflect the insurers losses, other than on a loan basis (which should be repaid).

7. The insurance should be restricted to perils that can easily be quantified, losses easily attributed and valued, and those which are not subjected to moral hazard problems.
8. Farmers should be compensated only for crop damage not their failure to achieve normal yields.
9. Insures must compile and maintain adequate data and loss records.
10. Insurer should develop a diversified insurance portfolio to spread its risks and minimise the chance of large losses
11. Adequate contingency arrangement for coping with large losses either through commercial reinsurance or contingency loan arrangement with the government should be made.
12. Premiums and indemnities should be tailored to the risk levels of individual and higher indemnities to be paid to the farmers.
13. The insurer should tightly control administrative costs, and should address seasonality problems in the work load.
14. Premium should be based on sound, actuarial calculations using available weather records and well maintained records of insured farmers. This should be reflected in risk levels of the faremrs. The premium should be set high enough to cover average indemnities, administration costs and a contribution towards building of a financial reserve. Without a government subsidy break even premium rates will probably fall in the range 10 to 20 per cent [Pomareda 1986].
15. The insurer should be voluntary and should be able to compete with the private sector. This will require the insurer to develop and market the types of insurance that farmer wants most.
16. To avoid adverse selection problems, premiums and indemnities should be tailored to the risk levels of individual farmers and not to the regional average.
17. Administration cost for small scale farmers can be reduced by insuring groups of farmers as well as individuals.

If group insurance rates are sufficiently lower, farmers will be encouraged to organise into insurance mutual. The insurer can also provide technical assistance as required.

Role of Private Sector Insurance

Another issue which require special attention of the policymakers that can crop insurance programmes be completely left to the public sector or private sector can also play an important role. Considering the changing socio-economic and political environment and economic reform process of globalisation and liberalisation of financial sectors private sector can also be encouraged to participate in insurance sector, especially rural and agriculture sector. However, it will require removal of certain constraints and effective control. Private sector insurance is legally restricted in some countries, where an existing publicly owned scheme is already operating. Even where the private sector is allowed to operate, they may find it hard to compete with heavily subsidised public scheme. This discourages private insurer to ensure middle size farms. In countries where insurance had been nationalised the absence of diversified private insurers with experience in health, home, life offers a week base for building up agriculture insurance. There are infant industry problems in establishing agriculture insurance particularly where the initiative is taken by farmers rather than by existing non-agriculture insurer. There are set of tasks in quantifying insurable risks and calculating premiums, more importantly the insurance portfolio is likely to be small and specialised in early years, and, started with limited financial reserves, the insurer is likely to go under the prevent of heavy losses. However, the potential amount of international reinsurance that can be obtained for agriculture seems to be very limited.

Policy Alternatives

Dryland region is a harsh environment and is characterised by low and unreliable rainfall, poor crop yield and often faces the problem of crop failure. During last two to three decades, agricultural scientists and farmers have made a significant contribution in making this country from food-deficit country to food-surplus country. India has a strong network of agricultural research network and highly trained manpower comparable to any other developed country. But it is unfortunate that still there is no comprehensive agricultural policy at the national level.

Farmers in dryland regions have many sources of income but crop, wage earnings, and livestock are the main sources of household income. Stabilisation of crop income helps more large farmers while stabilisation of labour income helps landless labour households as well as marginal and small farmers. Policies and investment that increase and enhance the stability of labour demand will be more "progressive" than those that focus on crop income stabilisation alone which will differently benefit large farm households. Crop insurance can shift cropping patterns that lead to higher average income. It can also encourage adoption of technology, and greater use of modern inputs, less depletion of assets during bad years, less shifting of risk adjustment to landless labour, and a decline in land fragmentation (Walker, Singh and Asokan 1986).

The land fragmentation due to splitting of families or even as a part of plot diversification strategy represent a significant cost in terms of income foregone or a material benefit in the form of enhanced crop income stability. Thus, a prospective land consolidation program would not compromise the risk-bearing capacity of farmers, nor it significantly increase crop income of farmers at existing levels of technology (Ballabh and Walker 1986). Non-farm income can also be a powerful force to compensate for lower-than-expected crop income. Access to non-farm incomes, occupational mobility, geographic mobility, and family remittances can help stabilise household income and consumption. Farmer's risk-management is conditioned by repeated weather cycle which translates into asset depletion and replenishment cycles. Reliance on liquidation of productive assets to even out fluctuation in farm income may have strong implications for economic growth and equity in risk-prone areas (Jodha 1978). Tenancy is actively used to spread production risk within and across cropping years. In the present economic scenario of globalisation of economy where mechanisation is highly subsidised and capital is under priced in the formal credit market, restriction on tenancy might not be in the interest of landless labourers who cultivate land on lease basis. This will also not be in the larger interest of agricultural production as a large part of land of absentee landlords will remain fallow.

It is also argued that Crop Insurance can be made compulsory for all the farmers so that they should actively participate in these programmes. But considering the level of income of most of the marginal and small farmers it would be difficult for them to regularly pay the premium. Also to collect premiums from and make payment of insured money to such a large number of farmers would not be an easy task and would not be very cost effective.

Farmers in dryland regions receive income from livestock also. Livestock-based farming system is the well established system. This has been distorted over time and policy emphasis is more on crop improvement. In dryland regions livestock plays a much more important role in improving not only income but also to support crop production in the form of farmyard manure and draft power. Hence there is a need to develop a comprehensive agricultural insurance scheme including livestock also a major component. Livestock insurance is equally important for dryland farmers.

For effective agricultural insurance programme some basic issues arise that which types of risks to ensure and to what extent. How can it be made cost effective? Can we insure for entrepreneurial risk if enough of individuals venture into some new risky technologies under uncertainty where probability of crop failure is too high. How efficiently various types of risks or losses/damage can be measured? Can a individual be compensated for that loss of his ignorance? In case if an individual succeeds in risky environment he receives profits for his entrepreneurial capabilities. In this case will he pay higher premiums? In other words can we have different types of premiums based on the risk bearing ability of individuals. How to incorporate social dimensions to risk rather than its loss by marginal and small farmers. Many of these marginal and small farmers contribute to production which is a gain to him as well as to the society and the nation also. Hence, risk loss cannot be seen only in terms of purely economic criterion. Often risk is associated with the extensive use of spurious improved seeds, fertilisers and pesticides. Can this type of loss to the farmers be compensated by the traders concerned who supplied the spurious inputs or the government has to bear this loss? This is a sensitive issue but require a clear agricultural policy that include not only increase in productivity but also complete insurance of farmers from such weather related risks as well as spurious input supply system.

Can all the aspects of risk or activities be covered under risk or only agricultural activities? How to insure some failure if the loss is due to negligence or ignorance of farmers? How actively insurance company and bankers will be able to improve the process of monitoring and guiding for or correction? How traditional mechanism of risk avoiding and risk minimising strategies can be incorporated into modern risk insurance mechanism? Can it be made into the policy of technological development ? How the methodology for measuring various types of covariate and noncovariate types of risk, damage/loss can be improved and what should be the unit of measurement. Will it be possible to develop some policy instruments by which a farmer will be automatically insured like the traveller to train and air are insured? This needs to be examined in the long term perspective with a social security concept.

REFERENCES

Anderson, Jock. A. 1979. Perspective on models of uncertain decisions, Risk, Uncertainty and Agricultural Development, Edited by James A. Roumasset, Jean-Marc Boussard and Inderjit Singh, Southeast Asian Regional Centre for Graduate Study and Research in Agriculture College, Laguna, Philippines and Agricultural Development Council, New York, USA

Ballabh, Vishwa, and Walker, T.S. 1986. Land Fragmentation, Sub-division, and consolidation in India's Semi-Arid Tropics. Economics Group Progress Report No.76, Patancheru, ICRISAT.

Binswanger, Hans, P. 1978. Risk attitude of rural households in Semi-Arid Tropics, Economic and Political Weekly, June 1978, Review of Agriculture, Pp A40-62.

Binswanger, H.P. 1980. Attitudes towards Risk: Experimental Measurement in Rural India. American Journal of Agricultural Economics, 62(3):395-407.

Binswanger, H.P. 1981. Attitudes towards Risk: Theoretical implications of an experiment in Rural India. Economic Journal, 91:867-890.

Binswanger, H.P. and Sillers, D.A. 1983. Risk Aversion and Credit Constant in Farmers Decision making: A re-interpretation, Journal of Developmental Studies, 20 (1): 5-21.

Binswanger, H.P. 1984. Risk aversion, collateral, requirements, and the markets for credit and insurance in rural areas. In Agricultural Risks and Insurance: Issues and Policies (Eds.) Hazell, P., Pomareda, C., and Valdes, A. Baltimore, John Hopkins University Press.

Binswanger, H. P. 1986. Risk Aversion, Collateral Requirements, and the markets for credit and Insurance in Rural India. In Crop Insurance for Agriculture Development: Issues and Experiences, edited by P.B. R. Hazell, C.Pomareda, and A Valdes, 67-86, Baltimore, Johns Hopkins University Press.

Gairola, Sangita. 1991, Crop Insurance in India, Agricultural Insurance in Asia: Planning and Prospects, Asian Productivity Organisation, Tokyo.

Hazell, Peter, B.R., 1991. Appropriate function of agricultural insurance in developing countries. Agricultural Insurance in Asia: Planning and Prospects, Asian Productivity Organisation, Tokyo.

Jodha, N.S. 1978. Effectiveness of Farmers adjustments to risk. Economic & Political Weekly, 13(25): A38-48.

Joshi, P.K. and Agnihotri, 1982. Impact of input subsidy on income and equity under land reclamation, Indian Journal of Agricultural Economics, Vol. XXXVII, Conference No. 3, July-September, 1982.

Rao, C. Hanumantha, 1978. Uncertainty, enterpreneurship and sharecropping in India, Journal of Political Economy, Vol. 79, P 578.

Roumasset, James. A., 1979. Introduction and State of the Arts, in Risk, Uncertainty and Agricultural Development, Edited by James A. Roumasset, Jean-Marc Boussard and Inderjit Singh, Southeast Asian Regional Centre for Graduate Study and Research in Agriculture College, Laguna, Philippines and Agricultural Development Council, New York, U.S.A.

Rothschild, M. and J.E. Stiglitz, 1970. Increasing risk: I. A definition, Journal of Economic Theory, 2(3), pp.225-243.

Stiglitz, J.E. 1974. Incentives and risk sharing in sharecropping, Review of Economic Studies, 41(2), pp. 219-256

Sharma, Kailash, and Singh, R.P. 1993. A Note on Crop-Weather Relationship: Case Study of Three Villages in dryland regions of India, Journal of Rural Development, Vol. 12, No. 5, September 1993.

Singh, R.P., and Walker, T.S. 1982. Determinants and its implications of crop failure in the semi-arid tropics of India. ICRISAT Economics Program Progress report no.46, Patancheru, A.P., 502 324, India: ICRISAT.

Singh, R.P., M. Asokan and T.S. Walker. 1982. Size, composition, and other aspects of rural income in the semi-arid tropics. ICRISAT Economics Program Progress report no.33, Patancheru, A.P., 502 324, India.

Singh, R.P. and Walker, T.S. 1984. Crop Failure in the Semi-arid Tropics of Peninsular India, Indian Journal of Agricultural Economics, 39(1)

Singh, R.P. and Jodha, N.S. 1990. Crop Rotation in Traditional Farming Systems in Selected Areas of SAT India, 1990. Economic and Political Weekly, March 31, 1990.

Singh, R.P. 1981. Crop Failure and Intercropping in the Semi-arid Tropics of India, Economics Programme Progress Report 21. ICRISAT, Patancheru, A.P. 502 324, India.

Singh, R.P. and Jodha, N.S. 1989. Determinants of Intercropping in Semi-Arid Tropics on India, Economics Group Progress Report No. 95, ICRISAT, Patancheru, A.P. 502 324, India.

Walker, T.S., Singh, R.P., and Jodha, N.S. 1983. Dimensions of Farm-level Diversification in the Semi-arid Tropics of Rural South India. Economics Programs Progress Report 51.ICRISAT, Patancheru , A.P. 502 324, India.

Walker, T.S., Ryan, James G. 1990. Village and household economies in India's Semi-arid Tropics. Johns Hopkins University Press.

Walker, T.S., Singh, R.P., Asokan, M, and Binswanger, H.P. 1983. Fluctuations in Income in Three Villages of Peninsular India, Economics Programme Progress Report No. 57. ICRISAT, Patancheru, A.P. 502 324, India.

Walker, T.S., Singh, R.P. and Asokan, N. 1986. Risk benefits crop insurance and dryland agriculture. Economic and Political Weekly, 21(25-26) : A81-A88.

Walker, T.S. and Jodh, N.S. 1986. How Small farm households adapt to risk. In Crop Insurance for Agriculture Development : Issues and Experiences, edited by P.B. R. Hazell, C.Pomarada, and A Valdes, 17-34, Baltimore, John Hopkins University Press

Walker, T.S. and Singh, R.P. 1983. Crop Failure and resource stability: Implications for assessing productivity in the Semi-Arid Tropics, ICRISAT Journal article No. 357, Patancheru, A.P. INDIA.

NOTES

1 Crop failure in simple terms can be defined as planted plot not harvested. It may be either partial or complete depending upon the harvest of main crop or fodder.

2 Short fall in income can be defined in different ways. In this paper shortfall in income has been estimated as less than half the median income of any particular household during a period of nine years, for which a continuous income data for each sample household was available.

2

RISK MANAGEMENT IN AGRICULTURAL INSURANCE

M.L.Lunawat

Faculty, National Insurance Academy, Pune

ABSTRACT

Risk Management is known to the mankind from time immemorial. Insurance protection is one of the tools of risk management in modern world. The significance of this is magnified particularly in agriculturally dominated economy like India as well as other developing countries.

Insurance protection deals with the law of averages and the spread of risks. In order to understand the risks and hazards involved, risk management becomes a necessary pre-requisite. The paper attempts to go into various issues related with concepts and the broad principles of risk management, as they apply in the developing world, in context of Agricultural Insurance.

Risk Management as a concept has to be looked at from the point of view of the insurers as well as that of the insured. In agricultural insurance sector, this poses a great challenge in as much as that the farm holdings and the other ancillary assets of a farmer are small in value. The variance of hazards and the risks to which these assets are exposed is tremendous. Therefore, looking at all such risk factors and fixing a premium rate which is compatible as well as affordable by a prospective buyer is quite a difficult proposition.

The financial implications, in agricultural insurance have been studied at great length by various experts and organisations and it has generally been found that matching the needs of customers and providing suitable protection is often quite difficult and accompanied by a large number of unresolved issues. The insurers, predicament in maintaining a balance between loss and the expenses therefore, has to be understood in greater details.

The insurability of the risk vis-a-vis pricing of product and the support through the reinsurance protection is another challenge in risk management of agricultural insurance. With the vast changing economic scenario in developing world, the governments also do not seem to be very keen on subsidising the agricultural insurance protection. Thus, transferring the risk to reinsured is often the only viable alternative though it may be available on a restricted scale.

A line of business in agricultural insurance such as crop insurance, cattle and livestock insurance, poultry insurance, horticultural and plantation insurance, thus need to be underwritten carefully with sound underwriting judgment and effective risk management dynamics.

Introduction

Risk management as a concept is as old as history, though this subject as is understood in modern world is being practiced for nearly a century now in various parts of the world. Risk management encompasses every walk of life and therefore is not bound by social, industrial and environmental issues only. As a matter of fact, in all these areas risk management is being adopted and needs to be adopted vigorously.

Risk management as a concept and practice entails the four basic principles:

1. Risk Identification
2. Risk Evaluation
3. Risk Retention
4. Risk Transfer

As can be seen, all the above principles, do have application in day-to-day life. The objectives of this paper is to superimpose these principles in the field of agricultural insurance and the resultant implications there of.

While deliberating on the subject of Risk management as a modern welfare measure particularly in the context of India, we cannot and should not forgot the other developing and under developed countries with which we have considerable similarities and thus we share a common relationship. While elaborating on the Indian situation, there could be a few examples from the developing countries which would be found mutually relevant and applicable.

In developing countries, up to 60% of the national income is generated through agriculture which indeed is a significant component contributing to the overall welfare and economic growth of any country. India is no exception to this. Thus, tracing a little bit into historical past, the need for agricultural insurance has been felt intensely in India immediately following nationalisation of General Insurance Industry in 1972. One of the prime objectives of nationalisation of the General Insurance Industry has been the spread of insurance to every nook and corner of the country. thus arose the need to extending protection to the various sections of the society in order to secure their assets, life and liabilities, etc. No doubt, various products in agricultural insurance were launched with social objectives having an undercurrent of political ideology. As such, the various products in agricultural insurance were broadly divided into following two categories:

i) Comprehensive Crop Insurance Scheme (CCIS)
ii) Commercial Agricultural Insurance Schemes (CAIS)

Over a period of last 2 1/2 decades, the experience on both the schemes has ranged from highly unsatisfactory to reasonable in terms of commercial viability as well as operational efficiency. A number of issues have arisen during this period, which could not be tackled effectively due to inadequate infrastructure as well as spread of knowledge and skill for practicing the agricultural insurance. However, it is noteworthy to find that among the developing countries India occupies a prominent place in terms of the product range and the availability of services. It is quite often said that the Indian example is a fair blend of social welfare responsibilities juxta-posed with commercial wisdom. With a sense of pride one can say that the India insurance industry has launched 30+

products for the agricultural sector identifying the needs of the agricultural and farming community vis-a-vis a protection needed by them in the form of insurance. Annex 'A' gives the various products that are operated in the Agricultural Insurance in India.

Indian General Insurance Industry has taken significant strides in the development of agricultural insurance in terms of efforts and the quantum of work done in designing new products and making them available to the members of public. However, in the context of premium income and the viability of the products, considerable progress needs to be achieved. From the total general insurance premium of Rs.1,800 million in the year 1974, only Rs.3.5 million came from agricultural insurance sector representing a little less than 0.2%. By the end of 1996-97 out of total premium income of Rs.68,000 million, the agricultural insurance premium contributes Rs.2,200 million which represents 0.33%. thus, the increase in agricultural insurance premium has gone up considerably over a period of nearly 25 years. this would apparently indicate that for a country of the size of India further potential remains untapped and unexplored. In order to find out an answer to this we need to study in-depth the issues of risk management in agricultural insurance. The issues are common and real and apply universally to all the developing countries. Various studies have been conducted by International organisations including United Nations Conference for Trade and Development (UNCTAD) as well as eminent experts have contributed papers on this subject in various international and national conference. I would therefore attempt to present the implications of this serious subject.

1. Risk Identification Introduction & Background

The activity of agriculture is often subject to enforceable perils of nature and hazards generally beyond the control of agricultural products. The yield in agriculture also varies considerably as compared to the manufacturing industries. Thus, the resultant income irregularity reduces the possibility of external financing and application of modern technology. This diminishes the commercial growth potential so closely linked with economic and social security and stability of agricultural sector.

Providing insurance for agricultural risks can contribute to increase efficiency and productivity of agricultural sectors and help to improve social and economic well-being of the agricultural community as a whole. This area therefore, has been identified as having considerable risks and also a potential growth market, particularly when liberalisation and foreign competition in insurance is envisaged in developing countries.

As of now, the provision of insurance services to agricultural sector are not as broad based as the manufacturing sector for two basic reasons. First, the values of agricultural risks in developing countries are very small in view of the small land-holdings, though associated with ancillary activities. It therefore, follows that commercially significant premium volume cannot be generated easily. An UNCTAD study while dealing with underwriting considerations for crops, livestock, poultry and aqua culture risks concludes that

" .... the difficulties to be overcome in introducing and propagating agricultural insurance in developing countries should not be underestimated. They are many and formidable. In a number of countries only a few lines have been introduced, their scope is limited. A more purposeful thrust will require conscious and concerted efforts and the process should be initiated sooner rather than later".

This study extensive definitions and commentaries on identification of risks, perils, hazards and insurable interest in agricultural insurance.

The fact that the insurance protection is needed in agricultural sector is beyond dispute. However, the simultaneous issue of commercial and financial aspects of introducing or increasing agricultural insurance operations also need to be looked into. The necessity of considerable technical knowledge and information to underwrite agricultural risks with reference to commercial performance is beyond doubt and therefore throws open the subject of technical co-operation and techniques.

Globally, the experience in agricultural insurance has brought mixed and variable results. This renders the job of risk identification quite difficult and perhaps insurmountable at times. The variance of the natural factors, hazards and perils is so very extensive that identification of risk possibly cannot be done on uniform basis. The major question that remains to be tackled effectively therefore is providing uniform protection through insurance covers for identified risks. This can possibly be attempted through risk evaluation as can be seen in the following.

2. Risk Evaluation - Risk Insurability:

One or two products such as crop or livestock do not necessarily cover the entire gamut of agricultural or agriculture related activities. This would mean that the evaluation of risks would have to be done in all areas connected with agricultural sector and can cover a broad range of activities such as dairy farming, poultry farming, aqua culture farming, floriculture farming and a large range of livestock contributing to the commercial and economic health of a farmer. In all these areas, due to advent of modern technology and processes involved risk evaluation assumes greater importance for understanding the commercial viability of insurance products and application thereof.

This gives rise to the question of insurability of the risks connected with agricultural sector and the accurate assessment of the likely implications. We can broadly identify six basic requirements of insurable risk as under:

i. The premium charged must be economically feasible for all parties;
ii. There should be a large number of homogenous objects exposed to the same peril;
iii. The probability of the occurrence of the peril insured against must be calculable.
iv. The loss should not be catastrophic;
v. The loss should be sufficiently large, determinable and measurable;
vi. The loss must be accidental and unintentional

The first requirement related to the price of the product along with the conditions attached to it. The foremost point is as to whether the farmers possess the necessary purchasing power to buy the insurance? Agriculture is often a cyclical business, exposing the farmers to the ups and downs in the income levels. This could easily result into difficulties for collecting premium. While pricing the product, insurer cannot overlook the likely claims, management expenses and the procurement costs. An insurer also has to keep in mind the economy of scale while charging the price as well as the protection of reinsurance. Apart from the normal losses, what needs to be borne in mind are the catastrophes which can bring in untold misery and destruction exposing the insurers to heavy losses.

The underwriting risk faced by the insurer is inversely related to the loss variance of the insurance portfolio since this principle is based on the law of large numbers. The homogeneity of the exposure unit can reduce the underwriting risks per insured unit though in totality the insurer may be exposed to increased volume or risk. This is offset by collection of large amount of premium. One more implication of this is that if loss events are independent the insurer can insure more farms resulting into enlarged underwriting ability and substantial premium volume. On the other hand, if the loss events are not independent, the insurer is exposed to much greater portfolio risk and therefore should not write more business and should attempt to reduce his own retention by more reinsurance protection.

The probability of occurrence of the peril insured against must be calculable in order to determine the expected frequency and determining the price accordingly. In agricultural insurance sector this proposition is rather difficult and suffers from a very wide spectrum since the perils that can affect are not only highly unsettled but fraught with devastating catastrophic losses on one side or very low losses as the other extreme.

If losses are catastrophic in nature, they can cause very extensive damages over large territories. During such an event the number of claims registered would be very large and there are hardly any measures to prevent losses of this magnitude. The following methods however can deal with the problem of catastrophic losses.

* Physical measures (prevention and loss minimisation) and
* Financial measures, such as;
    Establishing a catastrophe insurance pool, mutual or government insurance fund; and
    Allowing tax-free reserving for catastrophic losses over an extended period of time.

The loss must be sufficiently large and measurable. Thus if quantification is not possible, insurer would find it very difficult to estimate the loss. In agricultural insurance for normal losses this poses a big challenge to insurers. The risks are generally small in value, though claims assessment calls for high level of technical and insurance knowledge. It must therefore be understood clearly that

"..... The loss to be insured against should be important enough to warrant the existence of an insurance contract. Many policies of insurance exclude unimportant losses because the cost of insuring is greater than the value of protection given. Obviously, to cover every small loss would increase greatly the cost of protection".

The losses which are not accidental and are intentional involve the problem of moral hazard. Thus, if the business gets expanded with more moral hazard problems, the business turns out to be financially an unsound proposition failing the basic criteria of risk evaluation. It must therefore be clearly understood that the primary role of insurance is to eliminate future uncertainty.

The above factors of insurability if taken on very rigid lines, it is quite possible that very little agricultural insurance would be sold. One of the basic presumptions which insurers often make is improvement in insurability characteristic of particular risk in the near future. They would thus like to capture the market share where the other insurers may be hesitating to operate. In such a situation, it is possible that the risks with poor insurability may be underwritten at a loss in the beginning, though the real objective may be to capture insurance market offering more profitable business. this dimension is also applied extensively if the insurer is state-owned writing inferior risks connected with social development or political reasons.

3. Risk Retention:

The Financial Implications in terms of problems and practice need to be looked into. The foremost question : Is agricultural insurance large enough to be commercially viable of its own? The question has to be perceived from the view point of the farmer as well as that of an insurer. The statistical data indicates that the agricultural insurance generates a very small part of gross premium written in many developing countries . the following table which is only illustrative in nature presents this lop-sided picture.

Agricultural Insurance as a percent of gross premiums written

Country	Crop Insurance	Livestock Insurance
Algeria	1.18	0.58
Argentina	0.73	--
China	1.00	5.30
Colombia	0.01	--
Costa Rica	0.15	0.01
Cyprus	15.00	--
India	0.50	0.02
Madagascar	0.31	0.01
Mexico	0.80	0.03
Philippines	0.5	0.05
Thailand	--	0.10

The total premium volume of almost all developing countries amounted to US dollars 82.2 billion in 1991 and represented 5.81 per cent of the total world insurance business. Even if we demonstrate utmost optimism and estimate that crop and livestock insurance generates about 3 per cent of premiums in developing countries, the total business generated would not exceed US dollars 2.5 billion or 0.18 per cent of the total world premiums. The small volume of insurance premium is a large obstacle to managing a financially viable agricultural insurance line.

The data also illustrate a point that there is no definite relation between size of agricultural economy in the country and pervasiveness of agricultural insurance.

It is revealed that whereas there is need for agricultural insurance in so far as a farmer is concerned; this need is also curtailed by the premium paying capacity of an average farmer. It appears that whereas the farmer feels that his assets must be protected against various hazards, his ability to convert these risk factor into insurance protection is limited by the cyclical nature of agricultural business. In other words, the lower risks spread becomes an inhibiting factor for an insurer to underwrite these risks at a economic and affordable premium rate.

The implications of this reality are two fold. The concept of sharing the losses of unfortunate few by many suffers a serious setback in this proposition for both the parties. The farmer does feel that he must be adequately protected at an affordable price through an insurance product so as to enable him to retain very limited or nil risk. At the same time, an insurer is unable to retain big financial risk in agricultural insurance in view of a large number of variables and concomitant parameters. this vicious circle is ultimately governed by the following two factors:

i. High pure rates; the loss variance of agricultural exposure units is higher than those of extractive, manufacturing and services industries, and
ii. High loading for management, administration and distribution; as the values of the insured assets are small, the fixed costs of providing insurance grow disproportionately larger and force premium rates into levels not found in other sectors.

Thus it is to be determined in terms of the retention of risk if there is a relationship and trade off between the loss ratio and the expense ratio and the resultant underwriting results. In such a situation there would be considerable efforts on the part of the farmer and an insurer to retain as low a risk as possible. Conversely both will be seeking the route of risk transfer. Let us have a look at the ramifications of this principle.

4. Risk Transfer:

This principle entails the following major factors:

i. Premium rate compatibility
ii. Loss variance
iii. Government Assistance - Subsidy
iv. Reinsurance and Direct Capacity

The factor of premium rate compatibility has to be looked at in relation to all the factors as described above. As already narrated, it assumes great importance both for the buyer and the administrator of insurance. In other words, determi... g premium rates is not an annual ritual, but has much wider implications in terms of creating underwriting capacity and free reserves keeping future in mind.

Not with standing appropriate care that can be taken in determining the premium rates, there is always an unforeseen situation which can throw the financial projection out of gear. The high variability of losses and potentially very high peak loss ratios call for the need of government involvement as well as dependable reinsurance support for agricultural insurance.

Very often, however, the governments in developing countries indeed may not be in a position to accept the transfer of insurance risk in view of the constraints on their own resources. In fact, the experience reveals that the governments would like to withdraw its support wherever offered to state-owned insurers so as to channelise such funds to some other basic needs of their citizens.

Underwriting smaller number of risks poses a problem before direct insurers in retaining the risks with them. thus, there would be concerted efforts to seek reinsurance support from a specialist brand of reinsurers in agricultural insurance. Obviously being guided by pure economic considerations, such reinsurers would be looking for premium rate compatibility in relation to loss variance and the government participation, if any, for specifying their own terms and conditions.

The problem of risk transfer gets further compounded when seen from the point of view of catastrophic losses. These losses can upset the whole economics running agricultural insurance business and would thus require a much greater support in the form of alternative risk transfer. Incidentally, this support does not come in very easily. The main reason obviously is a large volume of loss compared with a small volume of premium generation.

Looking at the above dimensions, the government and the policy makers have to be very clear on the operation of agricultural insurance. It is important to undertake cost benefit analysis for wide participation and also a provision of financial source needs to be made for protection. Though reinsurers often see a very vast market for agricultural insurance, in actual effect translating the reinsurance support in the form of risk transfer does not present a very healthy picture. An argument often advanced by reinsurers is that the agricultural reinsurance is a specialised activity in which there are only a few interested operating specialists. If they have to take interest in any proposal, sound economic justification will guide their terms and conditions and they would not be motivated by social and political considerations.

CONCLUSION

In examining agricultural insurance portfolio each insurer and each government as well as each reinsurer needs to have adequate expertise in this Area in order to determine the cost and risks involved, which can impair the financial capacity of insurers with serious effects on policy holders as well as beneficiaries. It may not be altogether possible for the insurers to charge very high price in view of the regulatory aspects as well as consumer resistance. In simple words, agricultural insurance in reality is a necessity and this line of business may have to be supported with a multi product commercial expansion in the related areas. This would result into cross-subsidy of one range of products for another range of products and can help society at large by providing better protection.

The financial institutions play an important role in this entire activity. The principles of which the financial institutions operate:

i. Creation of Assets
ii. Protection of Assets
iii. Generation of Wealth From Assets

All over the developing world, the development oriented financial institutions have been instrumental in the principles as stated here-in-above. It therefore goes without saying that through mandatory requirements the financial institutions would call for insurance protection as a collateral security. though this is vastly applicable both to manufacturing sector, as well as agricultural sector, the need for protection in form of agricultural insurance is a much felt need. What therefore transpires is matching the expectations of such development assisted financial institutions by making available appropriate insurance products. This step logically has to conclude that the after-sales services from the insurers need to be equally satisfactory for the dual purpose of enhancement in safety and protection in the event of loss.

In brief, one can say that writing agricultural insurance is indeed a difficult proposition and has to be handled with care, caution and past data besides future expectations.

REFERENCE

1. Financial Implications of Agricultural Insurance - Background note prepared by United Nations Conference for Trade and Development Secretariat Ref.: UNCTAD/SDD/INS/9, 28th August 1995.

2. Role of Financial Institutions in creating Rural-Economic Infrastructure : Dr.K.P.Agarwal, Dr.B.N.Kulkarni, Mr.K.U.Viswanathan.

3. Live stock Insurance - An Opportunity for Versatile Niche Players : Thomas Hientz

4. Crop Insurance in India : Gulam Muntaqua

5. Reinsurance in Agricultural Insurance : P.P.Rao

6. An Overview of Agriculture Insurance in Developing Countries : Ashok Goenka

7. Agricultural Insurance in Developing Countries : Its Role in the Context of National Economies : Carlos Tovilla

PRODUCTS MARKED IN AGRICULTURAL INSURANCE SCHEMES IN INDIA

Rural Schemes

LIVESTOCK AND POULTRY

i. Cattle Insurance (Market Agreement)
ii. Sheep and Goat Insurance (Market agreement)
iii. Horse/Pony/Mule/Donkey Insurance scheme (Market agreement)
iv. Pig Insurance Scheme
v. Camel Insurance Scheme (Market agreement)
vi. Poultry Insurance Scheme (Market agreement)
vii. Livestock Insurance (Master Policy)
viii. Livestock & Poultry (Master Policy) (IRDP)
ix. Livestock Insurance (Master Policy agreement)
x. Duck Insurance Scheme
xi. Rabbit Insurance Scheme

xii. Elephant Insurance Scheme
xiii. Dog Insurance Scheme
xiv. Zoo and Circus Animal Insurance Scheme

OTHER SPECIES

xv. Bracish-water Prawn Insurance Scheme
xvi. Inland Fish Insurance Scheme
xvii. Silkworms Insurance Scheme
xviii. Honey Bee Insurance Scheme

PROPERTY INSURANCE

xix. Agricultural Pumpsets Insurance Scheme
xx. Animal Driven Cart Insurance Scheme
xxi. Hut Insurance
xxii. Gobar Gas Insurance Scheme
xxiii. New Well Insurance
xxiv. Lift Irrigation Insurance Scheme

PERSONAL

xxv Janata Personal Accident (Individual)
xxvi Janata Personal Accident (Group)
xxvii Gramin Personal Accident (Individual)
xxviii Gramin Personal Accident (Group)

* * *

3

CROP INSURANCE : AN OPTION FOR RISK AVERSION

Dr. A.Ranga Reddy, Sambasiva Rao, Ramachandra Reddy,

Associate Professor in Economics, S.V.University, Tirupati.

This paper highlights the dimensions of price stabilisation, risk aversion and crop insurance.

I

The Government intervention in farm produce sector was with two objectives - to protect the interests of consumers by keeping the domestic price below the import parity price and to protect the interests of producers by reducing price fluctuations and guaranteeing a support price.1

Developing Countries interest in market - based risk management techniques including the use of commodity futures, options and swaps, has grown significantly in recent years. Price risk of any crop has two objectives. First, it seeks to assess the risk management needs, if any, identifying the market participants and institutions exposed to risk and measuring the levels of those risks. Second, it seeks to evaluate whether market based financial instruments would provide a less distortionery method of managing price risks than the stabilisation methods currently used in the farm produce sector. Larson (1993) examined the management of price risk for maize imports in Mexico. Much of Larson concern was domestic price stabilisation using variable border tariffs and subsidies to keep domestic prices within a price band.2

Price stabilisation policies involving government procurement and pricing do not remove price risk from the economy as a whole but merely transfer risk within the economy.

II

James Tobin, Nobel Prize winner of USA in 1981 year in Macroeconomic management, formulated the Risk Aversion theory of liquidity preference on portfolio selection.3 His theory, which is superior to J.M.Keynes liquidity preference, does not depend on the elasticity of expectations of future interest rates but proceeds on the assumption that the expected value of capital gain or loss from holding interest - bearing assets is always Zero. Moreover it explains that an individuals portfolio holds both money and bonds rather than only one at a time. Tobin classifies three types of investors. The first category is of risk lovers, who enjoy putting all their wealth into bonds to maximise risk. They accept risk of loss in exchange for the income they expect from bonds. They are like gamblers. The second category is a plungers. They will either put all their wealth into bonds or will keep in cash. Thus plungers either go all the way or not at all. But the majority of investors belong to the third category. They are risk averters or diversifies. Risk averters prefer to avoid the risk of loss which is associated with holding bonds rather than money. They are prepared to bear some additional risk only, if they expect to receive some additional return on bonds, provided every increase in risk borne brings with it greater increases in returns. They will, therefore, diversify their portfolio, and hold both money and bonds. Although money neither brings any return nor any risk yet it is the most liquid form of assets, which can be used for buying bonds at any time.

It is fond that many of U.S.A. and European farmers were adopted Tobins third category of risk aversion as they practices, rotating of crops, on one side and markets provided a cushion of support price. Unfortunately, if any slump is formed, immediately the state comes forward to rescue the farmers by giving either subsidies or exports.

Whereas in Indian farming, the structure is such that 78 per cent of land holdings are owned and cultivated by marginal and small farmers with an area of holdings is 32.2 per cent for the year 1991.4 By examining the investment portfolio management of small and marginal farmers, they are following the first category of Tobins theory that is, risk lovers. In fact, 90 per cent of sown area, especially rainfed farmers, are found like in the casino of gambling with monsoons. Further, the Indian Farm markets are not cooperative to the mush of above farmers in getting profitable price. Generally it is observed that inputs markets are in escalation, leads to boon and produce sales markets are in slump. This brought the farming community in utter loss and was in discord of pessimism. The government - centre and states - did less concerted efforts to solve the farmers woes, at least the ultimate helping hand of remunerative price. In Andhra Pradesh, especially in Warangal and Karimnagar districts in the year 1997 more than 60 pesticide drank suicide deaths of farmers were taken place, due to non-remunerative price to hybrid cotton. Farmers were taken such a decision of ending of lives was the last resort as they made up their minds that they never repay borrowed compound interested loans.5 Investigations proved all deaths are occurred due to private money lenders exploitation. 6 The State Government merely announced Rupees one lakh for a family of suicide death and escaped from permanent solution like crop insurance, cheaper and adequate credit, low cost inputs, remuneration price, that is, holistic approach. The crop insurance scheme was introduced in mid 1980s with all loopholes to the farming sector, made the farmer as a victim of his own destiny.

III

IMPACT OF GREEN REVOLUTION

The first round of Green revolution had changed the rural economic scenario by HYV seeds, fertilisers, technology, water, cropping pattern, resulted raised the levels of income and employment. Further, irrigation component made the intensive and extensive agriculture. The green cover impact was spread to the dry land farmers, who switched over to sunflower, cotton, than traditional food grains. The cost of cultivation had become unbearable for small farmers than yields and remuneration. As long as farming community enjoyed profits from commercialisation agriculture, the major component of 'risk management' was never touched the hearts of farmers, farmers leaders, policy makers and Government. Nonetheless, since centuries rainfed farming was become a gamble of monsoons. As the farming is in the private sector, the Government never thought of seriously to insure farmer from natural calamities like drought, floods, cyclones. High cost of sensitive agriculture, that is, green revolution opened the eyes of farmers and Government, to go immediately for protecting the farmer from financial collapse. For any severe natural disaster was taken place, the concerned state and centre will provide a relief of re-scheduling the bank loans, interest write off, re-lending the new loans. Later states and centre realised insurance as a must in holistic policy of agriculture. Ninth Plan (1997-2002) Approach paper advocated that Marginal and small farmers are to be protected under crop insurance.7

Earlier, Pilot Crop Insurance Scheme (PCIS) has proposed elimination of subsidy in the premium. The new Pilot scheme at best attempted to reduce the State's burden of implementing the scheme.

COMPREHENSIVE CROP INSURANCE SCHEME

The present Comprehensive Crop Insurance Scheme (CCIS) launched in 1985 khariff is far from satisfactory and limiting its acceptance by farmers. This scheme is temporarily suspended in January 1988 but was re-introduced in September 1988 with limited insurance.

OBJECTIVES AND ELIGIBILITY

The basic objective of the CCIS was to financially support farmers in the event of crop failure due to drought or floods, to restore the credit eligibility of farmers after a crop failure for the next crop season and to support and stimulate the production of cereals, pulses and oil seeds. The states were free to opt in favour of it. The area and credit linked scheme was purely voluntary and continued on an ad hoc season to season basis. The CCIS supplies 50 per cent subsidy on premium rate of 2 per cent for wheat, rice and millets and one per cent for oil seeds and pulses for the small and marginal farmers. The criteria for eligibility of areas remained the same as that of past yield and number of crop cutting experiments. A slight modification has been made, however, in many crop cutting experiments, which has been specified for different areas as eight per stratum for Gram Panchayat, Firka; ten for mandal, blocks; twelve for Tehsil and sixteen for district, against the 16 per stratum in the CCIS.8

PROBLEMS AND PROSPECTS

From 400 lakh farmers in 1994 to 524 lakh farmers have been insured under the CCIS till July 1997, claims an amount of Rs.963 crore 1994 to Rs.1351 crore in the corresponding period were paid to farmers, against premium collection of Rs.231 crore upto Rabi 1995-96 season. The incurred claims ratio being 1:5.85, the scheme is extremely unviable. The premium loss ratio has been estimated at 1:8 and major beneficiaries under this were the farmers of Gujarat, Maharastra, Andhra Pradesh and Madhya Pradesh. Gujarat enjoyed a lion-share in it. However the scheme has no impact on Insurance companies because the expenditure on claims settlement is entirely met by Ministry of Agriculture.

It is found that lack of proper infrastructural facilities at states levels and inconsistent indemnity claims by few states leading to huge losses.

The states went on in non-uniform coverage of all areas and shifting of crop loans to non-insured crops was a glaring lacuna caused by primary Agricultural Credit Societies not preparing statement of crop-wise credit limits. By the by, many lending agencies disbursed the entire loan in cash at one point of time, instead of in two or three instalments. Further the lending agencies never cared for guidelines of successful implementation of the scheme. Perhaps, no financial stake to the credit agencies in the CCIS and do not share the loss with the Government. At best, it has focused on making the scheme self-supportive by proposing actuarial premium for all farmers.

As the scheme is voluntary in nature and adoption by states, selection of areas in some states by notifying high risk areas, especially predominance of rainfed crops such as oil seeds, millets, pulses and limited applicability to loanee farmers prompted the government to propose the new scheme. When centre brought to the notice of this issue before Chief Ministers, RBI, NABARD and Planning Commission, many states felt that the scheme should be made voluntary for all farmers against the proposal for making it compulsory for loanee farmers and leaving it the option to non-loanee farmers. The actuarial premium rate also proposed maximum from Rs.10,000 to Rs.45,000. The centre urged the states that the premium is to be revised as 2 per cent for Wheat, Paddy, Millets and one per cent for oil seeds and pulses. Subsidising the premia beyond a certain percentage also was rejected as it would not make the scheme as self-supporting.9

RECENT DEVELOPMENTS

There is an agreement in between centre and states on sum insured limit was Rs.25,000 subject to maximum Rs.45,000 per farmer, if cash crop are also covered. The ratio of sharing of indemnity claims remained un-resolved with the states demanding the continuance of the existing ratio of the centre sharing two parts and the states one, against the reverse proportion proposed in the CCIS. But the basic deficiencies of weak and inadequate crop cutting machinery and defects in credit institutions and inefficient monitoring of utilisation of loans remain unaddressed in the new scheme.

Of course, the increase in budgetary estimates for crop insurance has made to raise the incidence of indemnity claims. Thus the actuarial premium proposal may come as a relief to both the states and centre in off setting the loss incurred due to low premium and the subsidy paid to small and marginal farmers. This augurs well for the improved performance of the insurance scheme.. Finally, the representatives of farmers and states have been demanding the reduction of the unit area of crop insurance from the present level of Tehsil to Gram Panchayat. There is a need to improve the parameters of the scheme to make it financially feasible and successful. Further all farmers of states are to be associated, especially dry land farmers, to save their crops and incomes and make agricultural profession as a boon, but not a curse. Educating farmers and Government Servants is highly necessary at this juncture.

CONCLUSION

State intervention in farm produce and marketing is indisputable and inevitable, to bring remunerative price to the farmer, on one side and stabilisation of food and non-food stocks prices and exporting surplus produce, on the other, under the new economic policy. Further state has to inculcate the vision of risk aversion as a habit among all classes of farmers. Spreading risk of inputs and prices among state, traders, farmers and consumers is to be considered as an paramount important and scientific rational, than farm household alone. The crop insurance scheme is to be made as a leak-proof one, covering all classes of farmers, regions, crops, in view of sustainable agriculture and globalisation.

REFERENCES

1. Rashid Faruqu *et al* : Managing Price Risk in the Pakistan Wheat Market, The World Bank Economic Review, May 1997, p.263.

2. Larson, Donald F : Policies for coping with price certainty for Mexican wheat, working paper 1120, The World Bank 1993.

3. James Tobin : 'Liquidity preference as Behaviour towards risk' in *The Review of Economic Studies*, 1958.

4. Tata Services Ltd. : Statistical outline of India 1996-97, p.59.

5. N.Venugopal,Were suicides deaths of farmers avoidable? *The EconomicTimes*, Jan.1, 1998.

6. Burra Ramulu, Who are responsible for cotton farmers Suicides? *Vaartha*, Feb2, 1998.

7. Govt. of India, Economic Survey 1996-97, p.151.

8. Planning Commission,Approach paper to the Ninth Five Year Plan (1997-2002) p.56.

9. V.K.Varadarajan, Crop Insurance : Hurdles Aplenty in practice, The Hindu Survey of Indian Agriculture 1994, p.187.

* * *

4

NEED FOR CROP INSURANCE IN CYCLONE PRONE AREAS OF THE ANDHRA COAST, INDIA

Dr. M. Sambasiva Rao, Dr. Y. Nazeer Ahammed & J. Narendra Kumar,

Dr. Y. Nazeer Ahammed & J. Narendra Kumar

The Andhra coast has a total length of 910 kms with major deltaic regions like Godavari, Krishna and Pennar where paddy is the dominant crop during Kharif and Rabi seasons. These deltaic regions are constituted of abandoned river courses and ancient beach ridges. The disposition of abandoned channels in ancient river courses and beach ridges in ancient strandlines and their relative altitudinal variations are responsible for water logging and flooding during cyclonic periods. Four ancient strandlines and eight to ten abandoned meander lobes are traced in each delta. These deltas and the Andhra coast are frequently subjected to cyclonic activity during April, May, October, November and December months. Recently a number of aquafarms have been developed along the Andhra coast in lower reaches of deltaic regions, in marshy lands, mangroves and in and around tidal channel and tidal creek areas. These aquafarms are also subjected to cyclonic activity. A number of commercial crops like sugarcane, banana, turmeric, betelnet, etc. are cultivated in the natural levees and abandoned levees of the deltaic regions. These commercial crops are also subjected to cyclonic activity.

A cyclone is a huge rotating mass of moisture air, spiralling inward into the centre of the storm in tropical oceans, when developed fully it is a vast whirl wind of extra ordinary violence. The evolution of an average cyclone can be broadly divided into four phases namely formative, developing, mature and dissipating. During the formative stage the prevailing winds over the extensive oceanic region become variable and scattered showers of rain occur accompanied by thunders. Atmospheric pressure gradually falls and isobars take on closed shapes. The weather over the region is unsettled in this phase. During developing phase, the pressure fall continues and winds increase their velocity. Skies become thickly overcast and rainfall intensity increases. Winds spiral inward with a velocity of 20 Kms to 30 Kms per hour. This condition is described as 'Depression'. During the mature stage the area of low pressure and the associated weather region begin to move with a velocity ranging from 300 to 450 Kms per day. Many of the depressions thus formed do not develop any further and only a few of them pass through beyond mature stage and become severe cyclones. A depression is called as cyclonic storm when the wind exceeds 75 Kms per hour. In the mature stage the cyclone consists of fair district part. A calm central eye with 9 Kms to 30 Kms diameter with very light winds and partly cloudy skies, an inner ring of hurricane winds with a velocity of 75 Kms or more per hour. The width of inner ring varies from 45 Kms to 135 Kms in diameter with steep fall in pressure, fierce squalls and torrential rains. An outer ring with a diameter of 75 Kms to 225 Kms in which wind velocity ranges from 45 Kms to 75 Kms per hour and an outer most area of weak cyclonic circulation. During the dissipating phase the cyclonic storm after crossing the coast begins to dissipate due to increased frictional effects of land and lack of moisture supply from warm oceanic surface. The rainfall during this period will be continuous with very high intensity for a day or two. The zone of low pressure slowly dissipates as it further moves towards the land surface. The average rainfall during cyclonic storms vary from 300 mm to 800 mm. It is after this phase due to heavy downpour of rainfall, the swollen rivers, streams and channels bring unprecedented floods in the river valleys, deltaic plains and coastal plains. In the uplands the tanks are filled with run-off water from their catchment areas. Due to continuous flow of water for two to three days the tanks bunds are breached and result into splash floods.

An analysis of cyclones that struck over the Indian coast (Table 1) reveal that from 1901 to 1980 these are about 550 cyclones. Out of them 159 are severe cyclones. The monthly analysis of occurrence of cyclones reveal that the minimum number of one cyclone occurred in February month and the maximum number of cyclones of 98 occurred in October month. The number of cyclones occurred are less than ten in January, February and March months. During the months of April, August and

December the cyclones occurrence varied from 20 to 50. In May, June, July and September months they exceeded 80. The seasonal analysis of cyclones occurrence reveal that during winter period the minimum number of eight cyclones occurred and the maximum number of 236 cyclones occurred during north-east monsoon period. In south-west monsoon they are 221 and in summer period they are 85 over a period of eighty years. The severe cyclones occurred are 81 during north-east monsoon, 46 in summer, 30 in south-west monsoon and 2 in winter period. From the study of monthly analysis of cyclones occurrence it is found that during October and November their occurrence is very high and the seasonal analysis revealed that during north-east and south-west monsoon periods their occurrence is high.

Table 1: Cyclonic storms over the Indian Region (1901 to 1980) (Source: IMD)

Month	No. of Cyclones	No. of severe Cyclones
January	7	2
February	1	-
March	4	1
April	21	11
May	57	34
June	59	13
July	60	8
August	46	4
September	56	9
October	98	29
November	97	46
December	41	6
Total	550	159

The study of the severe cyclones that crossed the East coast of India during the last 25 years (Table 2) reveal that among the 14 devastating cyclones 6 each struck Tamil Nadu and Andhra coast and one each in Orissa and West Bengal coast. A few of the devastating cyclones that struck the coast in October 1942, December 1964 and November 1977 produced tidal waves and accounted to loss of life, livestock etc. About eleven devastating cyclones have struck Andhra coast from 1787 to 1986 (Table 3). Out of them two each devastating cyclones struck Coringa (May 1787 & December 1789), Kakinada (November 1969 and August

1986), Nizampatnam (May 1969 and November 1977) and Machalipatnam (November 1864 and November 1879). In Kalingapatnam coast (November 1966), Sriharikota coast (November 1972) and Kavali coast (November 1976) the severe cyclones which struck were one each.

Table 2: Some of the devastating cyclones which struck the East coast of India during the last 25 years in the months of November and December (Source: IMD)

S.No	Year	Date and month	Landfall	Coast
1	1964	20-24 December	Rameswaram Island	Tamilnadu Coast
2	1966	20-22 November	Near Kalingapatnam	Andhra Coast
3	1967	05-08 December	Near Nagapatnam	Tamilnadu Coast
4	1969	05-07 November	Near Kakinada	Andhra Coast
5	1972	18-23 November	Near Sriharikota	Andhra Coast
6	1972	04-06 December	North of Cuddalore	Tamilnadu Coast
7	1973	05-09 November	Near Paradeep	Orissa Coast
8	1976	15-17 November	Kavali	Andhra Coast
9	1977	14-20 November	Near Nizampatnam	Andhra Coast
10	1978	17-24 November	Near Kilakkarai	Tamilnadu Coast
11	1981	04-11 December	Near Sagar Island	West Bengal Coast
12	1984	09-14 November	South of Sriharikota	Tamilnadu Coast
13	1984	Nov.27 to Dec.2	Karaikal	Tamilnadu Coast
14	1986	12-16 August	Kakinada	Andhra Coast

Table 3: Some devastating cyclones which struck the Andhra coast (1787 to 1986) (Source: IMD)

S.No.	Year	Month	Landfall	District
1	1787	May	Coringa	East Godavari
2	1789	December	Coringa	East Godavari
3	1864	November	Machilipatnam	Krishna
4	1879	November	Machilipatnam	Krishna
5	1966	November	Kalingapatnam	Srikakulam
6	1969	May	Nizampatnam	Guntur
7	1969	November	Kakinada	East Godavari
8	1972	November	Sriharikota	Chittoor
9	1976	November	Kavali	Nellore
10	1977	November	Nizampatnam	Guntur
11	1986	August	Kakinada	East Godavari

From the study of average rainfall during cyclonic periods it has been found that lateral spread of influence of cyclones extended to a radius of 200 Kms to 300 Kms from the coastline of landfall. The rainfall gradually receded towards the western uplands. Based on the intensity of rainfall of the influenced areas the cyclones have been categorised into disastrous (>60 mm rainfall per day), very severe (45mm - 60 mm rainfall per day), severe (30 mm - 45 mm rainfall per day) moderate (15 mm - 30 mm rainfall per day) and less influenced area (<15 mm rainfall per day).

Impact of cyclonic on deltaic and coastal environment:

1. The devastating cyclones that struck Andhra coast brought huge quantities of rain water with fiercing winds and tidal waves.
2. The natural ecosystems are very much disturbed.
3. The fiercing winds have blown away poor huts, derooted the trees, twisted the electric poles and damaged the communications.
4. The unprecedented floods damaged the roads, bridges, culverts, houses, commercial and food crops, breached the tank bunds, and killed the livestock.
5. The tidal waves formed due to devastating cyclones washed away and killed the people, cattle, poultry, sheep, fishing ponds and prawn culture ponds.
6. The saline water encroached over the coastal aquifers and lands increased the salinity of fertile lands and choked the saline water into ponds, tanks, springs and wells.
7. The tidal waves crossed over the coastal environment to a distance of about 5 Kms to 20 Kms in land. The devastating cyclones of Coringa in 1787 and 1789, Machalipatnam in 1864 and 1879, Kalingapatnam in 1966, Nizampatnam in 1969 and 1977, Kakinada in 1969 and 1986, Sriharikota in 1972 and Kavali in 1976 have produced tidal waves and destructed the coastal life and environment.
8. The tidal flooding has generated drainage problems, siltation in ponds, tanks and drainage channels, water logging and increased salinity and alkalinity of soils and water.
9. It has also affected the physical properties of soils and brought down yield of crops.
10. The impact of devastating cyclones was also disastrous on the economy of the people living in coastal and deltaic environments. The damages caused to the property and standing commercial and food crops have

struck the living conditions of the people, ruined the standard of living and thrown the people and farmers into heavy debts. The people of cyclone prone areas take minimum of five years to recover to normal conditions.

11. The property loss to the government due to damage caused to communications, transportation, roads and bridges, runs to 100 to 500 crores every year to the centre and state.
12. The farmers incur a loss of about 200 to 500 crores due to damage of houses, loss of livestock, food and commercial crops every year in the cyclone influenced areas.

Technological management of flood water during cyclonic periods:

There is a need for technological management of flood water during cyclonic periods. Management has to be taken to divert the water to non cyclone prone areas and to store the water in under ground water tanks or quants. Each cyclone brings huge quantity of rain water (ranging from 300 mm to 800 mm). It is drained into sea wastefully. The broadening of the concept of technological management not only includes storage of flood water but also increases the environmental quantity for a sustainable long term feasibility and prevention of damage caused due to floods in the coastal and deltaic environment. The huge costs involved in execution of works initially may cause heavy chequer to the government but will minimise recurring losses every year. The state governments have taken steps to widen and deepen the drainage canals existing in the deltas with the financial support from world bank but the flood water is allowed to drain wastefully into Bay of Bengal. Contour canals have to be constructed along the coast to inter link the rivers at 5 meters, 10 meters, 20 meters and 30 meters above MSL to divert flood water to non cyclone influenced areas. The contour canals have to be linked with underground tanks to allow the flood water to drain into quants by gravity flow.

Some suggestions for better management of devastating cyclonic storms of Andhra coast:

1. Diversion of flood water from cyclone prone areas to non cyclone influenced area by inter linking the rivers through contour canals.
2. Construction of underground water storage tanks to store the flood water along the contour canals during flood periods.

3. Straightening, widening and deepening of the drainage canals in cyclone prone area to drain out excess water during flood water.
4. Raising of coastal bunds to a height and width of 10 meters in cyclone prone areas to minimise ill effects due to tidal waves.
5. Straightening the bunds of tanks/ponds in the coastal areas and up lands in cyclone influenced areas to minimise breaches during flood periods.
6. Development of green belts along the coastline to minimise the furiosity of the winds during cyclonic periods.
7. Construction of check dams near the confluence points of canals to minimise encroachment of sea water.
8. Construction of community shelter houses in villages in cyclone influenced areas at a height of about 10 to 20 meters above ground level to minimise loss of human life during tidal waves.
9. The farmers should be educated to raise flood resistant crops and the lands should be left fallow during cyclone influenced months April, May, October and November. Short term high yielding variety of paddy crop should be recommended for cultivation.
10. Farmers have to be educated about preventive measures and ill effects of cyclones to minimise economic losses through All India Radio, Doordarshan, documentary films etc.
11. The crops raised in the cyclone prone areas have to be insured every year to get back reimbursement from insurance companies if there is crop loss due to flood water inundation due to cyclonic activity. There is a need that the farmers should be educated about the advantages of crop insurance, house insurance, household articles insurance etc. The state and central governments should persuade the insurance companies to come forward to insure crops all along the coastal plains of Andhra coast. The government should make crop insurance compulsory, so that rehabilitation of people/farmers in cyclone prone areas could be carried out.
12. There are about 4,040,000 hectares of cultivable land along the Andhra coast raising paddy as the predominant crop besides commercial crop like banana, sugarcane, termeric, betelnet etc. All the farmers cultivating the above said crop insure their crops by paying a premium of Rs.100/- per acre per annum to an Insurance company. About a sum of Rs.40.04 crores will be collected every year by the Insurance company, which could be accumulated and paid to farmers who have been affected by cyclonic activity for the loss of crop, property etc. Every year about 500,000 hectares of

land is affected by cyclonic activity due to inundation. At least a sum of Rs.3,000/- could be reimbursed per acre to the farmer for rehabilitation in the cyclone prone area. Thus the crop insurance by the farmers living in cyclone affected areas would minimise the burden of compensation to be paid to` the farmer by the central and state governments.

***

5

NATIONAL AGRI - ASSURANCE POLICY (NAAP) FOR COMBATTING AGRICULTURE RISK

B.Ramachandra Reddy & L.Venugopal Reddy

Professors, S.K.Institute of Management,
S.K.University, Anantapur

INTRODUCTION

Risk Management has assumed tremendous importance over the last few decades and almost every human activity has been covered with some kind of insurance policy or the other. The Insurance service has spread like wild fire; it is a good business and also a good service.

Nature of Agriculture Risk

Agriculture in India exhibits a unique kind of risk caused by frequent changes in environment and market conditions. Failure of monsoon, out break of pests and insects, natural calamities like cyclones, theft of crop, unremunerative market prices etc., have a telling effect on the agriculture returns. Further, the substandard quality of inputs like, fertilizers, pesticides and seeds, intermittent supply of power and insufficient irrigation have complicated the problem of risk in agriculture. The recent incidence of farmers' deaths over the cotton crop failure in Andhra Pradesh is one such bizarre instances calling for an intensive debate and long lasting solution.

Agriculture Risk is a Social Problem

The dimensions of agriculture risk keeps on changing. It is not possible for the agriculturist to manage it. It is indeed, the problem of 85% of our population who live in villages and depend on agriculture for their lively hood. The returns from agriculture have become very meagre and uncertain. This forced the agriculturists to shift from cultivation of food crops to garden crops. Many have sold away their lands and migrated to towns and cities in search of better incomes; and in many cases vast stretches of agri-lands were not cultivated in view of prohibitive costs and cruel risk factors. If the present trend in agriculture is allowed to continue, the rural society is bound to be shattered into pieces.

Involvement of the Government

Government should wake upto the problem of majority of the population of the country. It must work tooth and nail to fight out the agriculture problems. Any half hearted attempt may provide temporary relief but aggravate the issue as the time passes. Since agriculture situation in the country has assumed alarming proportions, the Govt. should evolve a National Policy and assure sufficient income to the farmers. This exercise may even cause so much money for the Government but it should be realised that such a spending will be better than giving does and subsidies, exgratia, concessions etc.

A New Approach to the Agri Problem

In the wake of the new economic policy it is imperative that agriculture should also become market sensitive and adjust itself to the market forces. It is no more possible for the government to sustain agriculture by giving subsidies and concessions. In view of this, the agriculture industry must adjust itself to the changing environment for which a substantial lead must be provided by the Government. Agriculture must become and income stable industry so that farmers continue to remain in agriculture and the socio-economic fabric of Rural India remain unchanged.

The present system of providing credit to the agriculturist is only one single issue and it can not ensure stable returns in agriculture. The agriculturist need to be protected from the risks of all sorts and assure him of sufficient returns. Assurance of returns in agriculture must become the National Policy : As such National Agriculture Assurance Policy (NAAP) must be evolved to integrate Indian agriculture with rest of the world.

Redefine the role of NABARD

There is an immediate need for NABARD to redefine its role in the new economic policy, without any further loss of time. It must have through introspection of its policies. If agriculture and rural development is the objective of NABARD it must assume further responsibility of assuring a stable return for the agriculturist, besides providing credit. Such a course of action alone will help agriculture and rural society to develop. As long as agriculturist in subjected to unending risk factors he will not be in a position to escape from the clutches of poverty and emerge into an income sufficient farmer.

Twin Policies of NABARD

The development policies of NABARD should focus at two important issues ; viz., 1) Agriculture Assurance and 2) Agriculture credit : As such a National Agriculture Assurance Policy (NAAP) and a 'National Agriculture Finance Policy (NAFP) need to be evolved : Both these policies must be intertwined in implementation, with thorough market orientation.

Features of NAAP

NAAP is an agriculture assurance policy for different crops on the basis of support prices declared in advance. Yields can be calculated mandal wise. If the yield is falling short of the insured yield, the difference can be met out by the insurer, thereby assuring a full return to the agriculturist. The premium for agri-assurance policies of different crops can be worked out on a national level and subsidised by the Government to keep it under the reach of every agriculturist.

Features of NAFP

NAFP is an agriculture finance policy devoid of any concessions in rates of interest, write off of loans, raphasing of loans, does due problem etc. NAFP provides for an automatic facility of an over draft worked out on the basis of extent of cultivation of various crops as detailed in the pattadar pass books. Taking into account the cost of cultivation an amount sufficient for cultivation of crops at any period of time can be calculated and OD allowed by the financing bank at market rates of interest and upon mortgaging the entire extent of land as shown in the pass book and surrendering of the pass book. The balances for more than 30 days in the account of the farmer may be allowed an additional 2% rate of interest over the usual rate to serve as an incentive. This practice contains the features of voluntary enforcement of financial discipline on the part of the agriculture.

Intertwining NAAP with NAFP

The agriculture assurance policies can be sold by the agriculture financing bank itself, thus combining the two aspects of financing and insurance of agriculture. NABARD at the helm of affairs can over see the proper functioning of the system. It can refinance the agri-credit by raising funds on the securitisation of the mortgages of agriculturists and settle the insurance claims through instituting a fool proof system.

NAAP a Penetia for the Agriculturist

Though NAAP involves the sharing of the agri assurance premia, between the Government and the agriculturist, it works out cheaper for the Government than what it is spending otherwise at present. The scheme, has the biggest advantage of solving the agriculture problem permanently and on a continuing basis : The hope of rural India lies in the 'National Agricultural Assurance Policy'.

Let the economists, and financial experts deliberate further and arrive at a consensus to strike the agriculture problem from the angle of assuring the returns on a national level.

* * *

6

STRATEGIC DECISION MAKING FOR RISK MANAGEMENT IN SERICULTURE

Dr. C. Raja Gopal Reddy,
Inspector of Sericulture, Anantapur.

Prof. L. Venugopal Reddy,
Head, S.K.Institute of Management,
S.K.University, Anantapur.

ABSTRACT

Sericulture is an Agro based cottage Industry with an Agricultural base, now standing as the main occupation of the Farming community while absorbing the Rural labour giving direct employment through Silk Reeling, Twisting, Dyeing, Weaving and Printing, Sericulture Industrial equipment and Inputs manufacturers. It is the best among all the Agricultural crops for its low investment for a quick and high net returns of nearly Rs.20,000/- to 25,000/- per Acre / Annum. Silk is also one of the best items under export to different countries.

The aim of a farmer in opting Sericulture is to earn more income with his limited land and other resources. The management/Implementing Agency's aim is to produce the targeted silk production. Hence, it is the Co-ordinated effort of the farmer and the Management to achieve their set targets. At times the Sericulturists are said to be experienced with some risks/problems in their activity at different stages. It might be partly due to his poor understanding of the Technical know-how in Mulberry garden Management for quality leaf production and silkworm rearing, thereby resulting into poor yield, leaving a wide yield gap when compared with the expected yield (control). The main risk is with the distress sale of his produce (cocoons) to a lower price.

So, before attempting in bridging the yield gap, a thorough scanning has to be made with regard to the farmers potentiality, risks involved/ experienced and on the other side implementing agency's strategy in facilitating the farmer with timely assistance/supply of viz, location specific high yielding Mulberry varieties, Financial assistance for construction of Rearing house and purchase of Rearing equipment, quality seed supply, Technical Know- How, marketing of produce with a fair price and master coverage to the crop failures through Insurance Companies.

Basing on the scanning report, the Management has to change its strategy in the line of encouraging the farmer, otherwise he will adopt his own strategy. So a thorough study has to be made about the strategic management decisions adopted by the Beneficiary to avoid risk and the implementing Agency, to cover the risk of the Farmer with necessary Technical /Financial assistance,

Keeping in view of the above risks, the Government has to make a policy of Master coverage for the Sericulture Farmers who are well prepared to take the risks of high range to produce quality silk cocoons, the raw material for the Silk Industry in order to improve their Socio-Economic Status which inturn creates an indirect employment to the other Communities involved with Silk Industry.

Introduction

Sericulture is an Agro based cottage Industry with an agricultural base, now standing as a main occupation of the farming community while absorbing the Rural Labour giving direct employment and other communities through indirect employment through Silk Reeling, Twisting, Dyeing, weaving and Printing, Sericulture Industrial equipment and inputs manufacturers. It is the best among all the Agricultural crops for its low investment for a quick and high net returns of nearly Rs.20,000/- to 25,000/- Acre/Ann. Silk is also one of the best items under Export to different countries.

The Sericulture industry is covered by two activities i.e., Mulberry cultivation and Silkworm Rearing. Mulberry being a drought tolerant plant, following the recommended package of practices, the Sericulturists are raising the gardens under irrigated condition and harvesting improved quality leaf, the only feed of silkworms. Regarding silkworm rearing, besides the main requisites like quality mulberry leaf, Hygienic rearing condition with congenial climate, Disease free silkworm eggs are most essential for a success in sericulture.

The aim of a farmer in opting Sericulture is to earn more income with his limited land and other resources. The management/Implementing Agency 's aim is to produce the targeted silk production. Hence, it is the Co-ordinated effort of the farmer and the Management to achieve their set targets. At times the Sericulturists are said to be experienced with some risks/problems in their activity at different stages. It might be partly due to his poor understanding of the Technical know- how in Mulberry garden Management for quality leaf production and silkworm rearing, thereby resulting into poor yield, leaving a wide yield gap when compared with the expected yield (control). Studies in the line of yield gap were made and revealed that a gap of 15-20 Kg/100 Dfls is existing (Veeresham et al, 1977) . Here the question is , Is it the real yield gap or not ? If Yes/No,. What are the actual reasons behind this gap ?

The farmers are not in a position to get an average yield of 45-50 Kg/100 Dfls in a continuous periods of two to three years. It is because some farmers says that they are very much potential in getting the targeted cocoon yield, but for what ? When he does not get the expected income.

Is it due to the inferior quality cocoons or what else ? The reasons varies from place to place and case to case. He says that he has got the strategy of his own and is very much serious in his profession. But the reasons behind his becoming the non-serious be studied at different levels.

So, before attempting in bridging the yield gap, a thorough scanning has to be made with regard to the farmers potentiality, risks involved/ experienced and on the other side implementing agency's strategy in facilitating the farmer with timely assistance/ supply of viz, location specific Mulberry varieties, Financial assistance for construction of Rearing house and procuring Rearing equipment, quality seed supply, Technical know- how, marketing of produce with a fair price.

Basing on the scanning report, the Management has to change its strategy in the line of encouraging the farmer, otherwise he will adopt his own strategy. So a thorough study has to be made about the strategic management decisions adopted by the Beneficiary and the implementing Agency.

Some of the Factors that changes the Positive Attitude of the Farmer:

1) Quality leaf production management:

The farmer produces poor quality Mulberry leaf due to

1) Selection/maintenance of low yielding mulberry varieties
2) Poor application of Agronomic practices like maintenance of spacing , Fertilizer Manure Usage, Disease and pest control methods.

2) Rearing Management:

The Farmer gets a very poor cocoon yield due to

1) Delayed procurement / supply of seed
2) Brushing of poor quality seed
3) Untimely brushing
4) Usage of unsuitable poor quality feed to the silkworms
5) Poor provision of controlled climatic conditions like Temperature and Humidity
6) Poor understanding of disease/pest control methods
7) Total dependence on unskilled hired labour.

3) Cost of production:

When a rearer gets a crop of cocoons with the involvement of his men, material and machinery, naturally expects a good amount for his developed product. When the cost of production comes to around Rs. 60/- per Kg of cocoons, the farmer is supposed to get atleast Rs. 100/- a Kg to have some marginal profit atleast. Otherwise, the rearer becomes non-serious for the next crop when he is met with a bitter experience of seeing a very poor monetary returns i.e. not even the cost of production.

Hence, competitive rates play a crucial role to take up the activity in a serious way because a rearer always compares the income with the returns of the other cash crops.

4) Marketing of produce :

The seriousness of the farmer always depends upon the fair marketing of his produce. Buyer/Reeler may be a leader in the market. But the sellers are not at the mercy of the Buyer. It is only with the hard work of the farmers, rest of the post cocoon activities have got a link up programme.

So, if the farmer returns from the market with a sorry note, he will have a thorough discussion with his family members, the decision making Body about continuation of the activity. It is because the activity is a Co-ordinated one under their control connected with their yearly planning of their family welfare. So, naturally, marketing has got a direct effect on the survival of the industry. For example, during 1993-94 because of the easy availability of quality smuggled silk in India, the Industry was almost on the brink of precipice with the cocoon rates steeply fallen down to Rs.40/- to 50/- per Kg. Majority of the farmers have suspended their activity and some uprooted the gardens even.

A slab rate of Rs. 100/- per Kg atleast has to be fixed taking into account its cost of production, Otherwise, the farmers are with different options of moving out of the Industry and to opt for a better cash crop having ready marketing. So, cocoon rates are related to the yield gap.

Just like a Buyer who scans market environment before any purchase/ exploitation, after all a poor farmer applies his own strategy in selecting a crop of his own choice for assured income generation.

Strategic Decision

It is always the Rearer employs in-house Technology and applies Strategic Technology of his own either in the production of quality mulberry leaves for rearing of silkworms to get better quality cocoons.

A progressive farmer with seriousness in his profession having a well managed mulberry garden with a mastery over rearing with all infrastructure facilities, becomes non-serious when he realises poor returns for his produce. This situation ultimately leads to the development of negative thinking over the activity. A farmer as such tries to excel in achieving the results/yield but, he always expects net monetary returns on higher side.

Role of Insurance Agencies in Risk Coverage Silkworm Crop Insurance :

Since the Silkworm rearing is practiced by the Marginal, Small and Big Farmers of different communities like OC, BC, SC and ST. Inspite of using disease free eggs, feeding the worms with the quality Mulberry leaf, adopting improved rearing Technology and taking of preventive measures for control of Diseases and pests, the Sericulturists are encountered by sudden incidence of diseases and pests as well as the vagaries of nature like cyclone and hailstorms etc., which ultimately results into poor monetary returns. Seeing the risky nature of the activity, an utmost necessity is to have a crop coverage with a Insurance Scheme in order to contain loss and to see that the farmer should not move away from the Sericulture Industry.

Insurance Scheme for Silkworm Crop in Andhra Pradesh :

This scheme is implemented by United India Insurance Co. Ltd., in coordination with the Department of Sericulture, Govt. of A.P. in Anantapur Chittoor, Ranga Reddy, Vizag, Prakasam, Kurnool, Nalgonda and Karimnagar District. The premium per 100 layings is as follows.

Silkworm crop	Sum insured per 100 Dfls (in Rs.)	Premium Rate (in Rs.)	Premium amount per 100 Dfls
Bivoltine (Seed & Commercial)	1800/-	8%	144.00
Multivoltine	1500/-	7%	105.00
Multi x Bivoltine (C.B.)	1600/-	7%	122.00

Role of Sericulture Department :

The Department of Sericulture, arranges the premium amount of Rs.144/- as Rearer's contribution and Rs.144/- as Departmental contribution per every 100 Dfls brushing to the Insurance agency. The Extension staff records the silkworm rearing i.e., Crop's progress and informs the Agency immediately after the failure of the crop and claims will be sent to the Insurance company within week days for settlement of the compensation as per the norms of understanding.

Details of Stage wise Compensation :

Nature of Loss	Stage	Phase	Amount of Compensation
Eggs (Dfls)	[		
Ist stage	[I	Total	20% of sum insured
II nd stage	[		
IIIrd stage	[		
IVth stage	[		
Vth stage	[II	Total	80% for Bivoltine 75% ,, Multivoltine 75% ,, Multi X Biv.(CB)
Cocoon Stage	III	Partial	Difference of amount of i.e., lessening the amount realised through sale proceeds of the failed crop from the sum insured.

Role of Institutions in Risk Management :

The Department of Sericulture has to extent its Technical assistance to the Farmers and to cut down the risk range of the Farmers with its strategic decisions at times of emergencies like disease incidence and the Insurance Agencies have to support the programme in giving a life to the Rural poor Farmers at times of need/distress due to the failure of silkworm crop and the other Developmental organisations like District Rural Development Agency, Desert Development Programme (DDP), Integrated Tribal Development Agency (ITDA), S.C. Corporation, S.T.Corpoation to extend the subsidy amounts and commercial Banks to sanction matching Loan amounts and in order to give a support to the Farmers to raise good Mulberry gardens for quality leaf production, to construct an ideal Rearing houses and to purchase the Rearing equipment.

Range of Risk

Sericulture, being with two activities i.e. production of quality leaf and rearing of silkworms. The practices being followed for mulberry cultivation is similar to other Agricultural crops for production of quality leaf suitable for silkworms. But the Risk is involved in silkworm rearing, A Farmer always prepares to face the risk though the Income is relatively higher when compared to the other crops. So both the Risk and Monetary returns are on the higher side for which the Farmer has to be prepared with a clear mind.

Conclusion for Policy Implications

Indian Silk is one of the best items of export. In order to produce the export quality to compete in the Global Silk market Strategic decisions are to be taken by the Government to give an outright support to the farmers in the line of extending Technical and Financial assistance as follows.

1. Supply of improved disease resistant high yielding Mulberry varieties for production of Qualitative leaf.
2. Timely supply of Cross Breed disease free layings
3. Introduction of loose form of eggs into the field
4. Season wise/location specific supply of seed
5. Introduction of disease resistant silkworm races
6. New Technology of Rearing and preventive measures of diseases
7. Fair marketing of cocoons
8. Extension of need based Technical know-how
9. Master coverage to the Risks experienced by the Farmers
10. Involvement of Insurance agencies/Developmental organisations for the Risk coverage/ financial assistance.

Keeping in view of the above, the Central /State Government has to make a policy of master coverage for the Sericulturists who are well prepared for the risk of high range to produce quality silk cocoons , for higher Monetary returns to improve their Socio-Economic Status which inturn creates indirect employment to the other communities involved with Silk Industry.

* * *

7

CROP INSURANCE AS A RISK REDUCTION MEASURE :

An Evaluation of Comprehensive Crop Insurance Scheme (Ccis) In Andhra Pradesh

Prof. C.Sivarami Reddy, Dr. P. Mohan Reddy, Dr. P.V.Narasaiah, Prof. K.Ramakrishnaiah,

Faculty of Commerce, Sri Venkateswara University, Tirupati.

Abstract

Crop insurance offers protection against the risks caused by fluctuations in agricultural production. It is a device whereby the losses suffered by some farmers are shared by all the farmers exposed to the same risk. Greater popularity has been attributed to the concept of 'Crop Insurance', especially with the introduction of Comprehensive Crop Insurance Scheme (CCIS) in the year 1985. Presently the scheme covers only certain principal crops like rice, wheat, millets, pulses and oilseeds. But there is need to include cash and fruit-bearing crops under the scheme so as to protect the risk-prone farmers. In Andhra Pradesh, the CCIS has been doing a commendable job in protecting the farmers against the hazards in agricultural operations. At present the scheme covers only those who are availing loans from the commercial as well as Regional Rural Banks. But there is need to enlarge the scope of this scheme so as to cover all the farmers irrespective of their land holdings. The effective implementation of CCIS in Rayalaseema, a backward and drought-prone region in Andhra Pradesh is felt indispensable to save the farming community from the clutches of drought. The scheme must be given top priority both at Central and State level plans for benefiting the farming community. It would be more beneficial if the crop insurance scheme is exposed to the entire agriculture sector - a prime sector of the economy.

Introduction

The main objective of crop insurance is to cover and provide compensation for the risks involved in agricultural production. Crop insurance is a device whereby the losses suffered by some farmers are shared by all the farmers exposed to the same risk. The idea of crop insurance was first conceived by the American Statesman Benjamin Franklin in the year 1798 who suggested crop insurance for farmers in the U.S.A. against the damage that may occur to them by storm, rain, insects, floods and the like. Crop insurance registered greater momentum in India with the introduction of Comprehensive Crop Insurance Scheme (CCIS) in 1985-86. It was expected to cover all the willing states and union territories. The General Insurance Corporation of India is implementing the scheme on behalf of the Central and State Governments. By the end of 1989-90, the benefits of crop insurance were extended to about 1.94 million farmers and covered 3.41 million hectares.

Need for Crop Insurance

Crop Insurance offers protection against the risks covered by fluctuations in the output of a crop from one crop season to another. Farmers usually know that their crops are subject to losses either due to adverse climatic conditions or pests and diseases. They invest their money, often borrowed from banks for raising a crop. If the crop fails, they cannot recover their capital on it and will be unable to repay loans due to banks. Financial support to farmers in the event of crop failure makes them credit-worthy for the next crop season. If there is a mechanism to meet losses like in other insurances, the farmers will be benefited and the hazards in agricultural production can be overcome. This mechanism of getting compensation when the crops fail is called crop insurance. There is an urgent need to make crop insurance compulsory in all states, where agriculture is predominant. Effective implementation of crop insurance schemes not only save the farmers against the natural calamities but also make them financial viable. If there is no crop insurance, the poor farmers, especially the small and marginal cannot sustain against the hazards in agricultural production. Some times, in the absence of crop insurance the uncertainties and risks in agricultural production may lead to struggle for existence to the poor farmers. In this context, the distressing suicide cases of many of the cotton growers in Andhra Pradesh may be referred on a glaring example. Hence the need for crop insurance is strongly felt to overcome risks in agricultural operations.

Introduction of Comprehensive Crop Insurance Scheme (CCIS)

In order to provide financial support to the farmers in the event of crop failure, restore the credit eligibility of farmers after crop failure for the next crop season and support and stimulate production of cereals, pulses and oil seeds, the Central Government had introduced a country-wide crop insurance scheme commencing from the kharif season of 1985 called the "Comprehensive Crop Insurance Scheme"(CCIS).

Coverage

Presently the scheme covers the crops like rice, wheat, millets as well as pulses and oil seeds, whose production is short of the domestic demand. But sugarcane, jute, tobacco, chilies, potatoes, onions and other cash crops are not under the purview of the crop insurance scheme. the fruit bearing crops like apple, litchi, grape, mango and banana are also not covered by the CCIS.

Insurance Charges

Insurance charges would be 2 per cent of the sum insured in case of paddy, jowar, maize, ragi and one per cent of sum insured in case of blackgram, greengram, horsegram, groundnut, gingelly and sunflower. The coverage in respect of crops insured in any state will be shared between the GIC and the State Government concerned in the ratio of 2 : 1.

Limit of Coverage

All the farmers availing crop loans from commercial as well as Regional Rural Banks for the crops notified in the scheme are eligible for crop insurance. The scheme is operative in defined areas for each crop notified by the Ministry of Agriculture. However sum insured is 100 per cent of loan disbursed subject to Rs.10,000/- per farmer as the maximum, limit for all insurable crop loans.

Payment to Farmers

Payment of claims to farmers under the scheme is based on the average yield per hectare of the insured crop for the defined area determined on the basis of crop-cutting experiments in the insured season. If the average yield of a particular crop falls short of the specified threshold yield, all the insured farmer's growing that crop in the defined area are deemed to have suffered a shortfall and the scheme seeks to provide coverage against such a contingency. The original indefinable limit for all the identified crops under the scheme was 80 per cent since rabi season of 1986-87 and the limit was raised to 90 per cent for rice and wheat.

Subsidy on Insurance Charges

Keeping in view the small and marginal farmers the following subsidies have been provided under the scheme.

- 50 per cent of the insurance charges shall be subsidised to be shared equally by the Central Government and the respective State Governments
- The subsidy on insurance charges in respect of small and marginal farmers would be paid to the financial institutions by the State Government in advance on estimated loaning. The Central Government would remit its share to the state in advance on the same basis.

The Operation of CCIS in Andhra Pradesh - An Evaluation

The CCIS is implemented in Andhra Pradesh since1985. The scheme has been under implementation from the past 22 seasons without any break. An attempt has been made in the following pages to analyse the season-wise, crop-wise and region-wise operation of the CCIS in Andhra Pradesh.

Season-wise Operation

The particulars of sum insured, premium collected, claims paid, farmers covered and benefited under the CCIS during the period from 1985-86 to 1995-96 are shown in Table.1.

Table -1

OPERATION OF CCIS IN ANDHRA PRADESH

Season	Sum insured	Premiium collected	Claims paid (Rs.	Claims ratio	Farmers covered	benefited
Khariff	2,779.20 (82.77)	48.50 (83.02)	170.86 (91.84)	352.29	0.69 (82.14)	0.14 (87.5)
Rabi	578.70 (17.23)	9.92 (16.98)	15.18 (8.16)	153.02	0.15 (17.86)	0.02 (12.5)
Total	3357.90 (100)	58.42 (100)	186.04 (100)	318.45	0.84 (100)	0.16 (100)

Note: Figures in the paranthesis represent percentage to total
Source: State Legal Crop Insurance Cell, General Insurance Corporation of India, Hyderabad.

It is apparent from Table-I, that heavy claims have been paid during the khariff seasons of the period from 1985-86 to 1995-96. Bulk of these claims have been paid to the paddy growers in coastal districts, more particularly, West Godavari, East Godavari and Krishna who suffered crop losses due to severe cyclones and floods. The groundnut growers in Rayalaseema region have also been benefited substantially when the groundnut crops were affected due to severe drought. The farmers covred under the scheme during the period were 0.84 crore nos. of which 0.16 crore nos. were paid compensation. The claim ratio during the period ws 318.45. On the whole it can be said that during the Khariff seasons from 1985-86 to 1995-96 the sum assured, premium collected, claims paid, the farmers coverd and benefited are much more than that of the rabi seasons. Of the total farmers covered under the scheme, majority belong to small and marginal catagories.

——Crop-wise operation

During the period from 1985-86 to 1995-96 the premium collected and claims paid in respect of paddy crop are more when compared to groundnut and other crops (See Table-2)

TABLE - 2

Crop-wise Premium Collected and Claims Paid

Sl.No	Particulars	Paddy	Groundnut	Others	Total
1	Premium Collected (Rs. in crore)	48.44 (82.92)	8.46 (14.48)	1.52 (2.60)	58.42 (100)
2	Claims paid (Rs. in crore)	132.43 (71.18)	49.20 (26.44)	4.41 (2.38)	186.04 (100)
3	Claim ratio	273.42	581.56	290.13	18.45

Note: Figures in paranthesis represent percentage to total
Source: Ibid.

During this period the claims paid on paddy crop were Rs.132.43 crore, representing 71.18 per cent of the total claims paid on all crops. The premium collected from the paddy growers has also been high when compared to other crops. The claim ratio in respect of groundnut is as much high as 581.56 per cent as against 273.42 per cent in case of other crops. The paddy growers in Coastal Andhra and groundnut growers in Rayalaseema districts have been the major beneficiaries as for as insurance claims were concerned.

—— Region-wise Operation

Table-3 demonstrates the region-wise analysis of the operation of CCIS in Andhra Pradesh.

Table - 3
Region-wise Premium Collected And Claims Effected During The Period From 1985-86 To 1995-96

Sl. No	Name of the Region	Premium Collected	Claims Effected	claim ratio
1	Coastal Andhra	34.10 (58.37)	112.31(60.37)	329.33
2	Telangana	16.95 (29.01)	35.12 (18.88)	207.20
3	Rayalaseema	7.37 (12.62)	38.61 (20.75)	523.88
	Total	58.42 (100)	186.04 (100)	318.45

Note: Figures in parentheses represent percentage to total.
Source: Ibid.

A closer look at Table-3 reveals that the claim ratio in Rayalaseema region is much more than that of other regions. During the period, the total claim ratio in the state was 318.45 per cent, whereas in Rayalaseema region it was 523.88 per cent. The premium collected in Rayalaseema region was very meagre but the claims effected was at higher level when compared to other regions. This is the token of evidence that the risk envolvement in agricultural operations in the region is on higher side. It can be concluded that the effective implementation of the CCIS is very much significant int the Rayalaseema region when compared to other regions in the state.

Complication In Implementation Of Crop Insurance Scheme

Although the benefits that accrue from crop insurance are innumerable, its implementation is highly complicated. The difficulties involved in implementing a crop insurance scheme are:

- to introduce any insurance scheme, it has to be first dicided that what premium should be charged. To decide the premium, past statistics of losses are needed. But the collection of past yield statistics at farmer level or at village level is not an easy task.
- the farm lands are small and scattered. Hence it is very difficult to assess the yields at farmer level.
- the financial capacity of a farmer below the poverty line is extremely limited. He may not be in a position to pay aprropriate premium on the policy regularly.
- majority of the farmers in the country are illiterates. They are not aware of the significance of crop insurance. The illiteracy

and ignorance may lead to initial resistance and misunderstanding of the implementation of the scheme.

- the collection of premium from farmers regularly is very difficult as their liquidity position is unpredictable.

Conclusion

In the light of the foregoing discussion the following inferences have been drawn:

- the CCIS in Andhra Pradesh has been under implementation since 1985. During this period, claims amounting to Rs.186.04 crores. This works out to a claim ratio of 318.45 per cent. In other sense for every rupee of premium received approximately Rs.36/- has been paid to the farmers as claims under the scheme. This indicates that the financial commitment on the part of the institutional agencies and the government is much higher.
- the scheme covers only crop loanees who are availing loan facilities from Co-operative Commercial Banks and Regional Rural Banks. The non-loanee farmers are not eligible for insurance coverage. It is necessary that the entire agricultural credit structure is in urgent need of protection from agricultural hazards. It can be done only by means of an appropriate crop insurance scheme suitably linked to the agricultural credit structure.
- if the crop loan alone is insured, advantage to farmer will be limited to that extent only. As such it is better if the entire crop investment is insured at least in the case of small and marginal farmers. It would certainly to a longer extent help these category of farmers from the risks involved in agricultural operations. A thinking on these lines may be initiated by Governments at State and Central levels.
- the CCIS covers only small and marginal farmers. But medium and big farmers, who generally do not avail crop loan facilities from institutional agencies, should also be covered under the crop insurance scheme.
- in the amount of sum insured seems to be illogical and it needs reconsideration at the level of policy formulation. Otherwise, the crop insurance scheme would not a relief scheme and the purpose of it cannot be served.

- the scheme should be given top priority both at the Central and State level plans so that risk-prone farmers are motivated to participate in achieving the targets of agricultural production.
- efforts should be taken to make it a most practical and viable scheme by eliminating the inherent drawbacks of the scheme.
- it is also felt necessary to ensure co-operation and co-ordination between the General Insurance Corporation, Government, Banks and other institutional agencies fro an effective implementation of CCIS.
- the efficiency of the CCI scheme in Rayalaseema has been more significant as against the other regions in the State. The effective implementation of the scheme goes a long way in benefiting the poor farmers in the backward and drought prone areas of the state.
- it is also felt necessary to extend the crop insurance facility to the entire agricultural sector.

REFERENCES

1. Agarwal, A.N. 'Indian Agriculture, Vikas Publishing House Pvt., Ltd., New Delhi, 1980.
2. Subba Rao, U., "Marketing Problems of Cotton Growers', Book Links Co-operation, Hyderabad, 1994.
3. National Bank News Review, March-May, 1993, Vol.9, No.1, NABARD, Bombay.
4. Report of the Regional Workshop on Crop Insurance Scheme, 8th November 1997, General Insurance Corporation of India, (State Level Crop Insurance Cell).

* * *

8

RURAL INSURANCE SCHEMES IN INDIA

S.P.Deshpande

Research Associate, National Insurance Academy, Pune

India has a rural based economy with 76% of its population spread in the rural areas in nearly 5.76 lac villages. About 60% of rural income is from agriculture and nearly 65% of India's population is dependent on agricultural sector for livelihood, constituting nearly 40% of the National Income.

The policies adopted by the Govt. of India, RBI, NABARD have played a major role in diversification into allied activities of agriculture for rural development thus resulting in the growth of dairying, poultry, sheep and goat rearing, piggery, horticulture, aqua culture, etc. To support this policy of diversification into allied fields of agriculture, efforts have been made by the General Insurance Industry particularly from the year 1974 to provide insurance coverage for all such schemes. Thus, today we have a large number of insurance policies available and marketed by the General Insurance industry in India. Through this paper a brief attempt is made to discuss the various schemes available in India for the rural sector.

CATTLE INSURANCE SCHEME

The major part of the rural insurance schemes transacted in India belongs to this sector. Separate policies have been devised for beneficiaries under government subsidy scheme (IRDP etc.) and non-schemes (Bank financed, Co-operative dairies, private clients).

Scope

The word "Cattle" for the purpose of this policy refers to

a) Milch cows and buffaloes
b) Calves / Heifers
c) Bullocks (Castrated Bulls) and Castrated Male Buffaloes whether indigenous, exotic or cross bred.

Structure of Cattle Insurance

a) Bank Financed
   i) Non scheme
   ii) Scheme
b) Co-operative societies / dairies
c) Private Animals

Age Group

A	Milch Cow (Indigenous cross breed exotic)	2 years (age of 1st calving to 10 years
B	Milch Buffaloes	3 years (age at 1st calving) to 12 years
C	Stud Bulls (Cow/buff)	3 years (earlier age at sexual maturity) to 8 years
D	Bullocks (castrated bulls & male buff	3 years to 12 years
E	Indigenous / CB female calves / heifers	From 4 months upto the date of 1st calving or minimum age as I(a) and I (b)

Valuation and Sum Insured

As the market value varies from animal to animal and place to place, the examining veterinary Doctor's recommendation is considered for acceptance of insurance as well as for settlement of claims. The sum insured will not exceed 100% of market value.

Insurance coverage

This policy indemnifies the insured for death of cattle due to

a) Accident (Fire, Lightning, flood, earthquakes, cyclone, etc)
b) Diseases contracted or occurring during the period of the policy

c) Surgical operations
d) Riot and strike

The policy also provides for additional cover against permanent total disability (PTD) on payment of extra premium.

Permanent Total Disability is defined as

a) For Milch animals - total incapacity to conceive or yield milk.
b) Stud bulls - Permanent and total incapacity for breeding purpose.
c) Bullocks - Permanent and total incapacity for purpose of use mentioned in the proposal form.

Indemnity

a) Non-scheme animals: The indemnity is restricted to the sum insured or market value prior to illness which ever is less.
b) Scheme animals: The indemnity will be 100% of sum insured (Agreed value policy)
c) In case of Permanent Total Disability the indemnity is limited to 75% of sum insured.

Premium Rates

a) Non scheme animal	-	4% of sum insured
b) Scheme animal	-	2.25% of sum insured
c) For exotic animal	-	6% of sum insured
d) For P.T.D. extension		
i) Non Scheme		1% additional of S.I.
ii) Scheme		0.85% additional of S.I.

Identification of Animal

The cattle are ear tagged with Aluminum / Brass or Polyurethane ear tags for the purpose of identification.

Exclusions:

a) Common Exclusions: Theft, clandestine sale, malicious or willful injury, neglect, overloading, unskillful treatment, intentional slaughter, consequential loss, transport by sea and air, war, invasion, nuclear weapons. Accidents occurring / diseases contracted prior to commencement of policy. For non scheme cattle, claim occurring due to disease contracted within 15 days of inception of risk is excluded.

b) Specific exclusions: All claims received without ear tag are not payable. Pleuro pneumonia in Lakhimpur and Sibsagar districts of Assam.

Special Feature

The policy has provision for

a) group discount for animals above 5 from a single source (not banks)
b) Long Term discount for policies issued for 3 years and above
c) Transit cover is inbuilt in case of scheme animals from place of purchase to stabling. In case of non-scheme animals if distance is above 80 Km, 1% additional premium is charged

Procedure for acceptance

a) Duly completed proposed form.
b) Veterinary Health certificate
c) Ear tagging of animals
d) Premium

It may be noted here that in case of renewal on the date of expire or before no fresh veterinary health certificate is called for.

Procedure for claims.

a) Intimation to policy issuing office
b) Claim form
c) Veterinary death certificate and post mortem report (if called for) from a registered veterinary practitioner
d) Submission of ear tag

In case of Scheme animals claims procedure is much simplified.

OTHER LIVESTOCK INSURANCE

All livestock other than cattle is categorised into this class of business. This section covers sheep, goat, horse, mule, piggery, camel, elephant and rabbit insurance. These policies are similar to cattle policies subject to specific terms/conditions applicable to that particular class of business.

As in cattle insurance, separate terms and rates apply between Scheme and Non-scheme policies. The procedure for acceptance of insurance as well as for claims is similar to cattle insurance.

POULTRY INSURANCE

The policies marketed in India under this section include Comprehensive Poultry Insurance Policy for individual farmers and policy for the Parent Stock issued to the hatcheries. The policies cover loss of birds due to accident and disease subject to specific exclusions. The policy is applicable to broilers, layers and breeding stock) (Parent Stock of hatcheries)

Type of Bird	Period of —	Premium rate
Broilers (batch wise)	1 day to 8 weeks,	1.5% of S.I.
	1 day to 6 weeks	1.20% of S.I.
Broiler (annual premium)	1 day to 8 weeks,	6% of S.I.
	1 day to 6 weeks	4.80% of S.I.
Layers	1 days to 20 weeks	3.20% of S.I.
	21 weeks to 72 weeks	3.50% of S.I.
	1 day to 72 weeks	5.50% of S.I.
Parent Stock	1 day to 72 weeks	5%

For broilers financed under scheme the rate is Rs.0.25 per bird per batch or Rs.1.00 per bird p.a. For layers under scheme the rate is Rs.0.80 net per bird.

The sum insured is the peak value of the birds as per the valuation table.

Broilers	Non scheme Rs.45	Layers non scheme Rs.75
	Scheme Rs.15	Scheme Rs.25

Hatchery birds negotiable

Indemnity

A separate valuation chart is available for layers & broiler birds. In case of hatchery birds, valuation chart is prepared after mutual discussion with the hatchery. The valuation chart is prepared on the basis of a multiplier taking into consideration the chick cost and feed cost. The indemnification is on the basis of this valuation chart which is prepared age wise.

The policy has various specific exclusions and certain diseases are covered subject to proper vaccination and preventive measures.

The policy also provides for (1) No claim discount and (2) good feature discount.

BRACKISH WATER PRAWN INSURANCE

The policy covers prawns reared in brackish water. The period of cover is from the stage of transferring of post larvae to brackish water till actual harvesting (about 4 1/2 months). The insurance covers total loss or destruction of prawn due to accident and disease subject to standard exclusions. Any loss above 80% is treated as total loss. The policy can be extended to cover bunds too by changing additional premium against fire and allied risks.

The sum insured is on input cost basis and a fortnight wise valuation table is inbuilt in the policy. This is binding both for underwriting as well as claim settlement. The perils covered are summer kill, pollution, poisoning, riot and strike, malicious act of third party, earthquake, explosion / implosion, storm, tempest, cyclone, flood, inundation, viral or parasitic diseases. The premium charged is around 4% of peak value.

INLAND FRESH WATER FISH INSURANCE

This is applicable to fry/fingerlings/fish in stock ponds/breeders in fresh water only. The period of insurance is from 3 months to 12 months. It is a comprehensive policy covering death of fish due to disease, riot, strike, malicious act of third parties, poisoning earthquake, explosion, accident etc. The premium is collected on peak value of fish @ 3.4% including flood and 3.00% for scheme proposals. The sum insured is on input cost basis and a fortnight wise valuation table is inbuilt in the policy. This is binding both for underwriting as well as claim settlement. The policy can also be extended to cover bunds against fire and allied risks.

HONEY BEE INSURANCE

This insurance covers loss or damage to Hive & Bee colony. Theft risk is covered only on payment of additional premium. Sum insured is based on the cost of Hive and Bee colony as given by State or Central Khadi and Village Industries Board / Commission. The rate of premium is 4% for loss or damage to Hive / Bee colony and 6% if theft extension is opted.

SERICULTURE INSURANCE

The present policies cover the Mulberry & Tussar variety of silkworms. The period of cover is from egg stage to cocoon stage. This policy is marketed in collaboration with Central Silk Board and Department of Sericulture of respective governments.

AGRICULTURAL PUMPSET INSURANCE

This policy covers centrifugal pumpsets both electric or diesel used for agricultural purpose. The risks covered are mechanical / electrical breakdown, fire and lightning, theft & burglary (only if in permanent enclosure) riot, strike, malicious damage, terrorism, flood cover on payment of extra premium of 2%. The sum insured is 100% of market value and the premium is as per the H.P. capacity.

Indemnity

Limit of liability is cost of repair or damage. Maximum liability for rewinding charges are pre-decided in the policy.

The scheme has provisions for

a) No claim discount; b) Long term discount; c) Group discount

Submersible pumpsets can be covered under this policy for which the premium, sum insured, rewinding charges are pre-decided horsepower wise.

ANIMAL DRIVEN CART

This is a comprehensive policy covering the cart, the animal, the cart driver and third party liability (both TPPI and TPPD). The premium is 1.40% of sum insured per annum. The Sum Insured should include value of cart and animal. The animal however, is covered against accidental death only. If death due to disease is to be covered separate livestock policy is to be taken.

JANATA / GRAMIN PERSONAL ACCIDENT INSURANCE

These are simple Personal Accident Insurance Policies devised to cater to needs of common man. Gramin policy is specifically meant for rural masses. Policy covers death/permanent and partial disability (restricted to loss of limbs/eyes). Individuals in the age group of 5 to 80 years are covered. The sum insured is Rs.25,000/- and Rs.10,000/- for Janata and Gramin Policies, the premium being Rs.12.50 and Rs.5.00 respectively. Medical examination prior to taking the policy is not required. Insured can choose a sum insured upto a limit of Rs.10 lacs which should be commensurate with his income. The policy can be issued on long term basis at a stretch for a period upto 15 years. The premium for long term basis is worked taking into consideration long term discount. Group discount upto a maximum of 60% is available.

HORTICULTURE / PLANTATION INSURANCE

This policy covers citrus fruits, Pomegranates, Chikoo, banana, grapes, sugar cane, plantations such as Rubber, Eucalyptus, Poplar, Teakwood, oil palm, etc.

Coverage: The policy covers losses due to fire including forest fire and bush fires, lightning, storm, hailstorm, cyclone, typhoon, tempest, Hurricane, Tornado, flood and inundation, terrorist act, riot, strike, malicious damage. Additional / optional cover such as loss due to unseasonable rains, frost can be made available depending upon crop.

Period: The period of policy is crop duration or 12 months, whichever is shorter.

Premium: The basic rate for horticulture crop is 5% and that for plantation is 1.25%. This varies as per the crops involved and areas involved.

Sum insured: is the cost of cultivation or the input cost i.e., cost of raising/development of insured trees. The policy is for a fixed sum insured which is given separately under each crop.

Indemnity: The policy is a pre determined value policy. For calculating the amount of indemnity sliding scale of input is applied for each type of crop. The policy is subject to exclusions, franchise and excess.

Gober Gas Insurance: The policy covers loss or damage to the entire plant which includes the digester, gas holder and cost of construction against fire and applied perils. The premium is Rs.1/- per mille.

LIFT IRRIGATION INSURANCE

The policy provides indemnity against damages caused to lift irrigation system. This covers intake well, delivery chamber, jackwell, pump house, water storage tank, pipelines, cables, switches, gears as well as electric motor ranging from 3 H.P. to 200 H.P.

Risk covered: Fire, riot, strike, malicious damage, flood, earthquake, landslide, bursting of pipelines, accidental damage to machinery and pipelines, mechanical and electrical breakdown etc.

Sum insured: Will be equal to the cost of replacement of insured property by new property of the same kind and capacity. It should include freight, taxes and erection cost.

The premium rate is 1% of S.I. and the policy is governed by standard exclusions.

Policies are also available to cover zoo and circus animals, dogs, ducks, on similar lines to that of cattle and livestock policies.

Similarly, package policies are available wherein different sections of policy cater to the needs of farmers as well as tribals under a single policy.

Though the different covers have been discussed in brief, the same should give an idea of insurance covers available for the rural sector.

Many of these covers are still in the experimental stage. But with increase in insurance awareness on the basis of experience and feed back from insuring public, the existing covers can be improved and new covers can be innovated to meet the requirement of the rural sector.

* * *

9

CORPORATE RISK MANAGEMENT

S.R. Warrier, Ramaprasada Rao, Machiraju,

The New India Assurance Co. Ltd., Mumbai

In India Risk Management is yet to establish as an important item on the corporate agenda. The risk management philosophy seldom extends beyond the realms of insurance. In the West it has emerged from the shadows of insurance to claim recognition as a field of modern corporate management. This paper casts a glance at the risk management process and makes an attempt to understand the role of risk management in the business and social environment.

Risk Management - A social need

Risks enter into all aspects of our life. But its impact on the individuals and the society are not always fully understood. With the advancement of technology, risks have grown more complex, calling for more professional management. The response to risks varies widely. It is fascinating to observe the range of human response to risks which has the irresistible risk takers like gamblers at one end and those who rarely venture out of the armchair at the other. But the majority would go for the 'middle path. There is no 'one correct behavioural rsponse' to risky situations. Nevertheless, it should not be devoid of sensibility and common sense.

Events at Bhopal, Chernobyl and Flixborough have told us that the society has to bear heavy volts costs should be a catastrophe strike Fortunately such events are relatively infrequent. The low intensity -

high frequency. Risks also deserve equal attention, for, their impact on the society is considerable. The role of risk management its important here because these risks are more predictable and manageable.

Measuring the impact of risks on the society is a difficult task. While doing so, more often than not, the indirect effects go unrecognised. Statistics would tell us how much the country lost by the peril of fire. But it would not reflect the indirect loses suffered - the loss of profits, increased cost of working, loss of market and much more. The total effect would be many times the direct loss. The existence of a risk would cost the society the expenses for handling it and the cost imposed by the risk in addition to the cost of loss.

To effectively manage them. The development of professional risk management has helped to effectively manage The natural consequences of the high cost of risks on the society is the legal, social and morel pressure them. The development of professional risk management has helped to effectively respond to such pressures.

What is risk Management?

The popular perception of risk management is often that of insurance management. Insurance has been traditionally ' the answer' to risk. The transfer of risk to an insurance company is the simplest way of takcling risks. But it may not necessarily be the only possible option available. The effectiveness of insurance as an easy tool to transfer risks can not be slighted. Nor should the ease of operation be allowed to eclipse the other options like reduction and retention.

Risk management emerged from the shadows of insurance and has been recognized as a district field n modern management It is all about in modern management. It is all about identifying , analysing the controlling risks.

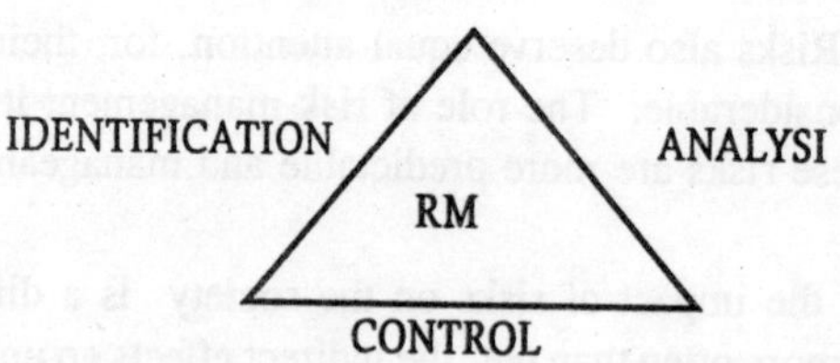

The Risk Management Process

The process of risk management is a continuous one requiring constant monitoring and periodic revision based on the changes in social political or legal environment.

Risk Identification

Any factor which would be an impediment on the path of the enterprise to acheve its objectives could be identified as a risk.

All enterprises are exposed to a spectrum of risks, It is always easier to identify the direct "material damage causing" risks. On e could always be guided by the available insurance covers in such cases. But the other risks are hard to identify. In-depth knowledge of the obbjectives and functioning of the enterprise as well as a good understanding of the trends of external factors are essential to effectively identify all the risks. It is easier said than done. Many a time the simplest risk escapes the eye. It is elementary that temporary pipe fittings could be weak points. Yet it failed to register itself as a potential risk at Flixborough and the result was devasting.

There are a host of methods available for risk identifiation. Physical inspection is a simple way. But it could be ineffective in the absence of a structured inspection system. However, this is very useful for preliminary risk identification. Check list is another simple but effective option if properly monitored. Flow charts, organisational charts and fault tree analysis are methods requiring more expertise. There are highly specialised and technical methods like Hazard indices and Hazop studies for areas like chemical industries.

Risk Analysis

The second phase of the risk management process is the analysis of risk identified in the first phase. Analysis is a Cause-Effect study of the risk.

Risk analysis would tell us the exact impact of the loss in financial terms. This is predominantly a mathematical exercise based on various statistical and probability techniques. Data base of the actual and "near miss" losses form the base for the analysis.

Risk Control

The third element of the risk management triad is control which refers to the activity of economically controlling the risk.

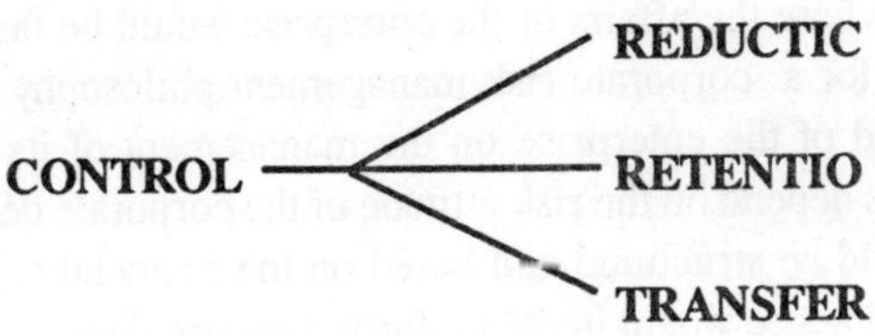

The risk control methods would fall into three categories as indicated above.

Reduction is all about having an effective loss control plan - both pre-loss and post-loss.

Retention is a tool for cost reduction by bearing a part of the risk. The estimation of retention on different types of risk would vary. The skills of the risk manager and the 'risk taking attitude' of the enterprise are the crucial factors influencing retention decisions.

Transfer is less complicated than the other methods and has the added the advantage of cost being known in advance. The most common transfer technique is insurance.

Risk Management Philosophy

Each human being has an innate attitude towards risks. It is an integral part of one's character. This attitude can be observed in the way an individual responds to a risky situation. Two people reaching a bus stop at the same time may see a bus just picking up speed. One ignores the risks of injury and becomes a 'flying bus catcher' whereas the other prefers to wait for the next bus. He is prepared to sacrifice the time lost in waiting for the arrival of the next bus in order to avoid the risk of injury. We can see two distinctly different behavioural patterns in this incident - One is a risk seeker and the other a risk avoider. This behaviour is reflected in other actions as well.

A corporate entity responds to risks based on the risk taking attitude of the decision makers. The decision making team may change from time to time changing their collective response also. This could lead to a chaotic situation where the affairs of the enterprise would be far from smooth. The need for a corporate risk management philosophy arises here. It is the stand of the enterprise on the management of its risks. The philosophy does depend on the risk attitude of the corporate decision makers. But it would be structured and based on the financial capacity of the enterprise and hence would invite uniform response from different individuals though their attitudes are not uniform.

The risk management philosophy is usually documented as 'Risk Management Statement' or as "Risk Management Policy'. Documentation citing the objectives and reasons for adopting the policy is absolutely essential to reduce the impact of individual attitude to a minimum. Usually the risk management statement would talk about:

* Objectives
* Potential risk exposures
* Suggested techniques of risk identification
* Evaluation/analysis of risks
* Legal requirements
* Levels of risk retention
* Insurance coverage
* Pre and Post-loss reduction methods
* Loss reporting procedures

A well defined risk management philosophy would ensure that response to risk situations would be uniform and well tuned. It also helps to create more awareness resulting in better preparedness.

Risk Management Department

Risk Management dept. is not very common in Indian corporate houses. The risk management functions are spread over various departments - insurance with finance dept., loss control with safety dept. etc. In effective functioning, it is essential that there is a corporate risk management dept. which would derive its functions mainly from the risk management policy.

Positioning of the dept. is very important. Risk management being a multidisciplinary function. It requires access to the information pertaining to all departments to implement its policy. Ideally risk management dept. should be placed at the corporate management level, reporting to the top management. This would give the risk manager the necessary momentum to make an impact on the operating managers.

Risk Management dept. would be more comfortable with a finance executive than operations executives. This is due to the inherent financial angle. The reports generated by the risk management dept. would be cost-benefit analysis, retention decision, insurance options etc., which appeal more to the finance executives.

In majority of the cases in developed countries Risk Management is in the corporate jurisdiction and operates either with the concurrence or under the supervision of the board. The day to day functions are usually decentralised. Many companies have a director holding functional responsibility of Risk Management. The primary reason for this is the incredible damage which Risk Management functions can cause to the bottom line should proper care be lacking.

Risk Manager

The implementation of Risk Management policies is the responsibility of the risk manager who heads the Risk Management dept. He is expected to foresee the losses, circumscribe or eliminate them or arrange for protection in the most economical way. He is essentially a manager and should possess all the necessary attributes and qualities of one. In additiion he should have a good base in insurance and the skills to identify, evaluate and control risks as well.

The emerging profile of a risk manager is that of a graduate with a masters in business administration or professional qualifications in insurance or risk management. The risk manager plays a key role in formulating the risk management policy and in effectively implementing it. The RM dept. is usually a much smaller dept., compared to others has less staffing.

The inter personal skill of the risk manager is viatal as his role requires constant liaisoning with other managers. The data base or the Risk Management dept. is about on the inputs from operations. A good understanding of the functions supported by an empathetic thinking would be the strength of a risk manager.

Good communication skills of the risk manager can help to create more risk awareness and would motivate employees to respond positively to the suggestions of the Risk Management dept.

Computerisation

The data base of the 'Risk Management dept. should be sufficient and suitably updated for assisting the corporate management dept. to develop its strategies ad to implement them systematically.

The "Potential Loss" information is the most vital data available with a riks manager, This would include the loss incidents, cost of loss, insurance recoveery etc. "Near misses" also should be properly recorded. In a large enterprise, computerisation is essential for proper storage of data, instant recalling and developing statistics and projections.

Easy access to loss information and insurance data with flexibility with to sort and classify it according to the need would highly enhance the objectivity in decision making.

Growing concerns of risk managers

The primary concern of risk managers has always been management of material damage marks, Subsequently 'worker safety' gained importance.

In the last decade of this millennium, the focus has shifted to the impact of the risks on society. The risk managers are growing more concerned about the suffering of the society than that of the enterprise. This transition has taken place owing to powerful social organisations which can build pressure by raising public opinion and stringent laws. The types of risk causing concern can change rapidly; for instance - environmental risks have risen to the top of the list in a short time. Exxon Valdez and the bruning oil wells in Kuwait have amply demonstrated that environmental risks need top priority.

Health care costs and workers' compensations form another area of concern. Social and legislative pressures act in these cases also and the risk managers need to watch such risks carefully.

The latest concern of risk managers is the complications which are expected to be caused by the 'Millennium bug'. The computer programmes, unless properly rewritten, would execute wrong commands or may simply crash taking down a host of operations with it. Y2K problem is a real challenge to 1st January, 2000. Risk identification itself is a massive task, for which the available time is too short.

CONCLUSION

All business enterprises operate in a dynamic risk environment. These risks need systematic and professional management. Risk manager is the centre of this branch of corporate management. He is a man with a purpose, assisted by a Risk Management dept. and guided by a corporate risk philosophy, striving toward efficient management of risks. He balances the needs of the society with the interests of the enterprise. He is yet to become a common feature in Indian corporate circles. But the wait is unlikely to be long.

10

PRODUCTIVITY LINKED INSURANCE

Dr. V. Reddappa Reddy

Associate Professor, Dept. of Rural Development, S.K.University, Anantapur. A.P.

INTRODUCTION

The insurance and agriculture hardly go together. Insurance basically aim at covering the risk that arise due to unforeseen accidents and incidents, which are normally uncommon. Whereas severe bumps and accidents are very common in agriculture. An agriculturist has to undergo the impact of these bumps and accidents. The effect of all these was so severe that, many farmers have to pay the price with self annihilation. It is called annihilation rather than suicide, because suicide is attempted, mostly based on emotions. This self annihilation seems to be the just result of the economic burden. This burden carry the tags of un-repayable levels of loans, non-compromising loan recovery methods of money lenders and business people, unresponsive Government and un-resolvable economic problems of the families.

This self annihilations are so many that, even the World Bank has to send a Team to analyse the problem. The has become an election issue too in recent elections. Government too had to respond with the compensation (or is it a reward) of one lakh each to the families of such annihilated.

The insurance agencies, banks and government departments which forgot the concept of crop- insurance have woken up and realised their role and are arguing the case of insurance after the self death sentences were pronounced and executed by many. In fact, when bank managers were contacted to collect information on the rates of crop insurance premiums and claims, it was told that, the crop insurance papers are dumped along with many old and unwanted circulars. This is an indication of the importance of crop insurance.

The crop insurance practice was in vogue in India since long. But the insurance cover, premiums collected and insurance payments are pathetically low to help any farmer to fill his losses and get back to the routine of crop raising. The insurance premiums are also so poor that, it is hardly possible to pay any amount of significance by the insuring agency to the farmer at the times of loss. This meagre rates of premiums and meagre rates of claims are so insignificant that, farmers many a time fail to meet their to and pro charges, necessary for collecting the claims. This name sake crop insurance is going to serve no purpose to any farmer. Few unpaid or half paid premiums and unclaimed policies are only to make the insurance agencies marginally rich. In all, it means, there is a need for collecting the reasonable premiums and settle the insurance claims of monetary significance. This calls for a reassessment of insurance premiums and insurance claims.

The rates of premiums and insurance claims are to be fixed based on the crop productivity levels. The fixation of rates of premiums and payment of claims need a thorough study of productivity levels which differ substantially from crop to crop, season to season, irrigated to dry crops and size to size farmers. More over, the productivity also do not deviate in the same rate, even for a similar natural calamity for example, with the farmers of different sizes and cultural practices. The present paper aims to discuss the differences in the productivity and rates of variations in productivity levels. Present paper tries to understand the differences in the productivity levels, if any, between seasons, size farmers, cultural practices and crops.

SAMPLE AND METHODOLOGY

To understand the variations in crop productivity an empirical study was conducted. A sample of 180 farmers were selected on sample basis drawn from six villages. The sample households belong to various socio-economic strata. The sample also covers the farmers who depend on irrigation and as well as dry cropping. The survey was conducted almost a decade ago. Though the survey was conducted long back the results are not going to be affected. Since the survey was conducted with other issues in focus, the data on all the crops are not available. The results of only two crops are considered in the analysis. The variations in productivity are examined in relation to season and size of holdings. This analysis is confined to rice and groundnut only. For this purpose, the productivity levels of rice and groundnut of all the sample households are computed by taking size of the holdings as a criteria. To understand the rate of deviations, the productivity levels of different sizes of holdings, the results of two consecutive years are considered i.e. current year (the year of survey) and previous year.

VARIATIONS IN RICE PRODUCTIVITY

Table I shows the season-wise yields of rice and their variations in relation to different size holdings. It can be seen that in both the years, the productivity levels of rice are higher for households whose holdings are between 2.0 to 5.0 hectares as compared to households cultivating more than 5.0 hectares. The yield levels of the smaller holdings are found to be low. For example, yield levels of 2.0 to 5.0 hectares size of holdings are higher by 13.2 per cent as compared to 1.0 hectare size of holdings during the current year.

It can further be seen that, the fluctuations are also of lower degree for households who have holdings between 2.0 to 5.0 hectares compared to other sizes of holdings during kharif season. But during Rabi season the fluctuations are of lower degree irrespective of size of holdings.

VARIATIONS IN GROUNDNUT PRODUCTIVITY

The variations in groundnut productivity in relation to size of holdings are shown in Table II. As in the case of rice, productivity of groundnut too was higher in the holdings between 2.0 to 5.0 hectares. For example, the groundnut productivity of 2.0 to 5.0 hectares size of holdings was more by 16.0 per cent as compared to the size of holdings of below 1.0 hectare. Further, the fluctuations in productivity of groundnut are lower in this category of holdings compared to either small or big holdings.

CONCLUSION

There is a need for assessing the differences in the crop productivity rates and rates of fluctuations of crop productivity for various sizes of holdings. The premiums are to be collected based on these productivity levels of the seasons, crops, size of holdings etc. and claims must also be settled accordingly. Unless significant premiums are collected, it may not be possible to pay claims of any monetary significance.

Table 1

Variations In Rice Productivity : Size Of Land Holding-wise

(Productivity in Kgs per hectare)

Size	Kharif Season			Rabi Season		
Holding (in hectares)	Current Year	Previous Year	Percentage Variation	Current Year	Previous Year	Percentage Variation
Below 1.0	1,501	1,591	+2.1	1,652	1,648	–0.2
1.0 to 2.0	1,500	1,597	+6.51	1,591	1,620	+1.8
2.0 to 3.0	1,699	1,701	+0.1	1,728	1,750	+1.3
3.0 to 5.0	1,677	1,698	+1.2	1,100	1,701	–1.5
5.0 to 10.0	1,590	1,491	–4.9	1,655	1,690	+2.1
10.0 and above	1,520	1,580	+3.9	1,620	1,595	–1.5

Note: In classifying the size of holdings, both dry and irrigated land is taken and 2 1/2 hectares of dry is equated to one hectare of irrigated and in terms of irrigated land only, size of holdings is fixed and households are accordingly classified.

TABLE 2

Variations In Groundnut Productivity : Land Holding-wise

(Productivity in Kgs per hectare)

Size of Holdings (in hectares)	Previous Year	Current Year	Variations in Percentage
Below 1.0	899	870	–3.3
1.0 to 2.0	898	929	+3.5
2.0 to 3.0	1,021	1,009	–1.2
3.0 to 5.0	1,007	997	–1.0
5.0 to 10.0	940	969	+3.1
10.0 and Above	901	890	–1.2

11

INSURANCE AS A RISK MANAGEMENT TOOL

P.Narayana Reddy

Head of the Department,School of Management Studies, C.B.I.T.,Gandipet, Hyderabad.

INTRODUCTION

In the broader context of life and the manner of its living risk is seen as a part of the basic exercise of survival. Risk is basically any type of loss. If risk implies something unwanted or to be avoided, risk is then associated with consequences that involve losses to risk taker.

Rowe defines "Risk" as the potential for realisation of unwanted negative consequences of an event and "risk aversion" as the action taken to control risk.

Willet defines "risk" as the objectified uncertainty regarding the occurrence of an undesirable event. Denvenbury further stressed this negative aspect of defining risk as the uncertainty of loss. Most risks cause loss of life and great damage. Risk is also a future event which results from actions taken now. If better risk management has been there major catastrophes would have been averted (Tale 1). Risks may be a part of life developmental process, risk must be maintained at a minimum level otherwise uncontrollable risks may have disastrous consequences.

Managing Risks

Academically there are risk important strategic elements of risk management shown in the following diagram. Management of risk in the business environment a historical review will shown that manages tended to deal with the phenomenon of risk as a matter of insurance and risks life assessed only in terms of possible cost. Insurance premiums are a form of loss prevention or self protection.

Table 1

Year	Event	Cause	Effects
1980	The north sea oil platform Alexander Keilland collapsed	One leg of the rig snapped in heavy seas	123 crewmen died.
1983	South Korean airplane shot down over kamchatka peninsula	Soviet Union fighter pilots shot the plane down	269 passengers including 61 Americans died.
1984	Toxic gas released at the Union Carbide Plant in Bhopal, India	Burst Valve	3,000-10,000 people died
1984	Famine in Ethiopia	Climatic change, over population, environmental destruction, civil war and political upheaval	Thousands of people died. Bob Geldorf raised 120 million pounds for famine relief
1985	Fire swept Bradford football stadium	Match or cigarette dropped on to rubbish underneath the stadium	56 people died
1986	Challenger space shuttle exploded on take off	Malfunctioning rocket seal	The three crew members died
1986	Nuclear reactor at Chernobyl exploded	Power surge caused the nuclear rods to disintegrate causing overheating and explosion	2,50,000 people may have died, plus damage to the agriculture and environment

{Cont.}.....

1986	Series of explosions on the Piper Alpha oil rig	Excessive flare from gas safety release led to fire	167 crew members died
1987	Herald of Free Enterprise ferry sank in zeebrugge harbor	Bow doors left open	193 people died
1988	Pan Am flight exploded over lockerbie	Terrorist bomb	259 passengers and crew died
1988	Iranian aeroplane shot down during the Iran-Iraq conflict	Us destroyer Vincennes mistook the airliner for a fighter plane	299 passengers died
1989	Hillsborough stadium disaster, Sheffield	Fans pushed into the stadium, where the match had started while many fans were outside	95 people died
1990	Exxon Valdez ship wrecked off Alaskan coast	Navigation error	2 million gallons of oil covered the coast 2000 sea birds and 300 others died
1991	Iraqis set fire to Kuwait's oil wells	Desire for economic sabotage at the end of the Gulf War	Environmental Catastrophe
1994	Estonia Ferry sank in the Baltic	Faulty Bow doors	900 people died

The Primary purpose of insurance is to cover the risk of uncertain losses by providing individuals and organizations with financial protection through the collection of a payment (premium). As this requires the spreading of risks as widely as possible, there is a clear international dimension to the insurance industry.

Insurance constitutes an important service segment accentuating economic development by resource mobilization, its utilization and to resource creation. It works on the principle of pooling risks and charging each customer a premium based only on the average risk of the pool. Insurance promises a compensation of monetary loss sustained by a particular person due to the damage or destruction of a particular piece of property owned by him, provided it happens due to certain causes.

Very large risks may also be covered through joint participation by a no. of companies where a major disaster could de stabilize or destroy a single insurer. The underlying principle of non-life insurance is the mutualisation of risks transferred by a wide range of insurance persons or institutions. Due to increasingly large industrial accidents, natural catastrophes, new types of pollution and liability claims, several interpretations of product and public liability laws, large claims arising from major risks such as chemical plants, oil platforms, world wide spending on insurance is rising.

Insurance business in India is in two forms. viz. life insurance and non-life insurance. Life insurance in its modern form came to India from English in 1818 with the establishment of oriental life insurance company. The 1st Indian Insurance company "Bombay mutual life Assurance Society" established in 1870. The Life Insurance Corporation Act 1912 was the 1st legislation to regulate Insurance business. However, the 1st comprehensive legislation, to govern not only life but also non-life insurance, came into existence in 1938 with the Insurance Act, 1938. The Life Insurance Corporation was established in the year 1956 by nationalizing the existing Insurance Businesses. The LIC is a financial intermediary which mobilizes people's savings and invests large amounts of premiums.

To take care of the non-life insurance business, Government of India nationalized the existing 107 companies and formed General Insurance Company in the year 1972 (with four subsidiary companies viz., a) National Insurance Company Ltd., b) New Indian Assurance Co. Ltd., c) Oriental Fire and General Insurance Co. Ltd., and d) United India Insurance Co. Ltd. The GIC does not collect savings, yet raise funds in the form of premiums.

COVERAGE OF INDIAN INSURANCE

Premium income from Indian Insurance Companies has increased 16 fold from Rs.184 crores to Rs.3100 crores in 1993-94. This represents an average compound growth of 17.1% per annum. The real growth excluding the impact of inflation would work around 8.5% per annum. LIC has 5 lakh agents and 18000 development offices. The aggregate premium generation in the GIC has growth from a paltry Rs.220 crores in 72-73 to Rs.6370 crores in 1995-96 incredible 29 fold increase. GIC has 2 lakh agents and 4000 development offices. Presently GIC is offering 160 policies with Rs.7,000 crores as premiums.

GIC - PERFORMANCE AT A GLANCE

	1972-73	1990-91	1995-96
Premium	220	38	6370
Profit	38	480	830
Capital of Free Reserve	98	1790	4275

Source: The Journal of Insurance of India. No.XXI, July-Dec.1996.

As per the world Bank reports Indian industry ranks 51 st in the world with annual growth rate of 13.2% with a total premium of 4652 million dollars which in turn consists of 1459 million dollars non-life premium and 3193 life premium. In other words the Life Insurance is more than 65% and non-life insurance is mere 30%. This obviously indicates that there are tremendous opportunities in non-life insurance field.

Despite the considerable growth in insurance industry in the country the spread of insurance in the country is very limited. The LIC covers insurable population of 320 million out of total population of 900 million amounting to little more than 22%. Obviously, this is very poor rate of coverage of eligible insurable lives in our country. The penetrating rate of insurance to GDP is only 1.8 per cent in India where as it is 12.6% in Japan, 11.6% in South Korea, 6.61% in New Zealand and 5.1% in Taiwan.

Problems with the existing Insurance Sector

Despite the significant growth and expansion of Insurance sector, this sector has various deficiencies. These are

1. There is a considerable gap between the expectations and the actual performance of the companies in delivering the service.
2. Insurance companies failed to come out with innovative service range despite having decades of experience.
3. Companies failed to adapt themselves to the changing market dynamics while transacting with the customers. A steep rise in motor insurance premium rates ranging from Rs.215 to Rs.759 with effect from 1st April 1997 just to overcome the losses substantiates the argument given above.
4. Companies failed to create insurance awareness among the people. That is why insurance penetration rate in the society is just 1.8% of the GDP. It is to be recalled here that the Indian insurers respond only when there is a demand. This is in contrast to the situation abroad where insurers themselves keep looking out for opportunities.
5. Insurance companies failed to simplify the procedures and practices in pre-and post acceptance of services.

LIBERALISATION AND CHALLENGES BEFORE INSURANCE INDUSTRY

Liberalisation in insurance sector would involve dumping of service by international giants equipped with new product, new idea, up-to-date technologies, strong currencies and cost effective methods of marketing. One of the important issues discussed at the Uruguay round of talks was service sector, where Insurance service sector was dominant. The Uruguay round of negotiations have highlighted the following as essential features.

*a) Transparency; b) market access; c) establishment; d) cross border provision of service; e) prudential regulations; f) most favoured nation treatment; g) national treatment, increasing; h) increasing participation of developing countries

REFORMS IN INSURANCE SECTOR

The Government of India is strongly inclined towards opening up of the insurance sector particularly general insurance. The Malhotra Committee appointed by the Government has made far reaching recommendations in 1994. Some of the recommendations are:

1. Allow private parties in life and general insurance sectors.
2. No single company be allowed to do business both in life and general insurance simultaneously.
3. Foreign insurance companies should be allowed in, by way of joint ventures.
4. The new entrants should bring in minimum capital of Rs.100 crores.
5. The new entrant must satisfy regulatory authority about its credentials and competence.
6. Set up an insurance regulatory authority to regulate the insurance industry.
7. New entrants in life insurance should be encouraged to transact a minimum business in rural areas.
8. Introduction of brokers for better professionalisation and improved customer services.

THE EMERGING SCENARIO

The following scenario may be emerging for the formation of strategies of the insurance industry.

1. Emerging integration of Indian Capital Market with global system.
2. End of present monopoly and emergence of fierce competition in the market place.
3. A change in the cost accounting and gradual move towards strategic costs management.
4. Emerging of competing products with dynamic features.
5. A growing competition among institutions for securities investment leading to sophistication in investment marketing.
6. Advent of more advanced technology - cyber space servicing, more aggressive and quantitative investment decisions with the aid of standard research.

7. Emergence of dynamic managerial culture removing many hierarchical bureaucracy in market-oriented, profit driven system with high degree of performance accountability.
8. An extra conscious and more demanding consumer class to satisfy.
9. Environment of prudential re-regulation with increased institutional accountability.

Strategy for the future

There are strong reasons for the eminent growth of Insurance industry in the country. The affluence of the people is increasing and so are their needs like safety and security, not only for the policy holder life but also for their family members. Similarly people doing business are serious to protect the property from the risk. Risk in even more in the liberalization due to innovative non-traditional emergence of industries. This trend is also seen in the agriculture, where the farmer started changing the cropping pattern to commercial crops. Therefore the insurance Companies have to re-assess their role in offering service by taking various steps. The following may be some of the positive steps.

1. The insurance companies have to develop innovative product range based on the market needs. The new product range must be able to deliver extra benefit to the customers. In the recent past, Insurance companies have developed new products like Industrial All Risk Policy, Health Insurance, Product liability Insurance etc.,. These products are certainly innovative products.
2. Companies have to concentrate on uncovered areas like semi-urban and rural areas as well as non-salaried class of people as potential market segments.
3. Companies have to take special efforts in creating awareness about the insurance schemes. Using local media in creating awareness is essential to attract people into their fold along with high bonus rates by efficient portfolio management of Insurance companies.
4. There are urgent need to eliminates procedures and formalities where common man can follow them easily.
5. Companies have to develop their employees (inefficiency) with last development. They must be able to create confidence and trust among the policy holders and to pay individualized services. Special effort has to be put in to inject professionalism among the agents.
6. Companies have to price the product based n the cost and market conditions rather than non-market elements.

7. Steps have to be taken to activate the loss prevention association to provide basic risk management services as well as loss prevention mechanism measures to reduce the insurance claims. As it is in the Indian environment there is a dearth of consultancy services in the risk management field.
8. 100% claims must be settled on the due day of maturity and special efforts must be put in to settle the death claims at the possible minimum time to reduce the trauma to the least possible level.

REFERENCES

1. Rowe W.D. Anatomy of risk, Wiley, 1977, New York.
2. Willett A H. The economic theory of risk and insurance, Irwin, 1951, Homewood.
3. Kit Sad grove: The complete guide to Business Risk Management, Gower, 1988.
4. Bob Ritchie and David Marshall : Business Risk Management, Chapman & Hall, 1993, London.
5. S.V.Mony : General Insurance as a financial service in the context of liberalization : The A.D.Shroff Memorial Trust, Piramal Mansion, 1992, Mumbai.
6. R.N.Malhotra : Liberalization India's Insurance Industry : The A.D.Shroff Memorial Trust, Mumbai, 1995.
7. Sadhak H. Life Insurance in India : Vision 2000 : Yogakshem - July 1997.
8. A new era in Insurance Coverage, Business World, 22nd June 1997.

* * *

12

COVERAGE OF LOSS OF PROFITS THROUGH INDUSTRIAL INSURANCE

A.G.Ravindranath Reddy

Practicing Company Secretary, Hyderabad

The storming surge of a progressive generation of those days dash feeble fencing, and gathering new momentum at each stride changed for itself its progressive course, discovering on its onward rush new beauties and tapping new resources from the secret chambers of Nature's inexhaustible treasure house, congratulating itself at every new invention and discovery. Science has thus grown in power and might, winning for man a thousand comforts which our forefathers would not have even dreamt of. The progress of science and the victory of materialism are, no doubt, greater achievements for man.

- *Swamy Chinmayananda*

INTRODUCTION

The advent of coverage of Loss of Profits (LOP) also called as 'Consequential Loss Insurance', help the most industrialists to enjoy themselves even after worst disastrous events. All of us know that 'Fire Insurance' covers the value of properties viz., Building, Plant & Machinery and its accessories, Stocks both raw materials and Closing stocks. But during the unfateful event of fire accident, production usually comes to a grinding halt for sometime depending on the gravity of the accident. When production is not there, one can imagine the trauma of management apart from financial burdens like interest, salaries electricity etc. Apart from the value of the property destroyed as a result of fire, the management will also loose profits and overheads which have not been earned. Unless, therefore, the management seeks protection under separate 'Consequential Loss (Fire) Insurance' or 'Loss of Profits Insurance', but management remain uncovered for consequential losses following occurrence of fire accident. Prudence therefore, demands that for a full protection, Insurance should be effected both against the material damage and Consequential Loss.

LOP Insurance is concerned with loss of earning power, consequent upon damage or destruction to the capital assets or stocks whereby insured is in a position to cover his total financial losses placing him as far as possible, in the same financial position as he held before occurrence of fire accident.

ASSESSMENT OF LOSS OF PROFITS

Both for insured and insurance Company, assessment of expenditure of damage is much easier, in case of assessment of loss of capital assets when damaged by fire. Since the loss is intangible in LOP Policy, the assessment of the sum is very complicated and time consuming. A person who is in the relevant field for a long time and sound knowledge of working, can assess the loss of profits little bit easily by comparing the turnover in the months following the damages with that in the corresponding period during the previous year, subject to the proper adjustments for special circumstances and trends of business. This method can be called Assessment of loss by 'Turnover Basis'. Under this method every Hundred rupees of Turnover or every unit of production earns its due proportion of Gross Profits. This Turnover consists of working expenses, overhead expenses and net profits. Because of damage by fire, the turnover will definitely fall which means variable expenses to the large extents will also proportionately be reduced and no loss will be sustained by the Insured under this head. However, the standing/fixed charges will not proportionately come down as these do not vary directly with turnover, which will result in reduction of net profit. At the same time there will be concurrent loss of net profit due to there being smaller volumes of turnover on which it can be earned. During the period of interruption caused by fire, the compensation is to be paid for standing/

fixed charges and concurrent loss of net profit by which business will be restored to the extent necessary. LOP Policy need not concern for loss of production costs, for example, if gross profit rate of 30% is applied the shortage in turnover can be ascertained accordingly and the loss of gross profit is to be reimbursed by the LOP Policy. The insurance Company will pay the additional expenditure not in excess of loss availed by means of that additional expenditure. To say precisely LOP Policy operates on the basic theory that every Rs.100/- of turnover or every unit of production bears its due portion of net profit and fixed costs.

One should keep in mind the LOP Policy is covered only for trading losses but not for capital losses. Profit earning capacity of any business depends upon its ability to produce money receipts greater than the total expenses. Thus the excess of revenue, over expenditure in broad terms called trading profit of the business. LOP Policy make good the loss of net profit, pays the continuing standing/fixed charges such as Rent rates, wages, interest and reimburse the additional expenditure subject to limitations under the policy.

ASSESSMENT OF PERIOD OF INTERRUPTION

Now the point come to one's mind that how long the coverage of LOP will be available to the insured. This period will be upto the time the particular business activity returns to its normal production capacity as was existing immediately presiding the occurrence of fire accident. The Consequential Losses during this period of interruption are indemnifiable under LOP Policy and therefore, it is necessary to specify this period while taking the insurance policy. This period is called "The Indemnity Period". It is very essential in specifying, indemnity period why because this period is directly linked in deciding the sum to be insured. A correct estimate is to be made of the time that may be required for the restoration of the damage which may involve reconstruction, procurement of indigenous and or imported machinery, erection and commissioning and finally procurement of raw materials, if damaged. The time factor in each of these items to be placed in order has to be assessed by the insured with his past experience and prudence.

Therefore there is a need to carry out a detailed analysis such as identification of critical factors of time of suppliers, lead time in receiving the machinery and time required to recommission. There were instances where interruption period has been two to three years as against the specified indemnity period of 12 months. Hence it is very very essential for the insured to arrive at a realistic estimate of the maximum probable period of interruption.

ALTERNATE METHODS

Apart from Turnover Basis Method wherein turnover is used as the index on activity, there are different ways by which loss can be assessed.

i) Input basis; ii) Productivity Wages basis; iii) Output basis;

It is possible at any stage to adopt the most convenient basis and ascertain its relation to Gross Profit so as to measure the loss. Though the turnover i.e., money realised on sale of goods is undoubtedly most satisfactory measure of loss, the shortage in production, at whatever stage from raw materials, finished goods, will not necessarily indicate the true loss in terms of money which would have been realised. For a particular industry output basis will be the best suitable method in measuring loss. There will be many businesses in view of their particular nature of production, it would be more sensible to use the unit of input of raw materials or output finished products or even in between. Most commonly it is found what the ultimate stage of production namely output, is the basis to be adopted. The loss is measured by applying the rate of gross profit per unit to the shortage in units following the fire accident. The output basis is employed where one kind of article or product is manufactured and where each unit can be said to earn a regular proportion of the gross profit.

Example: Breweries, Barrels of Beer or Flour Millers and Sacks Flour.

Whatever may be the different indices used or processed, the loss depending on the peculiarity of nature of business, it is always possible to ascertain the rate of gross profit on the basis of which loss of profit can be worked out.

CONTENTS OF LOP POLICY

LOP Policy has been designed by the insurance companies so as to indemnify the loss of gross profits because of fire accident so as to place the insured person as nearly as may be reasonably, practicable in the same financial health as if the damage had not occurred. The LOP Policy on the face of it may looks little cumbersome and elaborate but designed for practical convenience so as to understand the spirit behind the contract as a whole. The policy is meant only the profit resulting actually from insured's trading activities. One should keep in mind that LOP Policy is not concerned with Profit or loss resulting from any other sources such as Income from investments, commissions, royalties, dividends etc. While calculating, one should exclude these items from computation of insurable amount out of net profit. The Policy is also not covered for capital expenditure such as donations, non-recurring legal expenses, professional fee etc. While working out, the insurable amount of net profit, the above natured expenses, are to be added back. The nature of expenditure or income are to be analysed depending on the nature of industry while arriving True Net Trading Profit of the business at the premises, where its located. One should remember the point that since all taxes chargeable on profits are included under the definition of Net Profit these are not insurable as fixed charges. Another point is to be remembered is that premium paid on LOP Policy is a business expense for the purpose of income tax assessment and hence any claim received under the LOP Policy will be treated as earnings of the business and thus are taxable. Various types of adjustments are to be considered on merits to arrive at insurable net profit. The same kind of adjustments are to be carried out with the profit and loss account even if it shows a net loss also.

If business is conducted separately by independent department, the trading results of each departments are to be determined and LOP Policy can be modified appropriately so that provisions of the policy in respect of reduction in turnover and increase in cost of working shall be applied separately to each department effected by fire accident.

It is the duty of the insured to give to the insurance company a statement of claim soon after the event of fire accident and should provide additional information, records and should also allow the authorised persons of the insurance company to inspect as and when they require and help in assessing loss of profits.

DETERMINATION OF INSURED SUM

Before Policy is taken one should arrive at the sum to be insured since premium payable is directly linked to this factor. Some of the factors to be considered are

a) Net Profit; b) Standing/Fixed Costs; c) Trends of business; d) Indemnity period

The basis on which the insured sum can be arrived at is usually basing on previous accounting years Balance Sheet and Profit & Loss Account. It is also advisable to look into the accounts of previous two to three years, so as to gauge the real position and to make reliable estimate of future earnings. If half-yearly accounts are prepared by the insured then it will be a valuable guide for arriving at sum to be insured. The main aim should be to project prospective future earnings which is the real object of insurance under LOP Policy.

The insured can opt to insure all standing/fixed charges or only part of the such charges in which case those charges are opted for insurance must be specified by name in accordance with the head of account used in the insured's accounts. This will form part as insured charges which implies that the un-insured charges will not be taken into account while working out the rate of gross profit at the time of loss.

The important feature of insurance policy is that "Over insurance is not rewarded but, under insurance is penalised". The LOP Policy covers only the future profits, so one should be very careful in arriving at the insured sum and it is advisable to keep the gross profit figure sufficiently high to cover all anticipated increase in gross profit during the covered financial year. To encourage the insured not to under insurance an incentive has been provided in the LOP Policy. Upto 50% of the premium can be adjusted/refunded at the end of the policy period, if the sum proposed for insurance exceeds the actual insurable gross profit as per the audited accounts. This provision enables the insured to take a cover for a fairly high estimated projected figure and if the expectation did not fully materialise and the actual gross profit turns out to be lower, the insured can get a refund upto 50% of the premium paid.

As I mentioned earlier it is a time consuming and cumbersome process to arrive at the insured sum, in case the insured is in a hurry to take insurance and has no time to work out in detail as explained above, then an Thumb Rule Method can be adopted to project the provisional figure which should be rectified as soon as the correct figures are worked out. The Thumb Rule Method is that

i) Expected standard output per day in units of products multiplied by expected number of working days in the year multiplied by net expected realisation per unit = Expected Turnover.
ii) Multiply expected rate of Gross Profit = Insurable sum.

For a seasonable business special care must be taken in arriving the Sum to be insured when the Indemnity period is longer than 12 months. If the busy season is only Six months, during which the bulk of Annual Gross Profit is earned and a period of 18 months is considered and necessary to complete restoration of business to normal, it would be desirable for the sum insured to represent 2 years Gross Profit.

EXCLUSIVE CLAUSE

The LOP Policy will not cover the following losses even if directly or indirectly attributed to the occurrence of fire accident.

a) Loss of good-will; b) Spoilage of goods; c) Non recovery of debts; d) Third party claims; e) Litigation costs; f) Depreciation of undamaged stocks for fire; g) Under Insurance against material damaged policy; h) Difference value between stocks at the time of fire and subsequent replacement.

CONCLUSION

An attempt has been made by me in this article to analyse LOP Policy in a general manner. It is obvious that all contingents can not be dealt with item by item in a write up of this nature. If the method of approach is understood, a lot of confusion can be avoided to a large extent.

When all said and done 'Good House Keeping' is the best last control programme and this indeed is an indicator of healthy positive corporate attitude towards risk management.

*** * ***

13

MOTOR VEHICLE INSURANCE AGAINST THIRD PARTY RISKS INSURANCE COMPANY'S RIGHT TO DEFEND ITSELF

Dr. (Mrs) Lalitha Sreenath
Reader in Law, S.K.University, Anantapur

M.R. Sreenath
Advocate, Anantapur.

I. INTRODUCTION

1.1. Motor Vehicle Accidents and Compensation to Third Parties

Accidental deaths and disablements are an inevitable fall-out of our fast-paced modern civilization. Motor vehicles are the cause for a majority of these accidents. The 20th century has seen the birth of the motor car and its invasion into all the nooks and corners of the world. The automobile, which has brought about a revolution in transport by giving man the freedom to travel on a scale that could not have been imagined in the previous century, has also brought in its wake death and destruction on an unprecedented scale. The fatalities arising out of road accidents in our country have been showing a steady increase over the years. It is a pity that the same invention which is a boon to mankind in general should also be a bane to quite a few people. Justice Krishna Iyer, in his inimitable style, describes the situation thus: "An explosive escalation of automobile accidents accounting for more deaths than the most deadly diseases, has become a lethal phenomenon on Indian roads everywhere." [1]

Every accidental death and disablement brings in its wake untold suffering and misery not only to the victim but also to the victim's family, especially if it is the breadwinner who has been killed or severely maimed. An average Indian family, with its usual hand-to-mouth existence and virtual lack of savings to fall back upon, would find it extremely difficult to cope up with the financial hardships that result from its breadwinner's death or disablement. That's why, the law entitles the victims of motor accidents and/or their dependents to claim compensation from the drivers and owners of the offending vehicles by filing claim applications before the Motor Accidents Claims Tribunals which have been specifically set up for that purpose.

1.2. Compulsory Insurance Against Third-Party Risks

Realising the difficulty of the claimants in obtaining compensation from the drivers and owners of motor vehicles who might or might not be financially sound, our Legislature has enacted the Motor Vehicles Act, 1988 (hereinafter called 'the Act') which provides for all motor vehicles plying in public places to be compulsorily insured against third party risks. This compulsory motor vehicles insurance provides for protection to the owner of the motor vehicle against loss of three kinds: (1) against loss or damage to the vehicle and its accessories; (2) against loss arising out of personal injury to the owner; and (3) against loss arising from liability for death or injury caused to third parties or for damage to the property of third parties. Regarding the third species of protection, the insurance policy is a contract of indemnity under which the insurer agrees to reimburse the assured to the extent of the amount of damages which the latter may become liable to pay for the death or injury to a third party, or damages to his property caused in an accident. A claimant is entitled to recover from the insurer the amount of compensation which he is in law entitled to obtain from the insured.

1.3. Insurance Company's Right to Defend Itself

The Act makes the liability of the insurance companies in such third-party claims unlimited. The Act also stipulates that the insurance company, normally, be made a party before the Claims Tribunal so that it can defend itself. Under the common law an insurer has no right to be made a party to the action by the injured person against the insured. But such a right has been given to the insurer under section 149 of the Act. This right is not an absolute right; it is hedged by certain limitations. Since it is a right created by statute, its content necessarily depends on the provisions of the statute.

1.4. Objective of this Paper

In this paper, an attempt has been made to analyse, in the light of judicial decisions, the statutory provisions governing the insurer's right to defend himself before the Motor Accidents Claims Tribunal.

2. THE GENERAL RULE REGARDING DEFENCES OPEN TO AN INSURER

On the question of defences that are available to an insurer in a claim petition filed by the claimants before a Claims Tribunal claiming compensation for the death or injury caused in an accident involving the use of a motor vehicle that has been allegedly insured by the insurer, the leading authority is the following statement of law enunciated by the Supreme Court in *British India General Insurance Co. Ltd. v. Capt. Itbar Singh.*[7]

"The question is whether the defences available to an insurer added as a party under section 96(2) are only those mentioned there. ..... To start with it is necessary to remember that apart from the statute an insurer has no right to be made a party to the action by the injured person against the insured causing the injury. Sub-section (2) of section 96 however gives him the right to be made a party to the suit and to defend it. The right therefore is created by statute and its content necessarily depends on the provisions of the statute. The question then really is, what are the defences that sub-section (2) makes available to an insurer? That clearly is a question of interpretation of the sub-section.

Now the language of sub-section (2) seems to us to be perfectly plain and to admit of no doubt or confusion. It is that an insurer to whom the requisite notice of the action has been given "shall be entitled to be made a party thereto and to defend the action on any of the following grounds, namely", after which comes an enumeration of the grounds. It would follow that an insurer is entitled to defend on any of the grounds enumerated and no others. If it were not so, then of course no grounds need have been enumerated. When the grounds of defence have been specified they cannot be added to. To do that would be adding words to the statute.

Sub-section (6) also indicates clearly how sub-section (2) should be read. It says that no insurer to whom the notice of the action has been given shall be entitled to avoid his liability under sub-section (1) "otherwise than in the manner provided for in sub-section (2)". Now the only manner of avoiding liability provided for in sub-section (2) is by successfully raising any of the defences therein mentioned. It comes then to this that he cannot take any defence not mentioned in sub-section (2). If he could, then he would have been in a position to avoid his liability in a manner other than that provided for in sub-section (2). That is prohibited by sub-section (6).

We therefore think that sub-section (2) clearly provides that an insurer made a defendant to the action, is not entitled to take any defence which is not specified in it."

From the above mentioned passage, it is clear that the insurer is entitled to escape liability by saying that the policy is void because it was obtained by the insured on a false representation or non-disclosure of a material fact; or that the policy was cancelled before the accident; or that there has been a breach of a specified condition of the policy, being one of the conditions enumerated in sub-section (2) of section 149. The insurer is debarred from raising any other ground of defence to avoid his liability, if the insured is found to have incurred the liability.

3. STATUTORY DEFENCES

Sub-section (2) of section 149 mentions the grounds on which the insurer is entitled to defend a third-party claim. These grounds are firstly, that there has been breach of a specified condition of the policy, and secondly, that the policy had been obtained by non-disclosure of a material fact or by representation of a fact which was false in some material particular, thereby rendering the policy itself void. In the old Act, there had been one more defence dealing with cancellation of a policy by mutual consent or by virtue of any provisions contained in the policy of insurance before the accident had taken place. This defence has been deleted in the new Act.

3.1. Breach of a Specified Condition in the Policy

Clause (a) of sub-section (2) of section 149 of the new Act deals with a defence on the ground of breach of a specified condition of the policy. But it is not the breach of each and every condition embodied in the policy by the insured and the insurer that would provide the insurance company a defence to disclaim its liability. The said clause makes it clear that the condition which according to the insurance company has been violated should be one that is mentioned in the clause itself. Three kinds of conditions are mentioned therein. The first is a condition excluding the use of the vehicle for certain purposes and in certain ways; the second is a condition excluding driving of the motor vehicle by a named person or by certain specified categories of persons; and the third is a condition excluding liability of the insurer in times of war, civil war, riot, or civil commotion. Unless, therefore, the insurer establishes that the breach of the condition of the policy that he complains of comes within any one of the sub-clauses mentioned in clause (a) of sub-section (2) of section 149, the insurer cannot succeed, since the breach of any of the terms of the policy not mentioned in clause (a) would not be a defence to the insurer. It is significant that even violation of any of the provisions of the Act, violation of any of the rules framed under the Act, or violation of any of the terms of the permit under the Act, cannot be a defence, except when it falls within the ambit of sub-clauses (i), (ii) and (iii) of clause (a) of section 149(2) of the 1988 Act.[3]

An insurer and the insured may agree upon a number of conditions at the time of entering into a contract of insurance. The insured may subsequently breach one or more of such conditions. Then on the ground of such breach, it has been contended by the insurer that he is not bound to indemnify the insured in respect of any compensation that the insured may have to pay to the claimants in pursuance of an award made by the Claims Tribunal. But the Courts have not been convinced of this argument. No doubt, clause (a) of sub-section (2) of section 149 of the 1988 Act states that an insurer is entitled to defend the claim application before the Tribunal on the ground that there has been a breach of a specified condition of the policy. But such a breach must have been with reference to one of the conditions enumerated in sub-clauses (i) to (iii) therein. So if the breach is with reference to any one of the conditions mentioned in the said sub-clauses, the insurer is entitled to repudiate his liability; but if the breach is with reference to any condition other than the ones mentioned in the said sub-clauses, then the insurer cannot escape his liability.

3.2. Meaning of Breach

The expression 'breach' is of great significance. The dictionary meaning of 'breach' is 'infringement or violation of a promise or obligation'. (See *Collins English Dictionary)*. It is, therefore, abundantly clear that the insurer will have to establish that the insured is guilty of an infringement or violation of a promise made in the policy. The very concept of infringement or violation of the promise that the expression 'breach' carries within itself induces an inference that the violation or infringement on the part of the promisor must be a willful infringement or violation. If the insured is not at all at fault and has not done anything he should not have done or is not amiss in any respect how can it be conscientiously posited that he has committed a breach? It must be established by the insurance company that the breach was on the part of the insured and that it was the insured who was guilty of violating the promise or infringement of the contract. Unless the insured is at fault and is guilty of a breach the insurer cannot escape from the obligation to indemnify the insured and successfully contend that he is exonerated having regard to the fact that the promisor (the insured) committed a breach of his promise. Not when some mishap occurs by some mischance. And it is only in case of a breach or a violation of the promise on the part of the insured that the insurer can hide under the umbrella of the exclusion clause.[4]

3.3. Breach of Statutory Rules not a Defence

The High Court of Gujarat in *Bomanji Rustomji Ginwala v. Ibrahim Vali Master,* 1982 ACJ 380 (Guj), was called upon to decide whether the insurer could disclaim liability on the ground that the insured had violated some of the rules framed under the Motor Vehicles Act. A tractor, with a trolley and with a cultivator about 7 1/2 feet long, attached at the back of the tractor with a pointed hook, was being driven in a rash and negligent manner in the middle of the tar road, resulting in an accident, in which a car coming from the opposite direction suffered extensive damage. In a claim for damages by the owner of the car, insurer of the tractor pleaded that its liability under the policy of insurance was exonerated, since the driver of the tractor had committed breaches of certain rules under the Motor Vehicles Act, while driving the insured vehicle. Rule 264(2) of the Rules enjoined the driver, as far as possible to drive on the side strip of the metalloid road. Rule 266 dealing with projection of loads, had also been violated. The Court repelled this contention and held that the mere fact that while driving the tractor, the driver of the insured vehicle committed breaches of the statutory rules, cannot give a valid defence to the insurance company to escape its liability *qua* third parties, as admittedly none of the breaches of the statutory rules is covered by the conditions expressly mentioned in section 96(2) of the Motor Vehicles Act. The Court stated the legal position thus:

"It is now well settled that mere breach of statutory rules on the part of the driver of the insured vehicle would not automatically enable the insurance company to escape its liability to answer the claim of third parties as enjoined by the provisions of rules 95 and 96 of the Rules. It is also well settled that under section 96(2) of the Act, the insurance company has got limited defences. The insurance company can resist the claim of third party claimant if it can show that there has been breach of specific conditions of policy being one of the conditions expressly mentioned in section 96(2)(b)(i) to (iii)." (p.382)

4. EXCEPTIONS TO THE GENERAL RULE: WHEN ARE OTHER DEFENCES OPEN?

No doubt, the general rule is that the insurer can avail of only those defences that are mentioned in sub-section (2) of section 149. But the question is are there any exceptions to this general rule? In other words, are there any special circumstances that entitle the insurer to raise defences other than the ones mentioned in the statute? The answer to this question is in the affirmative. On two occasions, the insurer gets the right to step into the shoes of the insured and plead all the grounds that are available to the insured. One is when he had reserved to himself the right to do so in the policy itself[5], and second, when the insurer is impleaded as a party by the Tribunal under section 170 [old section 110-C(2A)][6].

5. SUMMING UP

The legal position regarding the defences that are open to an insurer to resist a third party claim, has been very neatly summed up by Dr.A.S.Anand, J. (as he then was), speaking for a Full Bench of the Jammu and Kashmir High Court in *United India Fire and General Insurance Co. Ltd. v. Lakshmi Shori Ganjoo.*[7]

"Before the Tribunal an insurer can resist the claim against him in two ways: (1) by urging that the insurer is not liable even though the insured may be liable, and (2) by pleading that the insurer is not liable because the insured is not liable.

Under the first head, an insurer is entitled to escape his liability by showing that the policy of insurance is void as it had been obtained on false representation or concealment of material facts or that the policy had been cancelled before the accident or that there had been a breach of any condition of the policy and the like grounds. The insurer is not entitled to raise any other ground of defence to avoid his liability, where the insured is found to have incurred the liability because of the simple reason that a policy of insurance being in the nature of a contract of indemnity, the insurer takes upon himself to discharge the liability of the insured arising out of a motor vehicle accident, subject of course to the terms and conditions of the policy and the maximum statutory liability. He cannot, under the first head avoid his liability except on the grounds mentioned above, when a party takes out a policy of insurance, it does so after paying the premium for the sum assured and unless the contract between him and the insurer can be avoided, the insurance company which has been benefited by the premium cannot back out of its commitment to indemnify the insured. This is manifest from the plain phraseology of section 95(5) of the Act, which reads thus: "Notwithstanding anything, elsewhere contained in any law, a person issuing a policy of insurance under this section shall be liable to indemnify the person or classes of persons specified in the policy in respect of any liability which the policy purports to cover in the case of that person or those classes of persons;"

However, no sum shall be payable by an insurer under section 96(1) in respect of any award unless before or after the commencement of the proceeding in which the award is given, the insurer had notice through the Tribunal of the bringing of those proceedings. It is only an insurer to whom notice of the bringing of any such proceeding is given who shall be entitled to be made a party to the proceedings and to defend the action on the grounds contained in section 96(2) of the Act, unless the insurer had reserved in the policy of insurance a right to defend the action in the name of the insured, in which event he can defend on all the grounds on which the insurer could defend.

Under the second head an insurer can plead that there was no negligence on the part of the insured and raise all such pleas in defence to the claim as are available to an insured to show that the insured had not incurred any liability. This however, can be done by the insurer only if the insurer had reserved, in the policy of insurance a right to defend the claim in the name of the insured. If there is not reservation made in the policy of insurance, then section 96(2) strictly debars an insurer from taking any defence, other than those enumerated therein, to show that the insurer was not liable although the insured has incurred liability.

Where an insurer finds that it has not reserved such a right but that the insured and the claimant have colluded with each other as it is a possibility that cannot be ignored, it is open to an insurer to bring that fact to the notice of the Tribunal and seek its permission under section 110-C (2A) to contest the claim on all the grounds available to an insured. On being satisfied that there is such a collusion, the Tribunal would grant permission and on such permission being granted, the insurer steps into the shoes of the insured and defends the claim on all available grounds, if the award goes against the insurer, it can challenge it in appeal also on all such grounds on which it had contended the claim before the Tribunal. Right of appeal against an award of the Tribunal is the creation of the statute. The Act had confined the right to avoid the liability of the insurer to the injured on certain grounds specified in it. It is not open to this Court to add to those grounds on the plea that hardship would be caused to an insurer. An insurer can avoid any hardship by remaining vigilant during the trial of the claim petition and also by providing, in the policy of insurance, for a right to defend the action in the name of the assured and that he had full liberty to do. Where the insurer has failed to do it, he cannot avoid the liability if the insured is found liable.

The aforesaid discussion leads to the conclusion that (1) an insurer is not entitled to resist the claim or the award, where the insured has been found liable, on grounds not enumerated under section 96(2) of the Act; (2) where the term of the policy of insurance provides that the insurer has the right to defend the action in the name of the insured, the insurer shall have the right to defend and if he does so, all the defences as are open to the insured can be urged by the insurer both to resist the claim as well as the award; (3) if it appears that the claimant and the insured have colluded, then after receiving permission of the Tribunal under section 110-C(2A) the insurer can defend the claim as well as the award on all grounds which are available to the insured; and (4) except for the aforesaid contingencies, an insurer cannot question an award in appeal and unless the case of the insurer is covered by (2) or (3) conclusions, as noticed above, an insurer cannot, in an appeal against the award, question the quantum of compensation only."

NOTES

1. *Concord of India Insurance Company Limited. v.Nirmala Devi*, 1980 ACJ 55.

2. 1958-65 1 (SC), at p.4.

3. See *National Insurance Co. Ltd. v. T.Elumalai*, 1990 ACJ 426 (Mad), at p.429.

4. *Skandia Insurance Co. Ltd. v. Kokilaben Chandravadan*, 1987 ACJ 411 (SC), at 417, per M.P.Thakkar;J.

5. *British India General Insurance Co. v. Itbar Singh*, AIR 1959 SC 1331.

6. Provided two conditions are satisfied. Firstly, there must be collusion between the claimants and the owner, or the owner might not have contested the claim. Secondly, the Tribunal must have directed the insurer to be impleaded as a party.

7. 1982 ACJ 470 (J&K) (FB), at p.482-3.

14

THE INSURANCE SECTOR IN INDIA - WHAT STAGE OF PRODUCT LIFE CYCLE IS IT AT?

M.S.Bhat

Professor & Head, School of Management, Jawaharlal Nehru Technological University, Hyderabad

---

The health and growth of insurance sector is closely linked to the general economy of the country. Though it is one of the relatively older sectors in the service sector of the economy contributing significantly to the Gross Domestic Product, thee is a great deal that can be accomplished in this sector. Though the growth potential of the insurance sector is often dependent on factor external to it, there are innumerable internal factors which contribute to the strength and weakness of the sector and a critical analysis would enable one to correct the situation and exploit the opportunities to the maximum extent. Indeed the issue becomes all the more relevant as in the Indian context it can emphatically be said that the insurance sector is still in the initial stages of growth and there is a long way to reach the maturity stage of product life cycle for the sector as a whole.

The business potential for the insurance sector is indeed quite vast judging from the fact that inspite of decades of growth of the sector the number of insurable population covered by insurance in the life category is just 22 per cent where as in the case of non life policies it is even less than one per cent. With a growth rate of seven per cent in economy and increasing population growth there is bound to be pressure for provision of insurance coverage both in life and non life category and therefore the insurance sector has a long fruitful march ahead.

The increasing shift from predominantly agriculture based economy to industrial and service sector as is the case with any developed economy would mean increasing demand fro various type of non life insurance policies. Various types of covers for transit of material and against risks in storage and safekeeping are all aspects of business linked insurance policies for which there is bound to be great demand with the increasing growth of industry and service. There is plenty of scope for innovation in product formulation and development with the emergence of high growth areas like software devolopment, marketing research, advertising and sales promotion services, financial services with innovative new instruments etc. All these make it abudantly clear that the growth stage in product life cycle stage of insurance sector is ripe with innumerable opportunities to be exploited and all that is needed to achieve this is a bit of marketing orientation.

While there was a strong case for nationalisation of insurance sector as also the banking sector in the initital stages of development of the economy, the situation now warrants an element of competition for all around efficiency and customer satisfaction. We shall discuss some of the measures that have been contemplated and suggested by planners and leading thinkers in this regard.

Privatisation of Insurance Service

The privatisation of both life and nonlife insurance sectors have been accepted in principle as part of the Common Minimum Programme of UF government and even Insurance Regulatory Authority has been setup. The Malhotra Committee Report has come up with a blue print for progressive privatisation. The background against which the privatisation is recommended along with the justification for the same as given by Mr.Malhotra is as follows.

"Over the years the nationalised companies have expanded their business and established an extensive presence throughout the country. They have developed financial strength and large reservoirs of trained manpower. However the lack of competition has engendered complascency in the insurance industry which is reflected among other things in insufficient responsiveness to customer need, high costs, instability of marketing networks, excessive lapsation of life policies, overstaffing, growth of restrictive staff practices. and serious lags in technology. Despite overall growth of insurance, several lines of business have not been sufficiently developed and there is a vast untapped potential. Since nationalisation, regulation of insurance industry has atrophied. High levels of directed investment of the funds of insurance companies have affected rates of insurance premia, as well as bonuses on most life policies".

"The Indian insurance market has large potential considering the country's huge and burgeoning population, a growing and increasingly affluent middle class, gross domestic savings of around 23 per cent over the 1980s and is expected to rise to 6-7 per cent in the second half of 1990, industrial output that could grow by 8 to 10 per cent p.a. and rising trade volumes. This should provide incrasing business opportunities to life and nonlife insurers. In a competitive environment, both the public and private sectors would vie for a share in a growing market".

Life Insurance Corporation with its 1900 and odd branches and General Insurance Corporation and its Subsidiaries with its more than 3000 branches have been presiding over the destiny of the insurance sector all these years. Once the Malhotra Committee's recommendation to privatise insurance sector is implemented we will have companies in the private sector with minimum investment of Rs.100 crores. The committee is of the view that there is enormous potential for growth in reinsurance sector also along with the growth of insurance sector. This is one area where the boundaries need not be limited to our country. With the kind of investment that is stipulated for the private sector to enter into insurance business the companies can aim for a place in the reinsurance sector as well. The reinsurance sector would find intself on the high growth path with a bit of push.

Product Varieties

The insurance sector has scope for offering nuber of packages. Even in the life sector LIC hascome up with innumerable policies including pension schemes. In the area of business, one can foresee demands for various packages such as for financial risk, transit risk, environmental risk, political risk, risk against nuclear projects, Research and Development, satelite failure etc.

At the growth stage of product life cycle it is apparent that there is enormous scope for introducing new product features and variety. This is an aspect the industry should not lose sight of.

The need for going hitech in insurance business

The growth in an industry is either due to market driven factors or technology driven factors. It is also true that one can trigger the other as in the case of say personal computer market of Email or Fax services. The level of technology currently in use in insurance sector is relatively quite low. There is urgent need to adapt information technology to the maximum extent for all aspects of business processing both in life and nonlife sector. A good data base about the existing product profile must be developed and should be readily accessible via internet. The information concerning the customers, their profile, demand pattern, behaviour of other indices which has good correlation on the growth pattern of business etc. must be readily available. Automation and Communication infrastructure are other two vital areas where technology can play a vital role in transforming the very fact of the industry.

Savings in cost through risk minimisation effort

While the insurance companies do concentrate their effort in covering their risks through reinsurance, other measures that can be effective in the long run is to analyse the cause of the basic risk for which customer insure themselves and invest in measures to reduce them at the root cause level. While this would certainly involve efforts at national and even global level such as for increasing the life expectancy, reducing road accidents etc. the insurance companies should endeavour to take up the role fo chief advocates and catalysts for the movement. This role would not only enable them to serve their own interest but also would project them as champion of wider interest concerning the society and bring a good public image which is so essential for any insurance company. The possibility of savings on these are quite immense thereby making the whole business cost efficient. This in turn would result in making policies less expensive for the customer thereby triggering additional demand and more turnover. There is every reason to believe that most of the products of insurance sector have high degree of elasticity of demand and growth can certainly be rapid by making the premium rate more and more attractive.

* * *

15

RISK MANAGEMENT AND FAMILY ECONOMICS:

Applications of Insurance Principle

Appa Rao Machiraju, Puranik, Sivarama Krishna Rao,

Founder Director College of Insurance and financial Planning, Secunderabad

---

The word"risk" derives from the early Italian 'risicare' which means "to dare". In this sense, risk is a choice than fate. The notion of bringing "Risk" under control is one of the central ideas that distinguishes modern times from the more distant point. The capacity to manage risk, and with it the appetite to take risk and make forward-looking choices, are key elements of the energy that drives the economic system forward. To study insurance without first studying 'risk' and 'uncertainty' is much the same as studying medicine without understanding anatomy.

INTRODUCTION

The vastness of the subject matter relating to risk is daunting. Risk touches on the most profound aspects of psychology, mathematics, statistics and history. The literature is monumental.

The Risk Management approach to the conservation of economic values of human life, is of relatively recently origin. This paper, however focuses only on the role of risk and its management confined to conservation of the economic value of the bread-winner during his life span in his family economic situation through application of life insurance princple. The economic value may be defined as the capitalized monetary worth of the earning potential resulting from the economic forces that are incorporated in our being: education, training and experience. No substantial difference, in fact, exists between the various types of insurance as regard their underlying economic purposes. Each household is treated as an 'isolated economic unit' which need to be affiliated to a group resource i.e., to an insurance company in the modern context to ensure the family economic security specially in the wake of disappearing joint family units and emergence of nuclear family units.

Any discussions of the need to conserve the economic values of heads of the family units - or for that matter any history of life insurance in particular - lacks validity unless it constantly bears in mind certain fundamental truths about 'risks'.

Discussion related 'risks' will address on

I. The nature of risk
II. (ii) The emergence of economic risk as a major concern for each member of modern individualistic society
III. Methods of dealing with risk
IV. Application of insurance principle as a device for meeting the risk.

The Nature of Risk

Risk may be called a threat to well-being. This definition has the merit of brevity, but it does nor sufficiently emphasize the essential element of chance which is present in all risks. A fuller definition might read: risk consists in the existing exposure of some entity to potential impairment of its well-being through the operation of chance.

Every form of life faced with risks of one kind or another. And, although there is great variety in the character and determinable magnitude of specific risk, all the risks are alike that, they threaten to limit economic life in particular. This generalization should be interpreted in its broadest sense.

Some risks are inherent in the nature of the physical universe. Other risks arise out of the system of living and working which men have formulated and thrust upon themselves. Of the latter group there are two types : ordinary and manufactured. Ordinary risks are such as have to do with the usual transactions of an individual within his community. Manufactured risks are those which are deliberately created. All gambling risks are manufactured. Risks having their source in nature, and the usual transactions between men, run against everyone whether he will or not. But gambling risks must be consciously sought and deliberately assumed.

Well-being, which we have said is threatened by risk, has a four-fold character: physical, economic, social and psychic. There is great interdependence between these several aspects of living, but the distinctions are none the less sharp and real. It is not correct to think of one risk spreading itself over all aspects of well-being. We should realize rather that there may be, usually are, four individual types of risk operating concurrently. The imporance of these risks is differently evaluated by different men. This is especially true in cases where the potential loss does not lend itself to absolute, or should we say mathematical measurement. Purely subjective values, while vastly important to each of use, defy appraisement by any of our common guages for reckoning differences in degree. 'Peace of mind', which is the ultimate insecurity from economic risks, in one and the same individual. Then too, safeguards against each type of risk must be of the same nature as the risk itself. Any finally, risk must be recognized as related to well-being at a given moment. These factors complicate the understanding and treatment of risk, yet we cannot afford to ignore them if we expect to think and act intelligently with regard to risk.

Risks may be ignored, or they may be recognized yet allowed to take their own course- which amounts to the same things so far as "costs" are concerned. Some losses will occur. The time of their occurrence cannot be known in advance, neither can the extent of the losses within a short period be predicted.

All positive treatments of risk may be called "safeguards". They are of three kinds : those which eliminate risk; those which reduce risk; and those which cncel the effect of impairment.

Emergence of Economic Risk as a Major Concern for Each Member of Modern Individualistic Society:

The most striking contrast between modern social organization and the earlier forms i.e., the patriarchal family, feudalism, the gild - each had its own pattern of limitations to imose upon the ndividual.

Today individual freedom is guaranteed but the individual is left isolated as an economic unit. It is this fact of economic isolation which is the sternest reality in modern social organization.

Today the well-informed man is aware of his isolated position in economic affairs. He knows that for his own economic well-being he must put an end to that isolation by associating himself with the group resources. He acts of his own violation. There is no compulsion. As he investigates, and finally selects, a job or an income-producing property from the wide range of work and investment opportunities which are available to hi, he may possibly appreciate the freedom of action. Of one thing he is certain, he must act for himself. He faces honestly the fact that society is not now organised to make certain a place for him and his family, today and indefinitely. He sees that it is organized one to give him freedom in making his own way.

If he must live by personal earnings, the individual gives consideration to three main problems and their respective solutions: (1) pressed by the need for almost continuous buying, (2) realizing that isolation is probably going to continue all his life, he sets about to provide for his economic well-being when he shall be unable too earn because of old age: (3) recognizing that he has oblications (toward those who are dependent upon him for their economic well-being) which may outlive him, he provides for their fulfillment by insuring the economic value of his life. With these protective measure, the well-informed and conscientious man meets personal economic risks in modern life.

Methods of Dealing with Risk

Unque among the modern means by which the individual may affiliate himself with group resources is the life insurance company. Throughout it he can acquire rights to assistance in any emergency. These rights must however, be voluntarily sought and accepted through the medium of private contract.

Economic well-being is a web of many standards each of which is threatened by diverse risks: and for most men their worth as earning machines is the strongest stand in the web. It is subject to many risks, chief of which are loss of work opportunity, inability to earn (owing to sickness, injury, or old age) and death. The latter is a peculiar item in economic risk. Death is no risk, it is a certainty. Nothing that is certain is a risk. We should say, therefore, that untimely death and financial consequences to the dependent family is the risk that we have in mind. Moreover, a dead man would seem to have no need for economic well-being. But we hve a way of disjoing a part of our economic self from the rest of our ebing and endowing it with a separate existence, even to the extent of arranging that it shall survive our physical self. Sometimes that economic self is referred to as a man's estate. It is treated like a person under the law, both before and after the death of the person with whom it is associated. It can own, owe, and be owed, wealth. That estate, as well as those persons to whom the living man is obligated, are presumed to have an economic interest in his life. Against the risk that death may (1) destroy his economic worth as an earning machine before, it is expended itself in a normal life-time of work, or (2) precipitate costs of transferring his estate to his heirs, that estate and those persons may be protected by the modern device known as life insurance. Under this plan of protection the individual may affiliate himself with others in a program guarantees against certain economic risks.

Application of Insurance Principle as a Device for Meeting the Risk

Insurance is, from certain points of view, a peak accomplishment in the long series of organizational devices to which men have devoted their creative talents down through centuries of social evolution. It is peculiarly modern in concept and method. To being with, it has little meaning. And practically no reason for being, in social orders earlier than our own. And until recent times the very sciences upon which it is founded were lacking.

What is needed are studies and research which shall take a broad and comprehensive view of all risks : Physical, economic, social, psychic.

Thereafter when economic risks are separately treated, they can be seen in truer, clear perspective.

Insurance an Integral Division of Economics

The science of Economic traditionally groups economic activities under such time-honoured classfications as "production", "exchange", "distribution", and "consumption without being ale to allocate insurance to any of these divisions. There is little emphasis on insurance in text books on economics, corporation finance, investments and other applied fields of economics. This gap will remain until the basic nature of insurance is more clearly understood and recognized.

Insurance involves activities and services that are intimately connected with all divisions of economics referred to. The outstanding and distinctive mission of insurance, which is 'risk-bearing' and risk elimination in our economic affairs is yet to be recognized. For its accomplishment there must be first leaders of thought, then leaders in action. When we have men who study and write about risk that they claim the attential of the community and leaders in action will surely be forthcoming. The insurance industry collaborating with the educational institutions should foster thinking and writing on risk with a view to building up a body of thinkers and a body of literature which shall be the beginning of more adequate recognition of the subject, in both our thinking and our acting leading ultimately to our contribution to the welfare of the society and country.

CONCLUSION

Perhaps we should proceed with the narrative more profitably if we formulated now certain questions which could be kept in mind a we further research and develop the subject.

1. How clearly ought men to understand their isolated position in modern individualistic, capitalistic, and competitive society?
2. How fully ought society to assume the obligation, if such it is, to inform its members, especially the young, of that position and the available means for safeguarding against the risks involved?

3. How far ought society to go in instilling the ideal of self-reliance, how for to show that adequate life insurance and financial planning is unique in its service?
4. Since these fundamental truths of economics and social philosophy could most logically and most effectively be given within the public education syste, how should insurance companies proceed to see that they are taught? Is this not the first and most important step in marketing methodology which all companies should unite to see taken.
5. How should the industry foster thinking and writing on risk with a view to building up a body of thinkers and body of literature which shall be the beginning of more adequate recognition of the subject, in both our thinking and our acting.
6. What immediate steps could and should be taken to educate the adult population on the truths which we have been considering?

REFERENCES

1. Against the Gods : The Remarkable Story of Risk
   * Peter L.Bernstein

2. Essays in the theory of Risk and Insurance
   * J.D.Hamond

3. The Economics of Life Insurance
   * S.S. Huebner

4. Marketing Lilfe Insurance
   *J.Ouness Stalson

* * *

16

CURRENCY RISK MANAGEMENT

Lessons from South Asian Economic Turmoil

Prof. C.Siva Rama Krishna Rao,

Professor, Department of Economics, Kakatiya University, Warangal - 506 009

This paper is divided into three parts. The first part deals with different exposures due to variations in exchange rates. The second part analyses the approaches in currency risk management. The third part presents the issues in risk management that had emerged in South-Asian Economic Turmoil.

I

Risk management is the identification, measurement and treatment of exposures to potential accidental losses, almost always in situations where the only possible outcomes are losses or no change in status quo[1]. The principal objective of risk management has been defined as "the effective planning of resources needed to recover financial balance and operating effectiveness after a fortuitous loss, thus obtaining a short-term loss of risk stability and long term risk minimization."[2] Hence risk management is essentially associated with losses and as the risk arising from currency fluctuations has assumed increasing importance in recent years, currency risk management has gained prominence in international risk management.

Exchange rate variations are no longer the exclusive concern of the corporate treasurer. As a result of their effect on international competitiveness, they are increasingly becoming the concern of corporate management. Firms exposed to the international economy have to realise that they are in two businesses at the same time.[3]

1) The business of producing and supplying goods and services;
2) the business of finance, in terms of understanding and managing financial risks. In fact, the finance function is being increasingly integrated with the various management and strategic decisions to create and sustain competitive advantages.

There are three types of foreign exchange exposures to which international firms are generally vulnerable : 1) transaction exposure; 2) Translation (or accounting) exposure and 3)economic exposure[4]. Transaction exposure arises when a company is committees to a foreign currency denominated transaction. In other words, on transactions that a firm has already entered into and that are denominated in a foreign currency, the firm could incur future gains or losses owing to unanticipated exchange rate fluctuations[5]. An example would highlight the management of the loss that may be incurred due to this exposure. Let us assume that State Trading Corporation imported fertilizers costing $50 millions in May 1996 when the dollar-rupee parity was 41=Rs.31.00. Payment was to be made in August 1997 when the dollar was quoted at Rs.32.00. The loss to STC due to transaction exposure is $50 million x (32.00 - 31.00) or Rs.50 million, a very significant loss.

Translation exposure, also referred to as accounting exposure, is the impact of currency fluctuations on a firm's balance sheet. This problem is particularly acute in the case of multinational corporation with operations in a number of countries around the world. At the time of the annual consolidation of accounts when subsidiary accounts have to be consolidated into the parent company's accounts, a serious problem generally arises. The accounts of subsidiaries, which are denominated in the currencies of their respective locations, must be translated into the parent company's currency in order to produce a world wide consolidated financial statement. Depending upon how the relevant currencies have moved in relation to the parent company's currency, consolidated accounts will show currency gains or losses resulting from these transactions. Although there are not many Indian companies with international operations, yet, there is a growing number of Indian firms with foreign currency borrowings. All these firms have a translation exposure arising from the need to report foreign currency borrowings in their published annual reports. While these appear to be transaction exposures, they also give rise to translation exposure of considerable importance[6].

A risk-information system that lays emphasis underlining the risks associated with exposures is essential. Apart from a dedicated risk information system, firms must ensure that the technical expertise of its managers matches the required level of technical expertise. Inadequate skills could inturn lead to inaccurate pricing that translate into losses. Lately, North West markets, the investment banking divisions of a British bank, announced that several years of inaccurate options had resulted in a loss of $124 million[7].

Another type of exposure, also referred to as competitive exposure, is the impact of currency fluctuations on a firm's future operating cash flows. It measures the extent to which the value of the firm, as measured by the present value of its expected future cash flows, will change when exchange rate fluctuates unexpectedly. Therefore, the economic exposure become the firm's operating exposure, as exchange rate changes after the firm's operating cash flows[8].

The steady appreciation of Japanese yen, in relation to the Indian rupee during 1983 to 1992, virtually knocked the bottom out of the light commercial vehicle industry in India, which consists of several collaborative ventures with Japanese firms. Some of these firms are DCM-Toyota, Eicher-Mistabishi, Allwyn-Nissan, Swaraj-Mazda. These joint ventures have both borrowings in Japanese yen and also recurring yen out flows on account of import of components and spare parts from their respective Japanese partners. The Japanese firms, being foresighted, have been absorbing a part of the currency losses along with their Indian partners. This has greatly helped the Indian firms in the tight situation but, it does not eliminate the problem. A strategic approach is needed involving a long-term restructuring of operations, speeding up the process of indigenisation and other similar strategies[9].

Economic exposure is by far the most pernicious and harmful exposure confronting businesses in a world of volatile exchange rates; yet it would seem that there is not enough appreciation of this phenomenon, particularly among Indian businesses. The curious thing about economic exposure is that, contrary to popular belief, it affects not only firms with international operations (or transactions in foreign currencies) but purely domestic firms as well. Economic exposure arises more from shifts in real exchange rates than in nominal exchange rates, the difference between the two exchange rates being inflation differentials[10].

II

Exchange rates volatility has been so great in recent years and exchange rates so unpredictable that firms not hedging against currency risk have some times come out ahead of those that did practice hedging. However, this can be no argument for a policy of no hedge, even if most of the time all that a hedge does is to "minimize our maximum regret[11]". Exchange risk is uncertainty of loss arising from devaluation or revaluation of foreign currencies. The potentials loss due to foreign exchange risk is that the value of the assets in the host country may decrease if the value of the local currency falls relative to the parent country's currency. Foreign exchange exposures are speculative loss exposures, not pure loss exposures[12]. When devaluation threatens losses from short term exchange risk, risk can be lessened by minimizing the amounts represented by debts to others in the soft currency country. Another technique is to speed up payments of dividends or other remittances due to the parent corporation, or to others in hard currency countries. When the risk is revaluation of a foreign currency these techniques should be reversed[13].

The firm may also hedge in the future market for foreign currencies. A futures contract is an agreement to deliver the specified currency to a buyer at some specified time in the future at a price determined at the time the contract is made. If the currency is later devalued before the expiration of the contract, the seller can purchase the needed currency at a reduced price in order to fulfill his contract. The profit made on this transaction offsets the loss. The firm has suffered because the seller must accept payment for his merchandise in a devalued currency. The hedging transaction thus protects the firm's normal operating margins. The weaker the currency the higher the cost[14].

Several European countries, France, Australia, Belgium, Germany, Spain and Switzerland have adopted exchange risk guarantee programs to handle the long-term risk. The exchange risk guarantee takes effect not sooner than one year after the contract is signed. A normal period is two years. The insured must retain the first 2 or 3 per cent of long-term exchange loss. Such contracts are designed to protect the long-term lender or the seller who as agreed to make deliveries will into the future at prices agreed to in advance. If the currency of payment is devalued, the seller or lender is protected against the ensuring loss[15].

Besides forward cover, a firm can take recourse to a spot hedge or a money market hedge, which is created through two different techniques, depending upon the specific needs of the firm. If a firm has an obligation to receive an amount denominated in a foreign currency at a later date, it can create a spot hedge by borrowing the present value of the amount of foreign currency and converting it to the currency of choice at the current spot rate. This amount can then either be deposited with a bank or applied to the current operations of the firm. When they receive payment in the foreign currency they can use it to pay off the amount of the loan besides the interest rate[16].

If a firm has an obligation to pay an amount denominated in a foreign currency at a later date, they can also create a spot hedge. They can do this by determining the present value of the amount that they will need, purchasing this amount of foreign currency at the current spot rate, and depositing this currency in the foreign capital market until it is needed to meet their obligation. This option is not yet available to firms in developing countries which, due to exchange controls, usually cannot borrow or lend foreign currency to guard against transaction exposure. However, this is a very popular option for firms in the industrially advanced nations where exchange controls are minimal and whose currencies are freely convertible[17].

Leads and lags are the procedures of "leading" or "lagging" receivables or payables as a part of managing a form's potential transaction exposure. This strategy is utilised particularly by the multinational corporations. Depending on the transaction debts and on how a particular functional currency is likely to move vis-a-vis, the parent company's reporting currency, multinational corporations frequently report to leading and lagging with the goal of minimizing transaction losses. The major aim in all such hedging action is to match, as much as possible, the currency denomination of assets and liabilities in a foreign currency. It also aims at minimizing their subsidiary units, hard currency liabilities in a situation where the respective local currencies are continually depreciating in relation to the reporting currency[18].

III

In spite of the currency risk management techniques, there could be certain situations like the recent Asian economic turmoil where these methods will be of no avail. The recent Asian turmoil had unraveled the risks involved in economic exposure. The Asian turmoil is a financial turmoil on the surface. But an insight into the turmoil will reveal the interplay of real factors, on hindsight, the risks involved in international capital flows are exerbated when short term capital flows are attracted to the asset markets. This had led to asset bubbles, with all the painful consequences of asset price deflation. But what is much more evident in Asia is that the process of hedging, arbitrage and "carry trade" whereby arbitrageurs borrow in one market and invest in another market that offers higher interest rates, has created both regional and global contagion. Portfolio shifts mean that when asset prices (that include consumer prices, interest rate, exchange rates, debt and equity prices and property prices) change, funds will flow in and out to follow the "law of one price". This suggests that open economies must adjust to global prices. The speed of such adjustments is only determined by the degree of openness of the domestic economy and financial markets. In other words, whether we like it or not we are being priced globally by the market[19].

The global contagion had manifested in the south-east Asian economic turmoil. From around mid 1997 onwards, the currency and the stock market crises which started in Thailand rapidly spread to other countries of the region - Malaysia, Indonesia, Philippines and then to North-East Asia and Latin America, notably Brazil. Week domestic monetary and fiscal fundamentals coupled with years of artificial currency rates have been the main reasons for the ruin on currencies of South East Asia. The Thai crisis was the result of an explosive mix of current account deficit, real estate speculation largely financed by foreign currency loans and failing banks and non-banking financial institutions. In India its banks are not allowed to invest significantly in real estate businesses[20].

Banks in Thailand, Indonesia and Malaysia resorted to extensive offshore funding of their balance sheets attracted by the low interest rates on foreign currencies. These funds were lent in domestic currency to take advantage of the wide differential between domestic and foreign interest rates. What gave encouragement and confidence to lenders and borrowers was the dollar peg that supported most South Asian Currencies. The peg eliminated the foreign exchange risk in offshore borrowings. These offshore borrowings were exploded to fund loans to the property sector and against shares. This fueled a boom in property and stock prices and as long as the exchange rate was pegged, this translated into healthy profits for all those that were involved. Foreigners were allowed to hold domestic currency deposits offering yet another arbitrage opportunity between local and foreign currency interest rates. But at the beginning of july, when Thai Baht and Philippines Peso were put on a free float and Indonesian Rupiah and Malaysian Ringgit were given a wider pegging, speculators who were waiting for such an opportunity moved in an hammered respective currencies down. However, in spite of making attempts to protect their currencies, Asian Central Banks were not successful[21].

The financial turmoil suggests that while the real sector causes of the stress is global competition, the financial effect is stress on domestic banking systems, as the banks intermediate the global portfolio adjustments. In an open economy, capital inflows will increase the deposit base of domestic banks which may be channeled through credit mistakes into funding domestic and asset price bubbles. There are two implications. First, asset price inflation eventually feeds into domestic inflation and erodes external competitiveness. Second, excessive lending concentration into less productive assets, either real estate or over investment in infrastructure and production capacity exposes the financial institutions to huge risks[22].

From the view point of financial inter mediation there are three major risks in Asia that underlay the shocks in Asia: first, maturity mismatch-Asian markets made the mistake of borrowing short term capital flows to finance illiquid non-tradable, such as property, thus exposing themselves to huge liquidity needs when capital flows reversed. Second, currency mismatch-corporations who borrowed foreign currency funds to finance investments that do not generate sufficient foreign currency funds to finance investments that do not generate sufficient foreign exchange to repay the debt sum - a currency mismatch. Third, credit risk - lending or investments ultimately must be against sound profits that generate long term returns higher than the borrowing rate or prospective dividends. Undue exuberance on the part of investors, when price earning ratios grow beyond fundamentals, or on the part of bankers who failed to assess the impact of high interest rates on collateral or cash flows, would expose both the investors and the lender to asset losses[23].

In this regard, Andrew Sheng, Deputy Chief Executive, Hong-Kong Monetary Authority suggested the need for national risk management. According to him,. aside from credit risks, market risks such as interest rate, exchange rate, legal risks, operational risks and systemic risks have to be managed both at micro level and at the macro level. Mistakes at the corporate or at the bank level will add upto national mistakes, which may now add upto regional or international crisis through contagion. Traditional risk management at corporate or sectoral level simply shift risks from one sector to another. Risks still remain in the economy as a whole and financial sector regulation was all about national risk management[24].

National risk management covers six major aspects[25]. They are as given here under:

1. Credible policies, with monetary and fiscal policies consistent with each other and are applied consistently:
2. Capital account liberalization should be phased appropriately:
3. Sound fundamentals include a high domestic savings rate, suitable fiscal and balance of payments positions, high foreign exchange reserves and prudent debt management;
4. Good supervision involves the maintenance of solid capital adequacy and liquidity requirements for the financial sector, as well as regular examination and monitoring of financial sector, as well as regular examination and monitoring of financial institutions and markets. The banking system must have the capacity to avoid excessive credit concentrations and risks, and to manage market risks will. In this regard, it had been suggested that banks should adopt asset liability management. This is basically a hedging operation in financial inter mediation. Value at risk models are catching on as the technique is to calculate methodically, the amount of risk inherent in a financial port-folio at any given time. The method opts out a number known as VAR, which is the maximum money a port-folio could possibly loose in, say, the next 24 hours with a level of confidence of 95 per

cent. It looks at how risk exposures in different parts of port-folio can either amplify each other or cancel each other out. Thus the impact of interest rate volatility on the asset/liability portfolios of banks can be worked out, while for those assets and liabilities that are non-tradable and do not have market values, it can be calculated in terms of the opportunity costs or benefits using the VAR methodology. This technique does through that older risk management technique cannot such as discover "hot spots" of risks[26].

5. A robust financial infrastructure would encompass an efficient payments and settlements system for domestic and international transactions. In essence, the world is moving towards Real Time Gross Settlement (RTGS) system, which supports Delivery versus Payment (DVP) and Payments versus Payments (PVP). RTGS reduces payment risks and allows central banks to monitor flows in domestic currency as well as exposure of banks on real time basis.
6. A non-distributive incentive structure, such as taxation or regulatory restrictions that would not encourage risk concentrations or excessive leverage in any economic sector.

Asia is now in a new growth league, with grater global competition. The adjustments will not be easy, especially building stronger and more robust financial systems to handle the new risks of globalisation. As competition intensifies at all levels, there can be no reversal to the globalisation. A time has come to adopt more innovative methods of risk management to mitigate exchange risk. India is at an advantageous position as its involvement was minimal in the Asian turmoil and it can now pursue new methods in currency risk management.

REFERENCES

1. C.Arthur Williams Jr & Richard M.Heins: Risk Management and Insurance, McGraw Hill Book Co., Newyork, 1988, P.4.

2. Mark R. Greene & Oscar N.Serbein : Risk Management :Text and Cases, Peston Pub.Co., Inc. A Prentice Hall Co., Peston, Virginia, 1978, P.4.

3. Vihand R. Errunza, Devi Singh & T.S.Srinivasan : International Business Finance, Global Business Press, Delhi, 1994, P.56.

MaMark R. Greene & Oscar N.Serbein : Risk Management :Text and Cases,

4. Ibid, P.58.

5. Ibid,

6. Ibid, P.59

7. Gaurav Jetley : "Risk Management for NBFCs", Chartered Financial Analyst, Sept.1997, P.80.

8. Vihang R. Errunza, et.al. : "International Business Finance", op.cit, P.63.

9. Ibid

10. Ibid. p.65

11. Ibid. p.69

12. C.Arthur Williams Jr & Richard M.Heins: Risk Management and Insurance, Op.cit: pp.711-712.

13. Mark R.Greene & Oscar N.Serbein : Risk Management: Text and Cases, Op.cit; p.422.

14. Ibid, P.423

15. Ibid

16. Vihang R.Errunza, Devi Singh & T.S. Srinivasan : International Business Finance, Op. cit; pp.73 & 74.

17. Ibid, p.74

18. Ibid, p.75

19. Andrew Sheng: "Asset prices, Capital Flows and Risk Management:, Chartered Financial Analyst, January 1988, P.40.

20. Kiran Nanda: "South East Economic Turmoil - Implications for India". Chartered Financial Analyst, 1997, P.32.

21. Ibid, P.23

22. Andrew Sheng: "Asset Prices, Capital Flows and Risk Management", op.cit: p.40.

23. Ibid

24. Ibid

25. Ibid, p.41.

26. Ch. Rajeshwar : "Asset Liability Management, walking the tight Rope" Chartered Financial Analyst, Nov. 1997.

* * *

17

INVESTORS RISK AND ELECTRONIC SHARE HOLDING

Dr. C.S.Rayudu, Associate Professor,

Dept. of Commerce, S.K.University, Anantapur

Backdrop

For decades Indian capital market is known for its conventional, traditional and outdated modes of operations. It lacks sophistication and mechanization. It is true because the then system of settlement based on physical delivery of paper certificates was probably adequate when there was just a handful of investors participating in the transactions of the market.

Present Complexity

Over the last decade the Indian capital market has been growing by leaps and bounds. The present corporate wealth evidenced by paper amount to Rs. 4,00,000 crores held by lakhs of investors. There are about 30 million investors spread across the country , 5000 issuers or listed companies, 6,000 member brokers spread across 22 stock exchanges. For instance , the UTI Master gain 1992 has the largest record of 65 lakhs folio holders.

Risk Fraught

The trade done by the institutional investors both domestic and foreign usually involve huge volume of certificates. The physical movement of these certificates and their transfers are associated with a number of problems and or usually cumbersome and time consuming . With the increase of volumes of trading there has been an increase in the number of bad deliveries and has introduced increased risks in settlement of trades.

The following are some of the trading risks in securities.

1. Tearing, torn certificates
2. Mutilation of share certificates due to careless and mishandling
3. Fake and forgery certificates
4. Loss of certificates
5. Stolen , lost, damage delay
6. Cumbersome and time consuming and other reasons have remained unresolved

In the light of these factors and various other known reasons it was felt that the setting up a depository and introduction of script less settlement would improve the efficiency of the markets, thus eliminating the various problems brought about by dealing in physical certificates. The Government of India promulgated the Depositories Ordinance in September 1995, thus paving the way for the setting up of depositories in the country. The Depositories Act has since been passed by both the houses of the Parliament in August 1996. SEBI notified Regulations under the Ordinance in May 1996 in order to provide the regulatory framework for the depositories.

Depository

A depository is an organization where the securities of a shareholders are held in the electronic form at the request of the shareholders through the medium of participant. A depository can be conceived as a bank for securities. The main objective of the depository is to minimize the risk involved in paper work with reference to ownership , trading and transfer of securities.

The Depositories Act 1996 makes a provision for the setting up of multiple depositories in India. The investors have been granted the option of holding the securities in a physical or dematerialised form. Thus it is a matter of choice for the investors as to whether he wants to avail of the depository services. The depository has been entrusted with the responsibility of indemnifying beneficial owners for any loss caused due to negligence of the depository or its participants.

For holding securities in the depository , the two routes that are adopted by depositories world over are:

1. Immobilization
2. Dematerialisation

National Securities Depository Limited (NSDL)

The NSDL has been registered by the Securities Exchange Board of India , on the seventh June , 1996 as India's first depository to facilitate trading and settlement of securities in dematerialised form. Settlement of securities in dematerialised form will eliminat problems that are normally associated with settlement through physical certificates like tearing/mutilation of share certificates due to careless handling, loss of certificates by postal authorities or registrars or investors`, problems of bad deliveries of shares. Cases of forgery of certificates will be eliminated in an electronic environment. Settlement of trades will be faster and hassle free leading to shorter settlement cycles.

The facilities offered by the NSDL are as follows:

1. Maintain investors holdings in the electronic form
2. Enable surrender and withdrawals of securities to and from the depository i.e., dematerialisation and rematerialisation.
3. Effect settlement of securities traded on the exchanges
4. Carry out settlement of trades not done on the stock exchanges i.e., off-market trades

Dematerialisation

It is a process by which the physical certificates of an investors taken back and actually destroyed and an equivalent number of securities are credited in the electronic holdings of that investor. This is done at the request of the investors. By converting the corresponding credit is made in the form of electronic balances which are maintained in the depository.

The entire dematerialisation process at a glance involves the following process:

1. Investor surrenders certificates for dematerialisation to depository participant
2. Depository participant intimates NSDL of the request through the system
3. Depository participant submits the certificates to the registrar.
4. Registrar confirms the dematerialisation request from NSDL
5. After dematerialising certificates Registrar, updates accounts and informs NSDL of the completion of the dematerialisation.
6. NSDL updates its accounts and informs the depository participant.
7. Depository participant updates its accounts and informs investors.

Rematerialisation

The process of conversion of electronic holding back into certificates is called rematerialisation.

The rematerialisation process at a glance involves the following process.

1. Beneficial owner requests for rematerialisation.
2. Depository participant intimates NSDL of the request through the system.
3. NSDL confirms rematerialisation request to the registrar.
4. Registrar updates accounts and prints certificates.
5. NSDL updates accounts and downloads details to depository participation
6. Registrar dispatches certificates to investor.

Immobilization

One of the routes in which the securities are held by the depositories in the physical form in its won vaults but transfer of securities takes place through book entries.

Depository Participants

Depository participants are market intermediaries through which depository will interface with the investor. According to SEBI regulations, financial institutions, banks, custodians, stock holders etc., can become participants in the depository.

Achievements

Total dematerialisation requests as on February 12, 1998 in eight securities specified by the SEBI was about 51 crore shares as compared to 23 crore shares as on October 15, 1997.

NSDL which commenced operations in November 1996 with ten companies, now has 176 companies. Of them 131 companies shares are available for trading as well. Market capitalization of companies signed up for dematerialisation has crossed Rs2320 billions. Demateriliasation has been accelerating in recent years and has now crossed Rs. 145 billions. The number of client accounts has increased to about 9,000 as on 13-2-1998 from 7,500 in 12-1-1998.

NSDL launched operations in 1996 with just five depository participants, all offering depository services at Mumbai, but today there are 43 fully operational depository participants offering depository services at more than 165 different locations across the country.

At present UTI financial institutions, foreign institutional investors and Indian mutual funds, amongst others participating in NSDL by way of dematerialisation and trading.

Besides these retailed investors are responsible for the dematerialisation of more than 13,00,000 shares. A number of client accounts have increased to more than 3,000.

Distinction between Bank and NSDL

Bank	NSDL
1. Holds funds in an account	1. Hold securities in an account
2. Transfer funds between accounts on the instruction of the account holder.	2. Transfer securities between accounts on the Iinstruction of the account holder.
3. Facilitates transfer without having to Handle money.	3. Facilitates transfer of ownership without having to handle securities.
4. Facilitates safe keeping of money.	4. Facilitates safekeeping of share.

Product Features

Depository is expected to serve the Investors , Issuer, Member Broker, Stock exchange, Depository Participants and Capital Markets in general. The service depository should address the specific needs of each of these clients such that they find immense benefit out of the sysytem The following points gives the client and service relationship :

	Client	Service
1.	Small Investor	* No risk of bad delivery * Simultaneous settlement and transfer
2.	Institutional Investor	* Custodial Service * Simultaneous settlement of transfer * Substantial reduction in paper work and follow up work
3.	Issuer	* Availability of frequent information on trading patterns of its shares * Distribution of securities
4.	Depository Participant	* A totally new business avenue, an opportunity for diversification. * For the eligible financial intermediaries, a new opportunity to provide complete basket of intermediary services.
5.	Member Broker	* Risk free settlement * Opportunity to expand client base
6.	Stock Exchange	* Efficient settlement of trades
7.	Capital Market	* Opportunity to increase settlement cycles * Reduction in transaction costs * Reduction in risks in trade settlement by eliminating bad delivery, reducing the period of exposure to the market. * Efficient distribution of securities leading to improved Liquidity.

* * *

18

RISK MANAGEMENT - FINANCE AND BANKING

Dr. P. Murali Krishna
Assistant Professor, Sri Krishnadevaraya Institute of Management, S.K.University, Anantapur

M.Sreenivasulu
Officer, Andhra Bank, Pamidi, Anantapur (A.P).

It gives me great pleasure to submit this paper on the above topic, one of the areas on which the present National Seminar that is being conducted by Sri Krishnadevara Institute of Management at Anantapur.

Risk Management has got much imprtance in the Indian Economy during this liberalisation period. The foremost among the challenges faced by the banking sector today is the challenge of understanding and managing the risk. The very nature of the banking business is having the threat of risk imbibed in it. Banks' main role is intermediation between those having resources and those requiring resources. The investors do not want to accept the risks attendant thereto. Hence Financial intermediation becomes necessary and banks came into the scene and assured prompt repayment of funds and accepted the risk of default. As a compensation, they earned a net interest margin between what they paid to the investors and what they charged from the borrowers.

Being a Banker, I would likek to present here, the existance of risk, to what extent the risk can be accepted, how to overcome the risk which we have accepted, the consequences of risk that is prevailing in the Finance and Banking Sector with some examples.

Meaning of Risk

While the banks assumed the role of financial intermediation and performed the different functions, they had to accept and manage different kinds of risks. Risk could be defined as danger, volatility of outcome of simply uncertainty. Risk is not simply the incidence of adverse outcomes. Unpredicatable favourable outcomes are also a form of risk. Opportunity looses can be as important as actual losses.

Banks are facing various types of risks and all those risks are linked to profitability.

RISK - ITS EXISTENCE AND EFFECT ON PROFITABILITY

Default (Credit) Risk

Credit risk has been around for centuries long and is thought for many to be the dominant financial service risk today. This risk can be defined as the risk of erosion of value due to simple default or non payment by the borrower. In fact intermediating the risk of default between borrowers and lenders dates to the origin of banking. If net lenders themselves were willing or able to bear the risk of net borrowers a primary purpose of banking would disappear. Banks intermediate the risk appetite of lendors (depositors) and the essential riskiness of borrowers.

Banks manage this risk by :

1. making intelligent lending decisions so that the expected risk of borrowers is both accurately assessed and prices.
2. diversifying across borrowers so that credit losses are not concentrated n time and
3. purchasing third party guarantees/credit issuance so that default risk is entirely or partially shifted away from the lenders. Accepting on appropriate level of credit risk is perhaps the single largest source of "value added" in the banking and financial intermediation business.

Strategic (Business) Risk

This is the risk that entire lines of business may succumb to competition or obsolescence. An example is the relative disappearnance of the traditional market for large, low risk corporate lending that has been largely replaced by commercial paper. In the language of strategic planners commercial paper is a "substitute" product for large corporate loans.

Human Resource Risk

The departure of an employee with specialised knowledge can bring certain systems to a halt. of course protecting against that requires paying for multiple individuals with similar knowledge and experience.

Concurrent with the risk of loss of key personnel is the risk of inadequate or misplaced motivation among management personnel. Absence of incentives - or presence of the wrong incentives can produce disastrous financial results when incentives are tied to individual performance, they can undermine co-operative effort.

Conversily, group incentives can undermine individual motivation. If incentives are tied to short term results, they can compromise the long terrm.

Risk due to Unhealthy Competition

New Private and Foreign Banks have entered and created competition among the Banks in Banking sector. In recent past due to liberal licence policy of RBI, in opening Non Banking Finance Companies and also the deregulated interest rates which were offered by NBFCs and their subsequent default in repaying the deposits, majority of the public was badly affected. Due to this un-healthy competition in the Banking sector, many banks were badly affected.

Interest rates are being deregulated and given autonomy to Banks to fix interest rates. With this, the Banks are increasing interest rates on deposits and reducing PLR (due to which interest rate on advances is reduced) to capture the business resulting in low spread. This is being done for Competing the business resulting in threatining the comfortable spreads in the interest income which were very good in past.

Earlier, during the era of protective economic policies - Banking also was not an exception to the general perception of the Government regarding the management of economy. Banks were mostly used as tools in the hands of the Government for carrying out the welfare programmes and for the social and economic upliftment of the down trodden int he society. Our Government and the buerocracy were popularly perceived as a monolithic structure with what is popularly known as red tapism attitude. Only after the advent of the liberalisation and the subsequent relaxation of the licence, quota and control as a result of the various measures taken as a measures of desperation by the Government - there was a change in the Banking sector also in the form of deregulation of interest rates, licencing policy, opening of the Banking sector for domestic private banks and foreign banks etc.

It must be remembered in this context, the opinion of the experts that the biggest scam in the Indian History in the financial sector has happened only because of the earlier controls, red tapism and outdated procedures which were more shrouded in secrecy and were easily exploited by the unscrupulous people than openness and clarity which could have easily prevented the occurence of such incidents.

Governments pre-emption of Banks resources through the statutory liquidity and Cash Reserve Ratios down in stages.

Government is reducing the SLR and CRR in a phased manner. Due to which banks lendable sources are increasing resulting in Buyers market forcing the banks to search for new borrowers which leads lending indiscriminately and which may raise levels of NPA (Non Performing Assets).

The risk prevailing at this stage is dangerous. Due to stiff competition among the Banks and also huge lendable resources with the Banks, the Borrowers are attempting frequently to take advantage of it.

Pressure by the customers to waive or violate the procedures stating that other banks are allowing. Some of the banks are creating unhealthy competition by extending facilities which are of off the record for shorter periods. In some cases though banks are not providing any of such facilities, the borrowers are demanding such facilities propogating that such services are being extended by other banks.

Most of the consortium advances are becoming sick due to lack of proper information exchange among the member banks and also taking advantage of communication gap among the member banks, some of the corporate accounts are becoming default.

Integration with global financial markets will raise uncertainities.

Entry into new business to boost non-interest income will increase risks.

Under the above circumstances, the present challenges in front of banks are:

- Preventing mismatch between low interest loans and high cost borrowings.
- Appraising and monitoring assets to systematically manage credit.
- Gathering data to anticipate financial market so as to protect customers as well as the bank.
- Evolving new strategies to meet priority sector lending
- Increasing lending to priority sector if necessary without hurting asset quality

Strategies

Improve custoer service and mobilise low cost deposits by using the Branch network (Fast Collection Centres) and providing good customer services. Launching a variety of products to staunch competition from Non Bank Players. Introduction of Insurance linked deposits, mobile loan facility against deposits, quich transfer of funds, cluster branch services etc.

Quick disposal of loan applications and timely disbursement of loan amounts.

Invest in technology wherever necessary to cater to the needs of customers immediately which results in increasing number of customers as well as deposit base.

Better HRD to develop specialised skills to compete others. Improve productivity per employee to improve profitability for which appraising personnel performance is required to reward the best performing employee for motivating.

CONCLUSION

Over the past few years in our country the performance of financial markets has been greatly undergone lot of changes and development of new technologies have made emerging of new areas in the Financial sector. Owing to Govt. liberalisation policies, many foreign and private organisations have entered into financial sector resulting in stiff competition in this sector.

At this juncture, the progress/growth of any organisation depends upon the capacity to accept the risk which is prevailing in the market. The extent of risk that can be accepted by any organisation again depends upon its financial soundness in order to withstand if the result of risk goes to loss, because the result of risk either may give profit or loss. Hence understanding the risk is the first step in risk management. For this it is advisable to apply ABC analysis by assigning priorities to selected areas of business which are having considerable share instead of concentrating on all areas. Providing better on job training programmes to the personnel keeping in view all the day to day developments in the market.

The need of the hour is a people strategy. The new strategy must address important human resources issues such as organisational structure, critical skills development and control procedures. Banks must adopt top to bottom approach in case of fixing up of responsibilities and information channels from bottom to top.

* * *

19

INDIAN STOCK MARKET:A TEST OF SEMI-STRONG FORM OF EFFICIENCY

Kamaiah, Ravindranath Reddy, Venugopal Rao, Allen Roy, S.Amanulla and Bandi Kamaiah,

Dept. of Economics, University of Hyderabad.

ABSTRACT

The objective of this paper is to test the semi-strong version of efficiency of the Indian stock market. The results based on a six variable VAR model running over the period 1990.01 to 1996.12 found evidence to the effect that the Indian stock market is not an efficient absorber of information especially in respect of Government's fiscal as well as monetary policy actions.

I. Introduction

In India it is generally perceived that movements in stock prices are mostly driven by speculative forces. The reasons for this have been attributed to the existence of weak market forces and underdeveloped financial sector. During the last several years however, there has been a continuous effort to promote the role of market forces and to develop the financial sector as well. In the context of the changed economic scenario it is interesting as well as important to test as to what extent the Indian stock market is efficient. In its semi-strong form the stock market efficiency (SME) implies that stock prices 'fully and rapidly' absorb all publicly available information (PAI) and reflect the same on their prices. Broadly speaking, the PAI set pertaining to stocks/equities consists of past and contemporaneous information about the movements of stock prices and discontinuous sequence of monetary, fiscal and other important macro policy changes as well. However, in the event of arrival of new information into the market, efficiency implies that stock prices not only absorb the new information rapidly but also reflect the same on prices, by way of the price changes taking place without any additional cost (or with least cost).

In his general equilibrium model of the financial sector, Tobin (1969) has emphasised stock returns as an important link between the real and financial sides of the economy. The movements of stock returns reflect the performance of both the real and financial sides of an economy, which may be monitored by maneuvering some macro economic variables. This takes the form of fiscal and monetary policy changes with regard to real and financial sides of the economy respectively. The returns from stock being sensitive to these policy changes, is expected to shed some light on the overall functioning of the economy. The movements in stock prices act as an important feedback for the policy formulators and hence decide the future course of direction for both monetary and fiscal policy.

Within the broad framework of the monetary and fiscal policies (e.g. Tobin-1969, Darrat-1988) in which these policies are expected to have an important effect on the returns of equities, this paper attempts to investigate the relationship between aggregate stock returns and a number of important macro variables including fiscal and monetary policy actions in the case of India. Having set the objective the next step is to select a model to test the efficiency of the Indian stock market. While a number of elegant macro models are now available none of them in isolation seems capable of explaining the intricate relationship between the movements of stock prices and important macro economic variables. Furthermore for a country like India, the exact specification of a model is very difficult, particularly in the face of recent paid structural changes taking place under the new economic policy. Faced with this difficulties and in the absence of any knowledge about the 'true 'model, we believe that the Vector Auto-Regression (VAR) technique (proposed by Sims-1980; Litterman-1979; Doan et al-1984) will be appropriate in this context to empirically test the efficiency of the Indian stock market.

The period of our study ranges from 1990.01 to 1996.12, which coincides with the period of liberalisation. This period marks the beginning of massive privatisation drive and deregulation of the financial sector on a large scale in a bid to globalise the economy as part of the structural adjustment programme. All these changes tactically shifted the public eye to the stock market. This resulted in a boom in the stock market which was short lived. This period also witnessed the country's biggest ever stock scam. During this period of seven years five Prime Ministers have ruled the country signifying the extent of political instability. Since political stability is considered to be prerequisite for efficient functioning of the stock market, the sample period assumes considerable importance. The results of the present study, will not only reflect the extent to which the Indian stock market integrates the real and financial sides of the economy, but also will shed some light on the extent and speed with which it (Indian stock market) absorbs the PAI and reflects the same on its price.

While analysing the efficiency of the stock market where stock prices are calculated on a daily basis, the monthly data seem relevant. It is possible that the fiscal and monetary policy effects may be relevant in the extended quarterly period stock returns, but when monthly data are used, this effects will also be captured.

The effects of fiscal policy, monetary policy and other important macro economic variables on stock returns are examined using the Impulse Response Functions (IRFs) obtained from the moving average representations of the VAR model. In fact this IRFs will enable us to analyse the dynamic behaviour of the stock returns (SP) due to unanticipated shocks given to the policy variables. If the IRFs of the stock returns (SP) due to a one standard deviation random shock in one of the policy variables turns out to be significant (insignificant) then the stock market will be deemed inefficient (efficient) with regard to that policy variable.

The rest of the paper is organised as follows. The methodology of the paper is discussed in section II. Section III presents the empirical analysis. In section IV the results are presented. The concluding remarks appear in section V.

II. Methodology

By the very construction each of the variables in a VAR system is related to lags of itself and of all other variables in the model. This provides a fairly unrestrictive approximation to a reduced form structural model without assuming beforehand any of the variables as exogenous. Thus by avoiding the imposition of a priori restrictions on the model the VARs add significantly to the flexibility of the model. Furthermore by incorporating the lagged terms of the variables, the VARs become useful in capturing the empirical regularities embedded in the data, which consequently enable one to obtain deeper insights into the channels through which the fiscal, monetary and other important macro policy variables percolate the system in influencing the stock returns.

The beginning step of the VAR estimation procedure is the selection of variables to be included in the system. Although a VAR system is theoretical in nature, the choice of variables that constitutes it cannot be arbitrary. In the absence of a precise theory to explain the inter-link between the policy variables and stock returns, the variables included in the model should fairly account for and explain the link between the real and financial sides of the economy. Since the present study deals with the Indian economy, the model formulated should be governed by considerations of major macro-economic variables affecting the Indian stock prices within the framework of a developing economy seriously pursuing the process of liberalisation.

It is known that the built-in disadvantage of a VAR specification lies in the cover parametrization of the model itself. With the addition of every variable into the system, the number of free parameters increases quadratically. Thus to avoid the degrees of freedom only six variables are included in this study. The variables are (i) return of stock prices (SP), (ii) narrowly defined money stock (MI), (iii) budget deficit (BD) as a proportion of gross domestic product, (iv) call money rate (CR) as a proxy for the short-term interest rate, (v) index of industrial production (IIP) as a proxy for real gross domestic product and (vi) whole-sale price index (WPI) to account for the general level of prices. These six variables taken together might represent the Indian macro economy to a considerable extent.

In this study the monthly return on stock prices (SP) is calculated by taking a percentage change in the BSE sensitive index. The adjustments is SP will be the determining factor in testing the efficiency of the Indian stock market. It is worth mentioning that the rate of stock returns is defined as the dividend plus the percentage change in stock prices. Thus the only difference between stock returns and growth rates of stock prices as Cooper (1974) showed is the mean of the dividend yield. Granger (1975) has also pointed out that the variance of dividends is almost entirely dominated by stock price changes. As an approximation therefore the growth rates of stock prices used above is referred to as nominal stock returns.

On purely theoretical grounds (Tobin-1969), (Blanchard-1981) fiscal policy could have important effects on the returns of equities. Therefore as a proxy for the fiscal policy measure, the percentage of budget deficit (BD) to gross domestic product is considered in this study. Because of the non-availability of the data for the monthly budget deficit figures in India, the annual rate is taken.

There has been much investigation in the finance literature (Kaul-1987, Murthy 1996) about the relationship between stock prices and inflation rate. A common conclusion that is reached is that real stock returns are negatively related to inflation. this result although holds good for the industrialised countries, might shed some light in the Indian context which is in the process of getting industrialised. The inclusion of WPI in the model is meant to capture the possible indirect effects of BD on SP via WPI. Because for a vastly populated country like India, where still a large segment of the population live below poverty line, developmental programmes have become imperative. This triggers up the government expenditure and ultimately leads to a large budget deficit. A high budget deficit ratio will mean higher rate of inflation which will eventually depress the real stock returns.

On the other hand, inclusion of narrowly defined money stock (MI) is expected to capture not only the impact of monetary policy on stock returns but also expected to help explain the indirect relationship between inflation and stock returns. With the increase in money stock if the real side of the economy fails to catch up with increased production, then in the short-run prices tend to rise. Assuming; that nominal returns from stock increases less than proportionately as compared to rise in prices, then it will have an adverse effect on the real stock returns. Moreover money stock measure (MI) is one of the important tools in the hands of monetary authority to regulate the economy.

Another important variable included in the model is the index of industrial production (IIP). Because of the non-availability of monthly data on real gross domestic production in India, IIP is used as a proxy. The fiscal policy variable is expected to influence the IIP, which is an important indicator of the performance of the economy. If the stock prices are sensitive to the economic conditions then the inclusion of IIP in the model may help to capture the possible indirect effects of the fiscal policy actions on the stock returns.

The model also incorporates short-term interest rate i.e., call money rate (CR). This variable is assumed to be a proxy for the required return on equity. Apart from the stock market, the commercial banks also mobilise capital. On this front, there is a direct competition between the stock market and the commercial banks. Supply and demand for funds by commercial banks determine the call rate. Similarly supply and demand for stocks determine their prices. Therefore short-term interest rate and returns from stock share a significant positive relationship, because the former is considered to be the opportunity cost for the latter.

The data related to all the macro variables are collected from various issue of RBI bulletins published by the Reserve Bank of India. Monthly averages of BSE sensitive index are collected from various issues of the bulletin of Centre for Industrial and Monetary Aggregates (CIMA). From the estimation point of view, all variables except SP, BD and CR are in natural logarithmic form. The data being used in this analysis were deseasonalised using an additive procedure.

III. Empirical Analysis

The next step in estimating a VAR system is fixing the lag length (in polynomials), i.e., the order of vector auto-regression. We have experimented with a lag length ranging from 3 to 8. The likelihood ratio test confirms that lag 4 is more appropriate for the estimated models and hence the results are presented only for lag 4. A lag of 4 months seems appropriate for an analysis of the stock market where stock prices are calculated on a daily basis. In the face that both fiscal and monetary policies being revised twice every year in India, a lag of more than 4 or 5 would be misleading. Furthermore in a bid to deregulate the economy and strengthen the market forces, policy changes have become frequent during the period of study. Under such circumstances a lag of 4 months is justifiable.

Having set the lag length for the model, the next step is to estimate the model. It may be noted that the coefficients obtained from the estimation of the VAR model cannot be interpreted directly. To overcome this problem, Litterman (1979) had suggested the use of Innovation Accounting Techniques (IAT) of which impulse response function is one. The IRFs are used to asses the impact of a temporary one standard deviation shock in each of the component variables in the system on the system itself. For computing the IRFs it is essential that the variables in the system be ordered and that the system be represented by a moving average (MA) process.

We also tried several orderings of the variables with policy variables appearing first and target variables at the bottom. Since varying the order did not substantially alter the results, in the present case, we have reported the results of only one ordering in this paper, which is as follows:

VAR : (BD, MI, WPI, CR, IPI and SP).

The implication for this ordering is that current innovations in BD can affect the entire system, but a shock in MI cannot affect the current period BD. Similarly by the assumed ordering a shock in WPI cannot affect the current period BD and MI but affects all the remaining variables in the system. With this logic the variable SP has been placed at the end of the ordering with the implication that current innovation in all variables affects the current period SP where as innovations in SP itself cannot affect the current period of all variables in the model except itself.

The above ordering is in conformity with the macro economic logic. Assuming that a positive shock is injected to BD, it will force the authorities to pump more money into the economy. With an increased MI, prices will tend to rise and simultaneously short-term interest rate will shoot downwards. Rising prices and low interest rates will promote investment as a result IPI will increase. The ultimate effect would be boom in the stock market resulting in higher returns from stocks.

In the event of arrival of new information pertaining to some policy variable, it acts like a shock to the stock market. The IRFs project the responses of all the variables in the VAR system due to the unanticipated shock, over a period of time. SME hypothesis contends that absorption of new information by the stock prices is almost instantaneous. Therefore, SME to be satisfied would necessarily mean that the IRF coefficients be equal to zero (insignificant) over the period of time.

IV. Discussion of Results

As mentioned earlier, the IRFs allow to trace the dynamic behaviour of each variable due to a one standard deviation random shock given to one of the variables in the system. If the IRFs of the stock return (SP) due to a policy variable (BD or MI) turned out to be significant (insignificant) then the stock market will be deemed inefficient (efficient). The following discussion is devoted to the analysis of IRFs.

Figure-1 presents the IRF of stock return (SP) due to a one standard deviation shock given to fiscal policy measure (BD). Inspection of figure-1 reveals that fiscal policy shocks produce fluctuating responses in stock returns within five quarters. this implies that during this period the IRF is significant. And after that the IRF of stock return due to BD becomes insignificant.

Figure-2 presents the IRF of stock return (SP) due to a one standard deviation shock given to monetary policy measure M1. In this case as well M1 produces fluctuating responses in stock returns for a little less than three quarters. And beyond that the IRF becomes insignificant.

Figures 3, 4 and 5 present the IRFs of stock return (SP) due to a one standard shock given to WPI, CR, and IIP respectively. On inspection these figures also reveal that there is considerable response of stock returns to contemporaneous shock given to the above mentioned variables. These evidences suggest that the stock returns do not fully reflect the available fiscal and monetary policy information. This evidence rejects the hypothesis of stock market efficiency in its semi-strong from for the Indian economy.

It is interesting to observe that for complete diffusion of a fiscal variable shock the stock market takes around five to six quarters, where as it takes even less than three quarters for the monetary variable shock to get completely disseminated into the stock returns. These periods for which the effects of shock persists are long enough to conclude that the Indian stock market is inefficient both with regard to fiscal and monetary news. But the very fact that monetary policy shocks get diffused relatively faster as compared to fiscal policy shocks provide some stylised facts particular to the Indian economy. To begin with fiscal policy being discretionary in nature are mostly politically motivated in India. But monetary policy being rule oriented seems to be atleast more streamlined as compared to the fiscal policy measure.

V. Conclusion

The objective of this paper is to test the efficiency of the Indian stock market employing the VAR technique, using a set of monthly data over the period 1990.01 to 1996.12. The findings of our study based on the impulse response functions reject the stock market efficiency hypothesis with regard to both fiscal and monetary policy measures. The results do not seem to support the proposition that the stock prices are an important link between the real and financial sides of an economy in the Indian context. The results further indicate that changes in the stance of fiscal and monetary policy play an important role in determining stock returns. Consequently it appears that a careful analysis of Indian fiscal and monetary policy could potentially increase the profit of a diligent investor. However, such profitable opportunities would gradually disappear as an increasing number of investors begin to utilise available information on fiscal and monetary policy, thereby leading to a more efficient stock market. It is also possible, one might argue, that the model specification, period of the study, non-availability of relevant data or any other estimation problems are responsible for the efficiency evidence reported in this paper.

REFERENCES

1. Darrat, A.F. (1988), "On fiscal Policy and stock market", Journal of Money, Credit and Banking, Vol.20, pp.353-362.

2. Davidson, Lawrence, S., Richard T. Froyen (1982), "Monetary policy and stock returns: Are stock markets efficient?" Federal Reserve Bank of St.Louis, Review 64 ,pp.3-12.

3. Doan, T., Litterman, R., and Sims, C. (1984), "Forecasting and conditional projection using realistic paired distribution", Econometric Review, Vol.3, pp.1-100.

4. Hakkio, Criag, S. and Charles, S.Morris., (1984), "Vector Auto regressions : A User Guide, Research Working paper"., Federal Reserve Bank of Cansas City.

5. Hassan, A. (1990), "Innovations and anticipated policy shocks and the Canadian macro economy : A Bayesian vector auto regression approach", Discussion paper, Acadia University.

6. Kaul, G. (1987), "Stock returns and inflation, the role of the monetary sector". Journal of Financial Economics, Vol.18, pp.53-275.

7. Litterman, R. (1979),. "Techniques of forecasting using vector auto regressions". Working paper No.115, Federal Reserve Bank of Minneapolis.

8. Litterman, R. Fall (1984),. "Forecasting and policy analysis with Bayesian vector auto regression models", Federal Reserve Bank of Minneapolis, Quarterly Review 30-41.

9. Murthy Y.S.R. (1966), Stock Prices, Money, Inflation and Real Activity : A Cross Spectral View, Arth Vijnana, Vol.1, pp.34-64.

10. Runkle, D.E. Oct (1987),. "Vector auto regression and reality",. Journal of Business and Economic Statistics. Vol.5, pp.437-442.

11. S.Amanullah, A.K.Giri, B.Kamaiah (1996), "Information Arrivals, Stock Price Variability and Market Efficiency in Indian Stock Market", Artha Vijnana, Vol. pp.20-33.

12. Syed, M. Ali and M.Aynul Hassan (1993), "Is the Canadian Stock Market Efficient with Respect to Fiscal Policy? Some Vector Auto regression Results". Journal of Economic and Business, Vol.45, pp.49-59.

13. Tobin, James (1969), "A General Equilibrium Approach to Monetary Theory", Journal of Money, Credit and Banking, Vol.1, pp.15-29.

14. Umstead, David A (1977), "Forecasting stock market prices", Journal of Finance. May, pp.427-41.

* * *

20

RISK MANAGEMENT AND TECHNIQUES

Dr. Ch. Rama Prasada Rao
Professor
Dr. P. Murali Krishna
Assistant Professor
Sri Krishnadevaraya Institute of Management, S.K.University, Anantapur (India)

Introduction

Everyone of us knows that human life and possession of assets are continually exposed to loss or damage because of various reasons. There is a great deal of uncertainty and risk in life as well as in industry. Since people are aware of this uncertainty and risk of their lives and possessions they show a strong desire for security. The desire for security is sought by taking all precautions possible to avoid or prevent the consequences of risk.

Inspite of all precautions, accidents, earthquakes, floods and cyclones do occur off and on causing loss of lives and damage to property. These natural calamities that descend on humanity catch man unaware and deride his precautions taken and throw all his plans into total disarray. Therefore, it is necessary to adopt more effective techniques or devices or methods to deal with the problems of 'risk' in modern society.

Definition and a brief review of literature

Webster's dictionary defines risk as 'the chance of injury, damage, or loss'. Several financial management experts have defined 'risk' in their own way. Peterson felt that though the terms risk and uncertainty are many times used to mean their outcome, uncertainty is not knowing what is going to happen, while risk is how we characterise how much uncertainty exists. He defined risk as ' the degree of uncertainty'. The investment thinkers have opined that risk is that the actual return from holding a security will deviate from the expected return. The psychologists (Kogan and Wallach, 1964, Slovic, 1987), economists (Knight,1921), anthropologist (Douglas and Wildavsky, 1982) and sociologists (Heiomer,1988) have examined the role of risk in their respective fields of analyses in different ways.

Importance of Risk Management

Willy-nilly risk and uncertainty are real. Everyone encounters uncertainty in everyday life - uncertainty about weather, uncertainty about the performance of one's investment, and uncertainty about one's health. As future is so abound in uncertainty that to live through it, despite the thrills it offers to man, this helpless man is compelled to make an all-out effort to counterbalance this future uncertainty. Men for several years have sought ways of controlling the risk to which mankind and business ventures are subjected to. However in recent years risk management has emerged as a distinct subject and as an arm of practical management in its own right. It brings together ideas and techniques drawn from many disciplines in order to provide a sound conceptual foundation and a set of tools for the analysis and control of risk. In view of the importance of risk management, an attempt is made to present the techniques of managing financial risk.

Risk Management Techniques

There are several techniques of managing risk. The following are some of them.

1. Insurance
2. Asset/Liability Management
3. Hedging
4. Transfer
5. Risk Retention
6. Avoiding
7. Risk reduction
8. Research
9. Combination/Portfolio Management

The financial risk can be managed through insurance and asset/ liability management.

Insurance

Insurance is liable for the management of certain types of financial risks. Such risk are said to be insurable. An insurable risk is a risk to which many firms or individuals are exposed for which manifestation of the risk is not highly correlated among those exposed, and for which probability of manifestation of the risk is known with a high degree certainty . Insurable risks include such risks as death, loss from fire, loss from theft, liability, medical expense. Consider the lose of fire, damage from fire results in financial loss and the risk of fire is therefore a financial risk.

The financial risk to which the firm is exposed from fire is a function of the probability of the firm experiencing a fire and the value of the assets of risk. The risk of losses from fire is an insurable risk because many firms experience a similar exposure and these individual exposures have a never zero correlation. That is, the probability of a fire at Firm A is the same whether or not Firm B experience a fire. Additionally, while we can not say that Firm A will or will not experience a fire, we do know with great certainty the statistical likelihood (probability) that Firm A will experience a fire. The latter is established through careful actuarial studies.

For the insured firms, the payment of insurance premium, even if in excess of the amount of the exposure, may be money well spent. First, the risk-averse nature of both the firms' owners and managers suggest that they will be willing to pay up to a point, for the removal of the risk. In the language of economics, that the firms or individuals enjoy a utility gain from risk reduction. Second the firms creditors will view the firms as more credit worthy if they minimise their risk. If they are more creditworthy, the creditors may be willing to extend credit to the firms at lower cost. This reduced financing cost offsets, to some degree, the cost of the insurance.

The insurer has assumed the risk of all the individual firms. It itself is not a significant risk, because the individual risks of fire are not highly correlated. That is, the risks are unsystematic in nature. If we assume zero correlation, the insurer's per firm risk is quite small. This is a rather application of portfolio theory. Since the risks are independent of one another, the premium received from all the firms tend to offset the payments to the firms that do experience a fire. The more policies the insurer writes, the greater the degree to which the premium and policy payouts are offsetting. From the insurers perspective, its average per firm risk decreases with each new firm added to its policy base. The average per firm risk to the insurer is as follows

$$PFR = IFE \sqrt{VN}$$

PFR: Average Per firm Risk to insurer

IFE: Individual Firm's Exposure.

N : Number of identical firm's insured

The relationship between the number of firms insured and the insurer's per rupee risk exposure is shown below.

INSURERS AVERAGE RISK EXPOSURE (PER FIRM INSURED)

How Insurance Works?

Insurance works because the insurer's risk, when spread across a large policy base, is a small fraction of the insured risk. The key to the principle of insurance is the independence of the individual exposure and the spreading of the risk across a large policy base. It is called the law of large numbers.

Asset/Liability Management

Asset/liability management is an effort to minimise exposure to price risk by holding the appropriate combination of assets and liabilities so as to meet the firm's objectives (such as achieving a stated earning target) and simultaneously minimise the firm's risk. The key to this form of risk management is holding the right combination of on-balance sheet assets and on-balance sheet liabilities.

Asset/Liability management is developed for managing interest-rate risk, exchange rate risk, commodity-price risk and stock-price risk. Despite its application to other forms of price-risk, it is explained here the asset/liability management to the management of interest-rate risk.

The users of asset/liability management techniques are long term bond issuers (such as IDBI, ICICI) banks, funds collectors (such as UTI) insurance companies etc. These companies are exposed to considerable interest rate risk and it is this risk that the funds needed to manage. Bond issuer or UTI sells bonds or plans to clients to create a fund which guarantee fixed stream of future income. The fund constitute liabilities of the company. The proceeds obtained from the sale of these bonds/plans are invested in financial assets that provide a return for the fund. Fluctuations in the market interest rate, however, can and will cause the return, on the firm's assets to deviate from the return promised to the bond holders. For example, if the rates decline, the fund might find itself an insufficient return on its assets to meet the funds obligations-as represented by the claims of the bond holders. An alternative way to look at this problem is to consider the market value of the firm's assets and the market value of the firm's liabilities. While these values should initially be the same, they may not be equally sensitive to changes in interest rates. Thus, a fluctuation in rates may impact the value of the funds assets more than the value of the funds liabilities or vice versa. The RISK is then that the fund's liabilities might be undefined at the time the fund is due to pay off.

Portfolio Immunisation

Portfolio Immunisation can be used to minimise the interest rate sensitivity of the difference between asset and liability value. The concept of immunisation and the strategy for implementing it were first developed by F.M.Redington in 1952. Since the goal of immunisation is to make the asset/liability mix insensitive to interest-rate fluctuations, the starting point is to measure the interest-rate sensitivity. A technique "duration" developed by Frederick Maculae can be used to measure the interest-rate sensitivity. Duration is calculated as a weighted average of the time to the investment's maturity. The weights are the present value of the individual cash flows divided by the present value of the entire stream of cash flows. The weights, denoted hereby w(t), are then multiplied by the time at which the cash flow will occur (t/m) (where 't' denotes the number of the cash flow and 'm' denotes the number of cash flows per year). The products are then added to get duration. The following equation will give duration value measured in years.

$$D = (W(t) . (t/m)$$

The duration value is often modified by dividing by 1 plus the investments yield (Y) divided by the number of cash flows per year(m).

The modified duration is

$$D^* = D/(1+ [Y/m])$$

The problem for the fund manager is how to invest the fund to earn assured return while assuring itself that the assets in which the fund investor will have a value of least equal to that of its liabilities at each and every point of time in future. The fund manager will have option of several instruments with different maturity and yieldings.

For constructing immunised asset Portfolio to match the fluctuations in the value of assets Portfolio and Liabilities Portfolio, combine the instruments (assets) weighing in such a fashion as to produce a Portfolio Duration precisely equal to the duration of liabilities. The weight must, of course, sum to 1. The following model W1 and W2 are weights on instruments, D1 and D2 are corresponding duration's and DL denotes overall duration of the liabilities.

$$W1 . D1 + W2 . D2 = DL$$

By substituting $W1 = 1 - W2$, we can calculate the percentage of amount to be invested in each instrument. Construction of such a portfolio of assets would match the value of assets portfolio and value of liabilities portfolio to a large extent.

CONCLUSION

Some financial risks can be managed by the purchase of insurance. Risks that can be managed in this way or said to be insurable. The most price-risk , however, are not insurable. For these risks, fund manager can employ asset/ Liability management technique. Immunisation strategy is developed for the management of interest rate risk.

* * *

21

INSURANCE EDUCATION AND TRAINING IN INDIA

S.D.Puranik,

Registrar, National Insurance Academy, Pune.

Need for Education and Training in Insurance

Insurance is still not fully developed as a boty of knowledge where education even at the university level can be pursued. Insurance is still learned through practice on the job. With the increase in the economic and industrial activity all over the world, the need for proper insurance coverages, both personal as well as for the property, has been increasing. This need has lead to development of a number of insurance policies leading to each aspect of insurance becoming more and more complex.

Since knowledge about insurance practices is not available through formal sources of education, separate facilities are essential for education and training in insurance.

Insurance operations are broadly concerned with following aspects-

I. Technical aspects of insurance - underwriting, claim settlement, risk management etc.
II. Marketing
III. Investment
IV. Management of Human Resources

These four broad areas are to be taken into account in the context of general economic and industrial conditions and its growth, legal aspects, and the socio-political aspects and development of a country.

Insurance education and training therefore has to be concerned with all these aspects. Additionally, insurance companies have to run their affairs as a business proposition - a profit making organisation. It is therefore required that insurance companies conduct their affairs in a scientific and business like manner and hence managing insurance business is also a very important area in which education and training is required.

Human resources is the most important component of any business and it is in the interest of each insurance company to ensure that proper attention is paid to the development of its human resources through education and training. Management education in insurance companies is therefore necessary for the supervisory and middle/senior levels of management. As a person grows in an organisation his job profile and responsibilities is necessary at periodical intervals. The need for insurance education and training therefore can be classified as follows:

1. Induction training
2. Knowledge about basic principles of insurance, various types and classes of insurance and its practices, underwriting and claim settlement.
3. Managing insurance business.

The objectives of training in insurance is towards achieving the following purposes:

1. People working n insurance companies need to learn the principles of insurance business.
2. People working in insurance companies need to upgrade their skill in functional areas like
   I. underwriting (selections, rating, retention limits, reinsurance, new product development etc.
   II. claims settlement (fair evaluation, administration and fraud prevention).
   III. managerial intermediaries, risk assessment, product knowledge
   IV. actuarial and statistical
   V. legal
   VI. investment of funds and accounts.

3. People working as intermediaries (agents, brokers etc.) need to learn to identify possible risks in the customers' situation and to match these risks with available insurance covers.
4. The public need to be aware of how to manage the risks to which they are exposed and how to avoid/reduce losses.

Growth of Human Resources in Insurance Sector in India:

Insurance companies have been functioning in India since the British rule. These companies have been composite companies transacting life and non-life business as well as specialised companies transacting either life or non-life business.

Before nationalisation of life business in 1956 and of general insurance business in 1971, some efforts of introducing training was made by New Indian Assurance Co. Ltd. through its apprenticeship course introduced in 1948.

The staff strength of employees in Life Insurance Corporation of India (LIC) at the time of nationalisation of life business in 1956 and now is given below:

	1957	1994
Class IV	4920	10693
Class III	19588	65581
Class II	5222	16580
Class I	1038	12064

In case of general insurance, the position in 1977 and now is given below:

	1977	1997
Class IV	3885	11179
Class III	17023	45059
Class II	6440	13160
Class I	3885	15294

The tremendous increase in the number of employees working in the insurance sector from the date of its nationalisation is an indicator of the need for insurance education and training for the professional development of manpower.

Present facilities available for education and training

The present position in regard to facilities available for education and training is as follows:

A. Industry Level

1. Insurance Institute of India
2. Actuarial Society of India
3. College of Insurance
4. National Insurance Academy

B. Life Insurance

1. Management Development Centre of LIC
2. Zonal Training Centres of LIC
3. Sales Training Centres of LIC

B1. Training of field staff in life insurance

1. Institute of Insurance & Financial Science Education Research & Training
2. Jeeva Vidya Trust
3. College of Insurance and Financial Planning

C. General Insurance

1. Learning centres of each subsidiary company (Corporate Training Centres)
2. Regional Training Centres of Subsidiary Companies
3. Development Training Centres of subsidiary companies

D. Facilities available in the University set up/other centres of higher learning

E. Training of industrial customers

A. 1. The Insurance Institute of India:

The Insurance Institute of India was established in 1955 for the purpose of imparting insurance education to persons engaged or interested in insurance. The Insurance Institute of India conducts examinations at various levels and arranges tuition services, both oral and postal. It is the only professional institute in India engaged in insurance education.

Scheme of Study:

A candidate is expected to study the course contents in depth and also assimilate general information relevant to the prescribed subject. However, the extent of study required to be made at each level of examination is general as follows:

i. CIS AND INSPECTORS' EXAMINATIONS:

These being courses to professionals the development personnel in the industry, the basics of principle and practices of Insurance (life and Non-life) (separately) and salesmanship are to be mastered.

ii. LICENTIATE EXAMINATION:

Only the fundamentals of Principles and practice of Insurance (Life and Non-life) and Elements of Modern Commerce are to be grasped fully. This is essentially an introductory course.

iii. ASSOCIATESHIP EXAMINATION:

Specialisation comprising of six technical subjects in any chosen branch is the approach at this level of examination. However, it is necessary that candidates should have comprehensive knowledge to technical subjects and related problems in each branch.

iv. FELLOWSHIP EXAMINATION:

This is the highest level and involves advanced studies of prescribed areas. Study courses form only the broad basis of examination. Further, stress is laid on application of acquired knowledge to a given situation or problem or case studies, involving additional reading as well.

The LIC and the General Insurance Corporation of India attach a great deal of importance to these examinations. A scheme of reward on passing such examinations is in existence currently in these organisations. It is regarded important for career development in these organisations. A large number of insurance employees appear for these examinations every year.

2. Actuarial Society of India:

Actuarial Society of India was established in 1944 to provide a central organisation for members of the actuarial profession in India for the purpose of elevating the attainments and status as also promoting the general efficiency of all who are engaged in occupations connected with the pursuits of an Actuary.

The ASI conducts examinations in actuarial science which are recognised by the Institute of Actuaries, London. The examinations held are as given below:

1. Entrance Examinations
2. Associateship Examination
3. Fellowship Examination

These examinations are the only source of supply of actuaries in the insurance industry. Actuaries are said to have good opportunities for career development in the insurance industry. A good number of candidates appear every year for these examination.

3. College of Insurance:

The College of Insurance, founded in 1966, is the training wing of the Insurance Institute of India. It is run by the Institute to cater to the training needs of insurance personnel at different levels. The college has a full time principal. the faculty consists of qualified and experienced officials of the insurance industry. Experts from outside the insurance industry are also invited as guest faculty.

The college has been recognised by the Government of India as an institution for higher learning in insurance. The Government of India has been sponsoring candidates to the college from several Afro-Asian countries under Colombo and SCAAP Plans. Admission to the courses structured and organised by the college is through sponsorship only.

4. National Insurance Academy

Structure: The National Insurance Academy was established in December registered as a Society, it is sponsored jointly by the Life

Insurance and General Insurance Organisations in India, with support of Government of India. the Academy is managed by a Governing Board consisting of persons representing the insurance industry, the Government of India and experts in the field of finance and management education.

Need for the establishment of the Academy

The organisations referred to in A to E catering to the education and training needs of the insurance industry were in existence and performing their role effectively when this Academy (NIA) was established in 1980. The need for such an Academy was felt on account of the following reasons:

i. There were no institutional facilities for training of middle/senior level executives in
   a. technical areas
   b. general management, policy formulation etc. areas
ii. Lack of availability research facilities

The NIA was therefore established in 1980, with the following objectives:

To promote and provide facilities for education and training in operations and management of insurance business

To provide consultancy and other advisory services to life and general insurance business in matters or improvement and economic betterment.

To promote and conduct research on problems of insurance management, training and development of insurance personnel, insurance policy etc.

To promote and undertake faculty development programmes to ensure and adequate supply of competent trainers to the training establishments of insurance companies

To disseminate information on management know-how and for furtherance to its objectives.

In line with the above mentioned objectives, the Academy has been effectively functioning in the following areas:

* Training
* Research
* Consultancy
* Publications

Training

As regards training, NIA has been conducting programmes for the following levels:

Life Insurance - Assistant Divisional Managers and above
General Insurance - Assistant Managers and above

In addition to the insurance organisations, a few financial institutions have also been participating at NIA programmes.

The programmes conducted by NIA are of following types:

i. Advanced Skills and knowledge in technical aspects of insurance.
ii. Managing insurance business
iii. Programmes for trainers
iv. Programmes for customers

The Programmes organised by NIA therefore could be classified under the following broad areas:

1. Programmes for Top Management
2. General Management, Education and Training
3. Marketing and public relations
4. Financial Management and Financial Services
5. Human Resources Management
6. Computers and Information Technology
7. Insurance (Technical)

As long as the Academy was located in Mumbai i.e. from 1980-90, the scale of activities undertaken was very modest on account of constraints by way of faculty resources, infrastructural facilities etc. the Academy shifted to its campus in 1990 and has been offering, since then, a large number of residential programmes. The scale of training now handle is reflected in the statistics given below:

Year	No. of programmes	No. of participants
1992-93	73	1550
1993-94	92	2250
1994-95	82	1887
1995-96	85	1864
1996-97	79	1797

Programmes organised overseas

The Academy gets invited from time to time to organise programmes for overseas companies in their own countries. In the past three years such programmes have been organised by NIA for the following companies/countries.

1. Ethiopian Insurance Corporation, Addis Ababa, Ethiopia
2. Fidelity Life Insurance of Zimbabwe (Private) Limited, Harare, Zimbabwe.
3. First Mutual Life Assurance Society of Zimbabwe, Harare, Zimbabwe
4. Lion of Zimbabwe Insurance Company Limited, Harare, Zimbabwe
5. National Bank of Ethiopia, Addis Ababa, Ethiopia
6. National Insurance Corporation of Tanzania Limited, Ear-se-Salaam,Tanzania
7. National Insurance Company of Zimbabwe Private Limited, Harare, Zimbabwe
8. Nyala Insurance Share Company, Addis Ababa, Ethiopia.
9. Oman United Insurance Company, Addis Ababa, Ethiopia.
10. PT (Persero) Reasuransi Umum Indonesia, Jakarta, Indonesia.
11. Professional Insurance Corporation Zambia Limited, Lusaka, Zambia.
12. Zimnath Life Assurance Company Limited, Harare, Zimbabwe
13. Zimnath Insurance Company Limited, Harare, Zimbabwe.

The subjects covered at such programmes included-

1. General Insurance - Technical Aspects,
2. Insurance Regulation and Supervision
3. Life Insurance - Technical Aspects
4. Marine, Cargo and Hull Insurance

5. Marketing of Insurance Services
6. Strategic Management

Faculty

The faculty of the Academy in multidisciplinary in composition drawn from insurance practitioners (life and non-life), academicians and professionals and cover a wide range of areas. The faculty also has a mix of full time as well as part time associate faculty members. In addition, faculty from international insurance companies are also drawn as and when required.

Funding

The entire capital expenditure for setting up this Academy in Mumbai and in Pune has been borne by the LIC and GIC and subsidiary companies. In the initial years, a major part of the recurring expenditure was also contributed by LIC, GIC and subsidiary companies. However, with the increase in the quantum of its activity, NIA has been able to attain self sufficiency in financial matters in 1992-93 and thereafter.

International Recognition

NIA is recognised as a premier institution for training in insurance in developing world by the following organisations:

i. African Insurance Organisation
ii. Federation of Afro-Asian Insurers and Reinsurers
iii. Third World Insurance Congress

B. LIFE INSURANCE

Life Insurance Corporation of India

Objectives of Training: One of the objectives of the LIC is to involve all people working in the corporation to the best of their ability in furthering the interests of the insurance public to provide efficient service with courtesy. Training *inter alia*, is an essential support to achieve this objective. Training is an integrated part of the Human Resources Development Programme of the Corporation. Training contributes in keeping people dynamic and provides an opportunity to employees to develop better understanding of what they do apart from enhancing their capability individually. Specially, the objectives of training are -

I. To acquire knowledge and skills necessary for the job, by understanding why the job is performed and how it can be improved
II. To acquire necessary supervisory/managerial skills in areas of decision-making, problem-solving, role clarity and role performance, inter-personal relationship etc.
III. Training to be seen as an important factor for managing change and achieving excellence.
IV. To develop internal faculty support on all areas, by a systematic faculty development
V. to develop expertise who shall guide the organisation through an effective internal consultancy system
VI. To identify the training needs of the entire personnel in consultation with operating managers.
VII. To dovetail training to the career-planning of the personnel in the industry
VIII. To achieve total effectiveness of training through tapping the in-house training facility as well as the sources available externally, in a balanced manner.

1. Management Development Centre

It runs the following type of courses for officers:

a) Management programmes and special seminars/workshops in identified areas.
b) Training of Trainers programmes
c) Functional programmes

2. Zonal Training Centres (Seven)

The ZTCs are expected to conduct the following kind of courses:

Courses on general management
Courses on supervision for categories listed n the schedule
Functional Training
Sale training
Seminars on special subjects
HGA, Section Head training

Staff training

3. Sales Training Centres (STCs)

STC holds programmes for development officers and other field staff. The nature of training is

ADOs training
Development Officers Training
Club members other than Chairman's & ZM's club members
Selected agents 'training

B1 Training of Field Staff in life insurance

There are three institutions in the country which are involved in the training of agents/development officers dealing in life insurance. These institutions are supported by Life Insurance Corporation of India by way of nominating agents and development officers for training at its cost. These institutions are

I. College of Insurance and Financial Planning, Secunderabad
II. Jeevan Vidya, Jaipur
III. Institute of Insurance and Financial Sciences Education, Research and Training (IFSERT), Pune.

C. GENERAL INSURANCE

The importance attached to training by the General Insurance Corporation of India, which is a holding company, for its four subsidiary companies viz.,

1. National Insurance Co.
2. New India Assurance Co.
3. Oriental Insurance Co.
4. United India Insurance Co.

is well illustrated in the preamble to its 'Training Research and Development Policy' as reproduced below-

Preamble:

General Insurance is a service industry; its key resource is competent and efficient manpower with a right attitude. The industry has been placing considerable stress on imparting effective and continual training to its employees, particularly after its nationalisation n 1973. It feels that it should continue to help its employees, in a planned and systematic manner, to acquire and sharpen capabilities required to perform various functions associated with their present or expected future rules and also to develop their strong organisational culture characterised by discipline, team work, collaborative practices, supportive and synergic superior-subordinate relationship, professional ethics, concern for customers, sense of belonging and a feeling a well-being on the part of all section of employees. A clearly laid-down Training Policy, therefore, becomes essential to give proper direction at all levels to achieve this mission.

The need to expand training activities in an orderly manner has, therefore, become accentuated in the context of -

I. changing insurance market, new legislative measures, consumer protection movement, globalisation markets, environmental issues, advances in computer technology, competition from unexpected sources, internal and external pressures faced by the industry.
II. Steady expansion of General Insurance Business by way of opening of large number of administrative and operating units viz. Regional Offices, Divisional Offices and Branch Offices, resulting in considerable growth of manpower in the industry.
III. Introduction on no-conventional types of insurance covers to suit the growing demands of Personal Insurance Business and in Industrial, Commercial, Agricultural sectors of the Indian Economy.
IV. Designing and marketing of new insurance covers for the benefit of economically weaker sections of the society both in rural and urban areas.
V. Developing a reinsurance market in India and formulating products to meet the requirements of technology changes in the context of the emerging mega-risks in the Indian scene.
VI. Improving the quality of service with professional approach aiming at creative customer satisfaction management
VII. Developing and enhancing versatility in the capabilities of individuals to achieve improved effectiveness in handling inter-functional / multi-dimensional jobs.

VIII. Evolving a culture of business and participative management leading to an institutional approach rather than an individualistic approach.

IX. It is, therefore, considered necessary to adopt a goal-oriented training policy with a view to developing human resources with adequate knowledge, attitude, sharpened skills and habits leading to effective professional approach and increased customer satisfaction and to relate it to the business needs of the general insurance industry.

2. OBJECTIVES OF TRAINING

1. To create constant awareness in the minds of all sections of employees of the mission of the industry, its objectives and goals.
2. To encourage self-development to achieve organisation goals with a sense of belonging and commitment to organisation and thereby ensuring development of a proper work ethos in the industry and fostering of team spirit.
3. To identify the training needs of the entire personnel in Industry in keeping with the corporate plans and in consultation with the user organisation.
4. To impart knowledge and skills necessary for performing the job efficiently and effectively and to help the employees to acquire necessary conceptual, technical, human and managerial skills in the areas of decision-making and problem-solving.
5. To make available in adequate number sufficiently trained manpower to meet to diverse needs of a rapidly growing industry.
6. To provide the Agents, Marketing Agents, Rural Representatives etc. with the required knowledge, skills, attitudes and habits for improving their marketing ability and better customer service.
7. To organise special training programmes to improve employment opportunities as well as career prospects of persons belonging SC/ ST, minorities, handicapped, ex-servicemen etc.
8. To organise training activities as aids to:
   i) Career Planning and growth ii) Succession planning
9. To educate and equip the employees to respond to the expectations of customers, and to accept responsibilities to attain a sense of achievement.
10. To achieve effectiveness of training through tapping the in-house training facilities as well as sources available externally in a balanced

manner so as to develop internal faculty support at all levels and disciplines

11. To promote research and development activities and to establish linkages with the operational front.

In pursuance of this policy and objectives as laid down by GIC, each of the companies as mentioned above has three types of training centres, vis., Corporate Training College (CTC), Development Training Centre (DTC) and Regional Training Centre (RTC). The training imparted at these institutions cater to the following categories of staff.

CTC - Assistant Administrative Officers to Managers
DTC - Development Officers, Marketing agents etc.
RTC - Supervisory, clerical and subordinate staff

The courses conducted include

CTC - Technical subjects
General Management and Human Relations Skills
Marketing Skills
Functional Knowledge
Computing skills
Customer servicing

RTC - Subject knowledge
Customer servicing
Office procedures
Conduct rules
Drafting skills
Communication skills

DTC - Product knowledge
Sales Planning
Sales Training
Supervisory skills etc.

For the levels of Assistant Managers and above the general insurance companies are dependent on NIA for technical subjects, managerial skills, policy formulation, economic and social environment scanning, planning and budgeting, decision making, problem solving, functional policies etc.

D. Facilities available in the University Setup / other centres

As stated in the beginning itself, insurance has still not developed as a body of knowledge even at the level of Universities and other institutes of higher learning. A few Universities have introduced some insurance related subjects as electives for masters course in the commerce faculty. The Indian Institute of Insurance and Risk Management organises a few workshops/Seminars/Conferences. It also sponsors students for examinations of Institute of Risk Management (U.K.)

E. Training of Industrial Customers

Insurance awareness is essential for spread of insurance business. To that extent, special efforts need to be undertaken. The aspects of insurance with which industrial customers are concerned are in the realm of general insurance as well as group and pension schemes.

A few programmes/workshops/seminars are being conducted from time to time by the general insurance companies as well as Indian Institute of Insurance and risk Management. National Insurance Academy also conducts a few such programmes every year.

SUMMARY

In the near future, insurance sector in India is likely to get opened up for other companies also. This may lead to increase in demand of training facilities offered by the above referred education and training organisations in India. The training system will therefore have to introduce qualitative changes as well as expand its capability.

(The above referred information covers the extent, spread and variety that is presently available in India in Insurance Education and Training mainly for the two public sector insurance organisations. No effort is made to go into the details of the quality of training imparted, course syllabus, training effectiveness, quality of trainers, infrastructural facilities available for training and all other administrative aspects).

* * *

22

EDUCATIONAL INSTITUTIONS CAN BE AN ALLY TO INSURANCE INDUSTRY

Appa Rao Machiraju

Founder Director, College of Insurance and financial Planning, Secunderabad

Insurance service serves the interests of a developing country in numerous ways. Insurance serves a social purpose by providing economic security to individual citizens, who purchase life insurance policies provide their families with a measure of protection against adverse financial consequences of premature death. In the process of providing indemnity of lost life values, of writing annuities and of furnishing many collateral services, the insurer accumulates capital funds. Thus, the insurer is at once an important social enterprise, a financial institution of colossal magnitude, and a provider of an economic device of far-reaching social significance.

Important as is life insurance today, its real progress is yet to come in our country. Education of the public through nation's educational force of importance because it has not had the "indoctrinating" influence from our educational system to the applications of the insurance principles in economic affairs.

Need-based Assessment

Insurance education through College and Universities can represent can represent a great teaching movement to spread the beneficient influence of life as well as general insurance to households and business enterprises.

We shall thus be able to add the most important educational force of all, the family unit itself.

Education as to principles, and economic purpose and mission of life insurance are equally important to the field contact personnel entrusted with the work of counselling the insuring public. The fact that proper understanding and interpretation of application of insurance principles to the best advantage of the insuring public underscores the need for early and continuing and frequent educational work to help every working man/woman towards an adequate comprehension of his/her economic position.

A collegiate/university level course, emphasizing the economic services of life insurance, is almost non-existent either as a part of economics or commerce curriculum in our country. It is important that students of social sciences and the public generally, and the practitioners in the insurance field should be exposed to the subject of insurance as an academic discipline with its fare reaching and manifold usefulness to the family, to business, and to the society. It deserves much more thought, planning and missionary zeal that has been bestowed upon the subject thus far in India.

As Vocational Education

Insurance and financial service counselling as a vocation involves a science and in its practice, an expert knowledge of that science. It is an inherently useful and noble callilng, and necessary for the public welfare. To be competent to serve as an adviser to the insuring public, the insurance counsellor, like the lawyer or accountant, must have familiarity with numerous subjects - economics, social problems, taxation, commercial and insurance law, wills, trusts and estates, business and family finance, banking and credit, and investments. Knowledge of human behaviour and marketing concepts must be joined with sound business training. A vocation does not make itself a profession overnight. Rather, the process is evolutionary, through the attainment of higher standards of skill and practice over a period of years.

Our time-honoured professions use colleges and universities as allies for the effective intial preparation of their practitioners and to provide opportunity for continued study. It has to be so with insurance subject as well which is a relative new comer on our socio- economic scene. Insurance and financial counselling as a vocation and profession could advance and acquire stature and dignity in direct proportion to the education received and success achieved by those in the business and with the pblic. Industry based inhouse education training programmes currently conducted for the benefit of the field practitioners nevertheless should continue but not to be treated as substitutes for the courses offered through independent educational institutions.

Imperative Need

Those who are qualified in the disciplines of actuarial sciences and accounting are well postioned now within the infrastructure of the insurance industry in our country. Facilities for study of these subjects are organised and available. The emphasis in the available study-material through the few publications is on mathematical principles andn operating practices. The imperative need now is for organised study programmes and study literature aimed at presenting comprehensively the service phases of life insurance to the students of economics, to vast field forces who should serve as counsellors to the public and to the public generally. The purpose of the educational facilities to be developed is to conceive, prepare and foster the study programmes assuring substantial mastery of the knowledge referred to. Emphasis should be on concepts and practical application of the required concepts. The educational infrastructure, when developed gradually through a network of several educational institutions, can be of aid to the insurance industry in developing public awareness that the counselling they receive is backed-up by good knowledge of the subject matter. Also, this approach will have tremendous impact in projecting insurance work as a vocation which can evolve, over a period of time, as a professional practice with satisfaction of rendering a useful service and securing monetary rewards.

The fundamental truths of economics and social philosophy of which application of insurance principles is an integral part, could most logically and effectively be given within the public education system. In fact, this should be the first and most important step taken in the process of developing marketing methodology and marketing orientation.

Public Opinion

It is time we recognise the urgent need to develop educational facilities for the benefit of the field contact personnel so that they can be advisors and counsellors instead of mere order taking salesman.

It is only through a comprehensive system of education, the 'concept' of insurance principle can spread vigorously and honestly. It is high time that a proper public opinion is developed and gradually the habit of thought moulded favourably to be receptive to economic security needs.

There is a core of knowledge of insurance which every citizen should possess and further there is a solid core of special fundamental knowledge, with which one who is to be an insurance counsellor must have to function effectively. A cooperative effort and attempt to find a place for it in educational institutions will be in the interest of the educational system, the industry and the society.

* * *

23

INSURANCE EDUCATION IN INDIA

N. V. Subbaraman

Senior Divisional Manager, LIC of India, Cuddapah.

I deem it a great privilege to participate in this UGC sponsored National Seminar on "Risk Management as modern Welfare Measure in India" under the auspices of Sri Krishnadevaraya Institute of Management held today in this great premises of S.K.University. My compliments to all the organisers of this Seminar for their farsightedness in choosing this theme which is increasingly becoming relevant and assumes greater significance in the light of the fact that this great country and the world around us is fast approaching the onset of the twenty first century.

As a person holding dear to the heart that peace, progress and prosperity in any area to a larger extent depends on the depth of education the society is provided with, I use to feel bad that we as a responsible lot have failed to provide necessary education in several fields and one such important area is "Insurance Education". No seminar on the theme chosen for the current occasion can be a comprehensive one without "Education" aspect and hence I chose this topic for presentation today and the result is this paper.

Risk Management is no doubt a technical topic comprising various facets and unless one has a basic knowledge about the same, one can not manage and much less one can not apply his mind. But the fact remains that "Risk Management" is a part of every individual, every institution and every business concern, because no matter how one lives, how a business is conducted or how an institution is managed, it is impossible to avoid all risks that they are exposed to. At best risk can be managed or minimised, if not totally avoided. For this an elementary knowledge of the risk - its source, dynamics, economics, approach, strategy is absolutely essential. Institutions and business concerns as they are conducted in a systematic manner realised the importance of risk management and began taking appropriate steps. As they have the paraphernalia, risk management by risk forecasting is not a difficult thing for institutions. But an individual who has to take care of his own life, his properties particularly against the background of increasing propensity of exposure to risks is left deficient in techniques of risk management. Therefore enlightening the public on areas of risk, ways to handle the risk is an important task before all the responsible forums like us. These forums can undertake the job of risk identification, risk evaluation, risk handling and finally risk management from the individual's viewpoint. By this I mean the educational institutions, universities, social service organisations who have got say in the society, whose message is respected by the society can suggest ways and means for risk management. It is like reading the pulse and giving the pill - what a doctor does without exactly informing the patient what he is ailing from or what drug he requires, because he may not fully understand the scientific aspect of the treatment.

The Playing field

If we consider the global population in this century we find that in 1925 the world population was 2 billion. It reached three billions in 1960, four in 1974 and five in 1987. While to take 25 years for increase of one billion the next and subsequent billions were added in shorter spans of 14, 13 years respectively. India too contributed for his growth of population. Thus a huge potential was available for the lone players in the Insurance industry. Economic conditions of the Nation also favoured rapid growth of the Industry. The economic reforms process initiated in 1991 has gained momentum year after year in the form of accelerated growth in manufacturing service and agricultural sectors like the GDP has moved from 5.4% to over 7% during the period 1991-96. The above analysis indicates that given the potential and the favourable market condition, it should have been a cakewalk for the industry to achieve this growth.

Yet it is of great interest to learn, read, and participate in the discussions on the various issues concerning the industry. In India right from 1992, we are talking about financial sector reforms. Since the formation of the Malhotra Committee there has been intense debate and speculation of the opening up of the Indian Insurance Industry. These had been accentuated and highlighted by the various pronouncements by the Finance Minister in his Budget speech in July '96 and Feb '97. The introduction of IRA Bill, its subsequent withdrawal and its aftermath may have apparently slowed down the progress but every one realises that a phased opening up of the Insurance sector is possibly around the corner whoever is going to govern the country.

Probably foreign Insurance companies see the vast potential and the vast uncovered ground in India as an opportunity to expand their markets.

Risk Management the LIC, GIC way:

When it is accepted that all risks can not be avoided, but can only be managed by minimising the loss, the immediate and best way to manage it is insuring the risk for indemnifying the loss to as great extent as possible. LIC and GIC are the lone players in the insurance market, which trades the concept of insurance, which is synonymous with "risk management". Risk Management has been practically rendered possible for the individuals and institutions in our country by the insurance industry. The basic objective of LIC is to provide insurance protection to all insurable persons and that of GIC is to cover all possible risks in general sector. In as much as the insurance industry is a service industry, its primary concern is to give the best possible service for the society's welfare. Here it is very relevant to the present topic that how do we go about looking after the welfare of the individuals, welfare of the society and welfare of the Nation.

Ours is a democratic country and a welfare state. Our former president Dr.S.Radhakrishnan observed that "we forget that the individual's welfare is the end of the State" and went on "when we call ourselves a democracy we mean that the state exists India through Life Insurance Corporation of India for promoting the good of its members".

True to his expectations the Government of India is providing free and otherwise Life Insurance Cover to the vast multitude of this country.

LIC and GIC since their nationalization in 1956 and 1971 respectively have grown in size and stature. LIC has spread its wings as a strong and vibrant organisation with a huge market spread in terms of both offices and representatives all over the country and abroad. In 40 years, it has increased to about 9 times in terms of number of Branches, 160 times in terms of total premium income and more importantly it has a strong rural base. The life fund has grown to astronomical 87000 crore. Bonuses have acquired a height over the last few years compared to the bonus being given at the time of nationalisation. GIC too has grown enormously spread its activities to over 30 countries across the globe. It has a varied product line, which covers a gamut of areas where risk management by insurance is possible. This phenomenal growth in the industry has become possible due to the huge potential and the monopoly enjoyed by the Corporations in their respective sectors of life and general insurance. But how good this growth has enabled us to extend the welfare measures is the question. Figures can speak more about it. (As I come from LIC, I can give very precise figures for the operations covered by LIC).

* LIC Operates from 1200 Rural Branches out of the total 2027 Branches in the country in tune with its objective of taking the message of insurance to the nook and corner of the country.
* There is an increase of rural share of business to 49.18% in policies & 42.78% in terms in terms of Sum Assured.
* The purpose behind nationalisation and creation of LIC was to take the benefit of life insurance to weaker sections of the Indian population at a reasonable cost. Providing protection to such sections of the society is our social commitment which LIC has been fulfilling though its increasing Group Insurance portfolio as well as through various Social Security Schemes it today administers. The total group insurance portfolio in force as at 31st March '97 increased to Rs.64, 606 crores of Sum Assured covering 238.97 lakhs lives under Group Insurance Schemes and 5.54 lakh lives for Rs.545.59 crores of annuity per annum under Group Superannuation Schemes.
* The Government of India set up Social Security Fund in 1989 and gave LIC the responsibility to manage this fund. The fund

is utilised to subsidise premium in respect of various social security group schemes providing life insurance cover of Rs.5000 per member (enhanced to Rs.25, 000/- in case of accidental death or total permanent disability due to accident) to 23 approved occupations amongst the weaker sections of the society. About 49.35 lakh people were enjoying this cover as at 31st March '97. In addition LIC also provides free insurance cover of Rs.2000/- to about 1.2 crores landless agricultural labourers under the LALGI Scheme. Besides LIC also manages the Social Security Scheme for over 1.28 crores IRDP beneficiaries which provides insurance cover of Rs.5, 000 on death enhanced to Rs.10, 000 in case of accidental death to every member.

* Under the Rural Group Life Insurance Scheme (RGLIS) during the year 1996-97 LIC extended coverage to 28,756 lives under the General Scheme and 5,87,477 lives under the subsidised scheme.
* The funds mobilised are invested in infrastructure development and in socially oriented schemes. Rs.2099 crores have so far been invested in socially oriented schemes with the objective of utilising people's money for people's welfare.

Inspite of the astonishing growth of LIC of India in its 40 years of existence, in its every facet of life insurance, it is to be deeply pondered over as to whether we have penetrated into the whole of Indian market. As per 1991 census the country had a total population of 91 crores which has in the last 7 years increased to 97 crores. Whereas the total life insurance policies in force as at 31.3.97 were 7.78 crores. A hooping gap between the total population and the life insurance policies in force.

Though the growth in industry has been quite satisfactory when considered independent of the monopolistic status enjoyed by its, the vast uncovered ground and the immediate necessity of the people to get insurance protection as a risk management measure tame the long strides made by the industry. This is where we find an abysmal bridge gap between the insurance needy population and the risk managers LIC and GIC. The bridge should naturally be to bring insurance consciousness among the people.

Insurance Education - Our Role

As far as LIC is concerned, we have been trying to impart Insurance education through various media. 5,60,000 strong agency force and probably half if its number in GIC is our primary force to bring insurance consciousness among the public. The publicity efforts in the form of advertisements in print media and electronic media do not still reach the nookest corner of the country. Literacy level is being very low, these efforts would not make much inroads. Those who show insight into the insurance needs, knowledge about the same and awareness to the public are mainly insurance agents - whose knowledge itself leaves much to be desired. LIC provides training to the agents through its sales training centres, Divisional training centres, Zonal training centers and through some of the outside training institutes recognized by the Corporation viz., IFSERT, Pune, CIFP, Secunderabad, JVT, Jaipur and PEACOCK, Thanjavur. LIC also provides in-house training facilities to other field and administrative staff, but this would only be useful for their administrative requirements.

After 50 years of independence lot of educational reforms and advancement of country, it is our misfortune that no concerted systematic and scientific system of providing insurance education, to bring about insurance consciousness right from the primary level is not available due to which conscience of risk management is practically zero in the society. On an experimental basis a few CBSE schools at Higher Secondary level provided insurance education with a well-defined syllabus but that is also discontinued today. At college levels insurance was kept as a subject in Commerce group in some of the Colleges but it has not made headway in creating insurance awareness among the general public.

What I want to picturise is that insurance consciousness is very much desired for risk management processes and unless we achieve this we are no way nearer to the goal.

Suggested action plan for short term and long term activity for providing insurance education in India in a broader and deeper way:

I. Periodic surveys on "insurance knowledge level" are to be conducted in the entire country utilising the educational institutions, research centres, Insurance Institutions, Social Service Organisations etc., and the study of the survey made by the specialists and draw conclusions.

II. Awareness on insurance, banking and other service organisation must be brought through regular studies in all the educational institutions right from primary class to university level.

III. Expert educationalists must involve themselves in consultation with Insurance industry officials in drawing up a syllabus at different levels.

IV. All educational institutions- Government, private, University controlled - should take it as an article of faith to bring in awareness of the "risk management" through insurance education and impart the same to all students.

V. In imparting informal, distance education also basic knowledge in these aspects must be provided.

VI. If it is decided by the Expert Committee that this education need not be taken into consideration for assessment of the individual for promotion etc., need not be but as a matter of 'self making education or 'social education' this should be included in the syllabus.

VII. Though advertisement and publicity through electronic and print media has its own limitations, awareness can be brought by greater utilisation with higher imagination.

Conclusion

I strongly believe that unless reinsure education is provided well in India, it is extremely difficult to make the people aware of 'Risk Management' as a personal measure or as a social welfare measure extended by the Government LIC & GIC by their own efforts can not bring out a revolution even in years to come - a revolution that will being every person and industry on the country out a revolution even in years to come - a revolution that will bring every person and industry in the country under the protective umbrella of the 'Risk Managers'. Towards that end if seminar of this type can help in crystalising thought and presenting plan for implementation at different levels, the objective of the seminar will be well fulfilled.

* * *

24

LIFE INSURANCE ACROSS THE FRONTIER

S. K. Kutty, Deshpande, Subbaraman,

Research Associate, National Insurance Academy, Pune.

Life insurance emerged more than two centuries ago as a child of industrialisation and the smock stack era. During this period it has largely been sold as a unique (death) protection cum savings instrument. Its archetype has been the standardised "bundled" contract (1), which provides for an assured sum at death or accrued cash value on maturity/ surrender.

The development of life insurance reveals a highly uneven pattern. In 1995 only seven OECD countries (2) had about 85% of the world's life insurance premiums. In the developing world we have a few other markets (3), which have been advancing in rapid strides. If we leave these out, the rest of the continents of Asia, Africa and Latin America together account for just about 1.5% of the world's life insurance premiums.

The major part of the industry's growth has been achieved through penetration among one segment of the population - the formal sector middle class. The formal sector has been defined as the non-agricultural wage-paying sector of the economy. Of course, a large formal sector alone is not a sufficient condition to ensure the spread of life insurance. This is seen for example in the case of Latin American countries, where severe inflationary pressures have adversely affected the demand for life insurance. It is however evident that the small size of this sector has acted as a barrier to spread of life insurance in many countries. This is seen from the following figures:

Country	Premium per capita ($)	Size of formal sector	Country	Premium per capita ($)	Size of formalsector
Indonesia	3.90	24.3	Venezuela	1.70	57.1
Philippines	6.00	35.9	S.Korea	782.1	59.5
Thailand	27.40	20.3	Malaysia	71.7	53.0
India	4.00	13.1	Singapore	569.3	85.5
Pakistan	1.50	30.0	Israel	354.1	73.2
Cameroon	0.10	12.9	Chile	72.6	58.5
Egypt	1.60	42.8	U.K.	1280.60	85.1
Nigeria	0.20	18.4	U.S.A.	964.60	89.7
Tunisia	2.20	56.7	Canada	570.50	89.1
Argentina	27.40	65.2	France	1204.70	83.9
Brazil	9.20	56.7	Japan	3817.30	77.9
Mexico	22.80	58.8	Australia	628.90	75.6
Panama	23.40	56.1			

Note: Figures of premium are for 1994: Source - SIGMA
Figures of formal sector are for latest years; source - World Development Report 1995, World Bank.

The informal sector falls outside this frontier. Its size may be seen from the following facts given in the World Development Report of 1995:

Out of an international work force of about 2.5 billion, about 1.4 billion are in the low-income countries. Of these, about 15% or 210 million are estimated to be engaged in wage contracts in the formal sector, giving us a whopping 1.2 billion in the informal sector. The middle income countries have about 660 million workers, of which about 46% are in the formal sector, giving another 357 million in the informal sector.

For much of mankind, life insurance then remains as alien and remote as ever. This failure to spread among the populace has apparently little to do with issues of ownership or control. Low density and penetration is evinced under both liberalised and competitive market conditions as under nationalised or highly regulated regimes. Nor does this indicate that the principles of mutuality and risk sharing - the foundations of insurance - are absent. Indeed, if that were the case, much of mankind might have perished at the first signs of misfortune.

Rather, life insurers appear to have set a frontier to their expansion by the particular way in which they have defined and conducted their business.

THE TRADITIONAL PARADIGM

Let us consider some of the main features of traditional contracts like the Endowment or Whole Life. We have:

1. A long drawn contract in which premiums are compulsorily paid for 20-25 years. Maturity date may generally correspond to retirement from service.
2. A level annual premium is charged on the basis of conservative assumptions about mortality, interest and expenses of the insurer. The principle is to charge an adequate premium with sufficient loading to meet all kinds of contingencies.
3. The excess of premium, over that required to meet outgo for expenses and policy holders' payments, goes into a pooled life fund, which is kept invested largely in government/social sector and corporate securities and loans. Investment is governed prudential norms, keeping the objectives of income and capital certainty prime.
4. Yield on the policy is made available for distribution (4) in the form of reversionary and terminal bonus, which accrues at the date of maturity or surrender. The bonuses are declared through a periodic valuation of assets and liabilities. the valuation is done on conservative basis with the intention of achieving a graduated but consistent rise in surplus available for distribution.
5. Surrender values are low in the early years of the policy and get graduated upwards as one reaches the maturity date. There are strong built in safeguards and deterrents against early surrender.

The Uniqueness of these contracts is given by their particular application of the mutuality principle in two areas.

Firstly, with regard to mortality risk, it provides for immediate creation of an asset to be made available to dependents on one's untimely death.

Secondly, the pooling and averaging of funds over numerous contracts creates a relatively riskless financial asset, which contribute to reduce portfolio risk over the long run.

As a financial product, the traditional contract thus contributes to optimal inter temporal allocation of resources for an individual facing two sources of income discontinuity during his/her economic lifetime - death and retirement. Life insurance policies have been positioned to meet these uncertainties. Other features which have made the product attractive include its tax saving aspects and its role as a compulsory form of savings.

Theoretical approaches to life insurance demand (5) general assume a life cycle framework of savings where savings behaviour appears as a residual to the income - consumption decision and savings is done with the purpose of making provision for the long term future. The life cycle framework assumes that:

* Expected future income and consumption streams are assumed stable, including the rate at which they are discounted.
* Perfect capital markets are assumed with free borrowing and lending at given rates and no credit rationing. In other words this implies an absence of liquidity constraints in meeting short-term needs as and when they arise.

A significant result of this conceptual setting is known as the SEPARATION THEOREM, which yields that the choice of investment, as a decision, is separate from personal consumption preferences of individuals. The theorem implies that individuals are free to choose the manner of holding their wealth - this does not depend on the pattern of their income - consumption streams. Rational choice behaviour then involves optimising risk adjusted rates of return of a portfolio of assets. Two parameter (mean-variance) models of portfolio behaviour have emerged as the dominant frame of reference for such portfolio optimisation.

Life Insurance, like mutual funds and other instruments, has been seen as vehicles for mopping up the (residual) surplus available with households. A major concern in actuarial and other literature has been with regard to arriving at an appropriate yield-risk trade-off. This has been particularly evinced in the debate (6) on "reasonable expectations of customers" where the smoothing mechanism of the uniform reversionary bonus system (of traditional contracts) has been compared with the individual treatment of risk, seen in unit linked and other variable contracts.

Conditions in informal markets may adversely impinge on this conceptual decision making framework in three respects:

1. Firstly, they have a large number of households with low level of surplus (or residual) income after consumption.
2. Secondly these households are characterised by a state of fluctuating income streams - this may be on account of unemployment, business ups and downs, seasonal fluctuations in agriculture etc.
3. Thirdly, their difficulty of access to credit, to meet short-term liquidity needs.

Let us consider the implications of the above:

Firstly, a relative lack of surplus income does not mean that informal households do not save. Indeed, there is much evidence from Asia and elsewhere (7) to indicate large savings generated by rural farmers etc. Conceptually, this becomes plausible when we treat savings not as passive residual behaviour but as an active function in which one consciously cuts consumption and creates assets to increase net worth.

The logic of the process is provided by the situation of fluctuating income streams. It is seen that people with uncertain incomes have a greater marginal propensity to save than others.

It is also seen that the separation theorem breaks down in this situation. The choice of savings vehicles is no longer separate from the income - consumption decision. Indeed the purpose of savings (building net worth) is now strongly related to the need to shield consumption against the vagaries of income, with assets being selected to serve as buffers in this regard. Liquidity preference rules in this domain and assets that build protective liquidity crowd out others from the portfolio.

While protection against death may be a major need of informal sector households, it would be rational for such households to reject cash value life assurance contracts, which do not meet this need for liquidity.

They may also not be disposed to buy pure term insurance with an all or nothing payoff. While protection from death is important, it may not necessarily be that urgent. The key issue is thus of how death cover may be combined with other attributes to provide a customised product for this sector.

FEATURES OF INFORMAL MARKETS

Let us now throw some spotlight on the informal sector and consider some issues, which arise.

1. Firstly, it is not obvious that economic growth would automatically lead to displacement of the informal economy. In many economies, the trend appears to be different (8). Again, as we have indicated earlier, thrift comes naturally to informal households having irregular income streams and needing to build up net worth even more than others do. It makes little sense to ignore this segment with its vast untapped potential.
2. Secondly, while the liquidity preference of these households is well known, what is less realised is the fact that they may also have high illiquidity preference. When they come to acquire lump sum cash and liquid resources, they would like to convert it into illiquid assets, before it is frittered away or borrowed by relative's etc. This may be particularly true of women workers in the informal sector, whose very purpose of entering the work force may be to have a supplementary source of income and savings to provide for their children and their old age.
3. Thirdly let us examine the process of financing. In general we understand it as the transfer of surplus resources from households (surplus units) to firms and government (the deficit units). The financial inter mediation role of life insurers and other financial institutions generally involve the principle of separation of markets - savings are mopped up from one market and invested in another.

The essence of the financial inter mediation process in rural informal markets is the transfer of funds from households who have surplus cash at certain points of time to other households who are in deficit and need the funds at that point. There are two types of transfers taking place here - from one household to another; and across time, when the household parts with liquidity now in order to have access to the same, when they need it latter.

Informal financial markets in the rural sector are thus governed by the principle that CREDIT IS THE OTHER SIDE OF THE COIN OF SAVINGS. It may not be easily possible to mop up purchasing power from the informal market unless one pumps in purchasing power to households in the same market.

4. Fourthly there may be a difference in perception about what constitutes a safe contractual agreement. In our parlance, safety is generally defined in terms of absence of default (on capital) and interest rate (income) risk. For the informal sector household, uncertainty largely looms in two ways - the risk that they would not be able to meet their contractual obligations as stipulated in the contract and secondly, the risk that they would not have access to liquidity when they need it most.
5. Finally there is a major difference in the character of the relation between the life insurer and the insured from that found among members of an informal sector financial institution like ROSCA (Rotating Savings and Credit Association). The former is in the nature of a strictly contractual transaction whose structure is rigidly defined and scope limited to what is agreed while signing on the dotted line. The information asymmetry, which is prevalent between the parties to the contract, may be addressed through elaborate procedure and paper work.

Informal institutions work on basis of the "lemon principle" - models of an economy in which trust and first hand knowledge of the customer is important. We have less of a transactional contractual and more of an ongoing relationship here. Again, the ROSCA involves a relationship of mutuality between members of a group rather than a one to one relationship between individual and an institution. Agreements are made and honoured more by peer and group pressure rather than through legal recourse.

It is obvious from above that a different logic and set of rules operate in the informal and rural sector.

THE INDIAN CASE

In 1991, only about 13.1% of India's work force were estimated to be engaged in the formal sector. About 62% of the work force were engaged in agriculture. Another large section was estimated engaged in small and marginal rural enterprises. The massive size of the rural informal sector is obvious from the above figures.

Meanwhile the in force business of the Life Insurance Corporation of India has grown over the last four decades to 77.75 million individual policies and another 23.9 million lives under Group Insurance. Assuming that about 30% of policyholders may have more than one policy and also a population of about 900 million, we may thus have coverage of less than 10% of the population.

LIC of India has divided the Indian market into four segments. The exact extent of coverage under each segment is difficult to ascertain. It is however well known that the main thrust has been among the first two segments (namely, the professional and managerial group and the regular income wage and salaried group). A large part of the population in these segments have been covered. The last two segments (consisting of the self-employed including agriculturists and the agricultural labour segment) may have coverage of less than five per cent. The informal market is mainly centred among these segments.

It may be instructive here to examine some of the findings of studies conducted on life insurance and savings in the informal sector.

1. The study of NCAER in 1975-76, sponsored by LIC and covering about 5125 households spread out in rural and urban areas. Fixed income earners had the major share of life insurance. About three fourths of the earners were not aware about LIC. This was particularly seen in the rural areas. Among the reasons for taking LIC policies the majority were attracted by its risk covering nature and build-up of a lump sum for old age. About 10% were attracted by its tax saving provisions.

Among those non-insured earners who were aware about LIC, about three fourths opted out because they felt they could not afford to pay the premium. About 11% preferred alternative forms of investment while another 10% stated that no insurance agent had approached them. At lower income groups affordability was seen as the main impediment to purchase while at higher incomes, it was choice of alternative investment sources. The main objection of rural earners to life insurance was its lack of flexibility while poor servicing was seen as the deterrent factor among urban earners.

2. Another study, quoted by R.Jayaraman (Journal of the federation of Insurance Institutes Vol.5, 1979), was conducted in Malavalli and Pandavapura Talukas of Mandya district. This study stressed that the main needs of rural prospects included:
   * Awareness of the necessity of life insurance protection;
   * Insurance plans which provided for simple procedures and flexibility in the payment of premia;
   * Presence of LIC in a conveniently approachable place in the area;
   * Trustworthy representatives of LIC to deal with, who are not often transferred.
3. Dr Mishra's UGC sponsored study (1983). It showed that among those who purchased life insurance in rural areas, the purposes of such purchase were, in order of preference - old age provision; insurance of children; insurance for marriage; family provision and insurance for education.

Among the reasons for non-purchase of life insurance by those who were aware about it, we have in order of preference, that:

* They were unable to afford insurance:
* They preferred other forms of savings because of higher returns;
* Insurance agents had not approached them;
* They could use the money more profitably in other business;
* They depend more on their children for their old age;
* There is no flexibility in the life insurance contract.

It was found that non-banking companies were competing and progressing faster than LIC due to their personal attention and higher returns. Banks were also preferred due to their inherent qualities of savings deposits, loans and advances and flexibility.

4. The study by Kirloskar Cummins Consultants in the late eighties. It covered a sample of 3000 respondents spread out in 15 blocks of Maharashtra. About 72% of these were engaged in agriculture and

12% were agricultural labourers. Around 8% were in service occupations and 5% were self-employed.

Nearly 80% of the respondents were inclined to utilise savings for development of agriculture. Only 4% were inclined to have specific old age provisions. About 6% of the respondents were policyholders.

Among the reasons given for not taking LIC policies, about 47% respondents stated that they did not know about them. Another 13% stated that no one had approached them and another 40% cited money and liquidity problems.

5. The study by Madhoo Pavaskar and others for Tata Consultancy Services in 1985. It covered about 1000 affluent farmer households in Maharashtra, Gujarat and Andhra Pradesh. Savings rate was found to be as high as 38% and wasteful expenditure did not exceed 10% of income. Financial assets absorbed nearly two thirds of the investment and half of these were in bank deposits. The major finding of the study was the high preference for assets with high liquidity. About 1.8% of the sample respondents had life insurance.
6. Coming to the urban informal sector we have two significant studies conducted in recent years. One was the National Housing Bank Study (sponsored by the Ministry of Urban Development) and the other was conducted by the Society of Development Studies for the Government of Maharashtra. The results were broadly similar and may be summarised as below:
   * Informal sector respondents were aware about the desirability of saving regularly. However due to fluctuating nature of income and expenses, they found it more realistic to save periodically.
   * They also wanted the amount of deposit to be flexible. though not averse to make a pre-stipulated amount of deposit, they did not prefer a mandatory stipulation of this amount on a month to month basis.
   * Though interest rate (return) was deemed important, it was not so significant as assurance of safety of deposit and a flexible withdrawal system for temporary and permanent withdrawal. A yield of 10% was generally considered satisfactory.
   * A fourth motivating factor was linkage with a future line of credit which could help finance acquisition of an asset.

7. Finally, the author's own survey of 75 rural policy holders of LIC, conducted in Trichur district of Kerala in 1990. Some of they key findings were:
   * A majority of respondents were concerned with specific savings needs like building a house and marriage of children. A smaller number were concerned with general needs like old age provision.
   * Life Insurance was felt to be a dominant need (among top three needs for savings) by a majority of respondents. However LIC as an institution ranked far below banks and Kuri companies in their pattern of preferences. the main reasons cited for popularity of the latter was their easy accessibility and the personal relationship which they maintained with the client.
   * A large number were concerned with safety of investment. But they understood security mainly in terms of the ease with which they could get their money when they wanted it urgently.
   * An overwhelming majority was inclined towards short term investments, for a period of seven years or less.

The distinctive pattern of expectations of the informal market is fairly apparent in the above studies.

INFORMAL MARKETS - A MODEL OF INTERVENTION

Life insurers have left rural informal markets will alone in the past. They may not have that luxury in future. There is a clear need to address the issue of how to intervene in these markets. One or two points may be considered in this regard.

Firstly, there are two ways in which the informal market may be approached. The first is for the life insurer to informalise its own structure and operations so as to take, more and more, the desirable features of informal financial institutions. The other course is for the insurer to have tie ups with a range of both formal and informal sector organisations as well as individuals. One may indeed have a mixture of both.

Secondly it may be imperative to see the rural market as a separate system in which one has to participate with a range of intervention mechanisms, including credit and other services. A system of incomplete of incomplete market contracts, which provide a hedge for only a few contingencies, may be of limited relevance to these households. The working out of the extended family system on a community scale as it operates here represents the principle of mutuality. The question is where does the life insurer fit in.

In the last part of this paper, we shall consider a model of intervention in the informal market. It conceives an institutional framework, which has both the features of a long-term insurer and of a banking type institution with depository and credit functions. The model is hypothetical and tentative - the purpose is to highlight how different principles may be combined.

* Consider a community of craftsmen each having an income of Rs.2000 per month. Assume the entire community is covered under insurance linked saving scheme and divided into groups of ten members each for the purpose. The institution, which intervenes, is known as the insurer.
* To begin with, each member pays a membership contribution of Rs.2000 each. The amount is assumed paid in lump sum at the beginning of the process. It is analogous to an initial share capital paid by the member. The principle, which operates here, is that of the credit union -credit is not a free sop to be pumped in from outside but the resources for the same should be generated from within the community and members should share both ownership and accountability for the same.
* It is intended to offer life insurance cover of Rs.50, 000 to each member. This is roughly about twice the annual income of the household. Assume that all members are aged around thirty and that the term of the contract expires on reaching age 60. A net level annual premium of Rs.3.00 per thousand sum assured is assumed payable by each member, so that the total annual premium for insurance cover is Rs.150.00 Though members part of a group, contracts of insurance are separately entered into and selection is individual. The idea is derived from the French system of the open group contracts. The first year premium is paid at the time of the contract and subsequent premiums are deductible from the fund accumulated with the insurer.
* Now assume that each member household sets aside 15% of household income from immediate consumption. This is about Rs.300 per month. The amount may be typically set aside on

the basis of a few rupees each day. The group designates one member to collect the amount from other members on a daily or weekly basis. The group has meetings regularly. Collections are deposited with the insurer once a month when its representative meets the group. While the 15% savings target is suggested it is not mandatory. Individual members are free to decide how much they wish and are able to set aside. The only stipulation is that the member should be able to set aside a minimum contribution of say Rs.200 a year - to meet the cost of insurance cover and some additional expenses.

* The members are also allowed to withdraw upto 505 of the amount they have deposited in a certain year. This is to meet certain transaction and unforeseen contingency needs, which are expected to arise in the short run. The balance at the end of the year gets transferred to a long-term fund, which earns interest at 10% per year. We shall assume that interest is earned only from the beginning of the second year.

Let us now assume that our representative member puts in 15% of income on average. We also assume that 50% of what is deposited is removed during the year. The balance to the credit of the individual at the end of five years would thus be as shown below.

Fund at beginning of year	Fund after payment of insurance premium	Interest @10%	Amount of new deposit @15% of income	Total amount accumulated	Balance of fund after withdrawal
2000	.....	200	3600	5800	4000
4000	3800	380	3600	7780	5980
5980	5960	596	3600	10156	8356
8356	8156	816	3600	12572	10772
10772	10572	1057	3600	15229	13429

As we can see above, a sum of Rs.13429 has been accumulated at the end of five years.

Let us assume that the member wishes to avail of a loan at the end of five years. The insurer may set a limit of say 2 1/2 of the total amount accrued to the member's credit as the maximum loan payable. In the present case, the loan amount would thus be around Rs.33570. The actual amount allowed may also be determined by other considerations like assessment of credit worthiness etc.

The significant point of this credit system is that the group as a whole may be made responsible for the loan repayment performance of the individual member. The group's s accountability may be achieved in two ways. Firstly, any further credit to the members may be made liable as guarantors atleast upto the extent of the portion of assets they have built up with the insurer. The Grameen Bank experiment of Bangladesh and other similar interventions have revealed the advantages that such group lending can yield. This is both in terms of reduction of information asymmetry and also the role of peer pressure in ensuring repayment performance. It is of course imperative that the profits made through such loan transactions is shared with the members as a reward for risk taking on their part.

The welfare enhancing impact of such an intervention would depend on the extent to which the credit cum savings mechanism converts savings into a means by which latent productive resources of the community (in particular labour power) is drawn forth and put to active use. This could set a circular spiral of productivity and income generation in motion. As the saying goes, "give a man a loaf of fish and you feed him for a day. Teach him how to fish and you feed him for life".

The idea we have tried to demonstrate above is the synergy, which may be made possible through combining risk management with savings and credit as part of an integrated programme of intervention. Once the basic idea is grasped, it may be possible to extend it to other areas like health care and property/casualty insurance. The key issue here is the partnership relation thatthe insurer builds with the community as a whole, by means of which, risks is shared and managed collectively with members of the community.

No doubt, it would need a certain amount of imagination and romanticising to take on this kind of a role. We are aware that this may be counter to the tenets that are derived from the formal logic, which governs life insurers today. The realities of tomorrow begin as dreams today.

NOTES

1. Examples of such bundled contracts are the Endowment and Whole Life Policies of traditional life insurance.
2. All figures of premium income for different countries are derived from SIGMA. The seven countries are Australia, Canada, France, Germany, Japan, UK and USA.
3. Other markets include S.Korea, Taiwan, Malaysia, Singapore, Israel, South Africa and Chile.
4. This pattern has been followed in UK for traditional policies. It is not applicable to the more current unit linked products of UK. The US pattern of distribution is also quite different. In India, as in many other third world countries, we have the traditional reversionary bonus system.
5. Theories of demand for life insurance generally take Huberner's Human life value approach as their starting point. Following Year (1965) and others we have a good deal of theoretical literature on the role of life insurance in meeting the needs of optimal inter temporal allocation of consumption.
6. The concept of "reasonable expectations" was first introduced by Skerman in his paper to the institute of actuaries (1973). The debate on the subject has been elaborately discussed in Marshall Field's presidential address to the institute of actuaries (1986).
7. Asian Productivity Organisation, Symposium of Mobilisation of Rural Savings in Asia and Pacific, December 1990.
8. ILO - World Employment 1995.

* * *

25

LIFE INSURANCE AS A MEASURE OF SOCIAL SECURITY

Dr. A.Raghunadha Reddy, Rayudu, Srinivasulu, Ramakrishna Reddy, Narayana Reddy,

Asst. Professor Dept. of Law,S.K.University, Anantapur

I. INTRODUCTION

The Concept of Welfare State

The Constitution of India envisages the establishment of a welfare state. In a welfare state the primary duty of the government is to secure the welfare and promote the prosperity and well being of the people.[1] A welfare state is to ensure social, economic and political justice, equality, freedom and dignity of life to every citizen.[2] It has to bestow welfare benefits on the teeming millions of poor, weak and downtrodden in order to harness the powers of all in an equal manner for common good and collective well being. Therefore, a welfare state has to be a social security state, such as Britain in Pre-Thatcher era or with its assurance of minimum standard of life and egalitarian social welfare state like Sweden. A corporate- oriented positive state like the U.S. is not a welfare state at all because its primary aim is to protect the holders of property from problems of unregulated markets and from potential redistributive demands.[3]

There is a need for welfare state that will be active throughout our lives i.e., providing safety, security and decent standard of living from cradle to the grave. It should help people to negotiate unpredictable change at work and home. Instead of a safety net to relieve poverty, we need a social security system that can prevent poverty. In other words, the welfare state must not only look after people when they cannot look after themselves, it must also enable them to achieve self-employment and self-support. It must offer a hand up rather than a hand out.[4]

II. SOCIAL SECURITY SYSTEM

Too many people in this country are not in employment and work for too many no longer guarantees income security. Several millions are part-time, self-employed and low-earning workers living under pitiable circumstances where there is no security cover against risk. Further the inherent changing employment risks, the prospect of continual change in the work place with its attendant threats of unemployment and low pay especially after the adoption of New Economic Policy and the imminent life cycle risks - a new source of insecurity which includes the changing demands of family life, separation, divorce and elderly dependents - are tormenting the society. Risk has become central to one's life. It is within this background life insurance policy has been introduced by the LIC covering risks at various levels.

Life insurance coverage is against disablement or in the event of death of the insured, economic support for the dependents. It is a measure of social security to livelihood of the insured or dependents. This is to make the right to life meaningful, worth living and right to livelihood a means for sustenance.[5] Therefore, it goes without saying appropriate life insurance policy within the paying capacity and means of the insured to pay premia is one of the social security measures envisaged under the Indian Constitution. Hence, right to social security, protection of the family, economic empowerment to the poor and disadvantaged are integral part of the right to life and dignity of the person guaranteed in the Constitution.[6] Social security is a facet of socio-economic justice to the people in particular to the middle class and lower middle class.[7]

But the problem is whether life insurance premium is within the means of a common man. Is the life insurance policy designed for and confined to government employees or those working in semi-government or reputed commercial firms only whose sources of income may be easily tapable source? What is the spirit behind the policy? Do the people of this country have a right to know about the working, discriminatory practices, drawbacks and shortcomings of the LIC? The insurance being a social security measure should it not be consistent with the conscience of socio-economic justice adumbrated in the Constitution? It is precisely with a view to tackle and enlighten on the issues raised above an attempt is made in this paper. At the end, some suggestions are also mooted for remedying the situation.

III. THE ROLE OF THE SUPREME COURT AND THE FUNCTIONING OF THE LIFE INSURANCE CORPORATION

The LIC is a 'state' within the meaning of Art. 12 of the Constitution[8]. It is created under an Act, namely The Life Insurance Corporation Act, 1956. It is charged with the duty 'to carry on life insurance business', within and outside India. It is further charged with the duty to so exercise its powers under the Act as 'to secure that life insurance business is developed to the best advantage of the community.'[9] It is therefore, obvious that the LIC must function in the best interest of the community. The community is, therefore, entitled to know whether or not this requirement of the statute is being satisfied in the functioning of the LIC.

The respondent namely Prof. Manubhai, D. Shaw who was the executive trustee of the Consumer Education and Research Centre, Ahmedabad after undertaking research into the working of the LIC published on 10th July, 1978 a study paper entitled A Fraud on Policy Holders - A Shocking Story.[10] This paper portrayed the discriminatory practices adopted by the LIC, which adversely affected the interest of a large number of policyholders. The respondent's effort in preparing study paper was to bring to the notice of the community that the LIC had strayed from its path by pointing out that its premium rates were unduly high when they could be low if the LIC avoided wasteful indulgences. The endeavour was to enlighten the community of the drawbacks and shortcomings of the Corporation and to pin point the areas where improvement was needed and possible; so that the general public will have an access into the functioning of the LIC. The informed public opinion would operate as the most potent of all checks on the actions/working of the LIC. As a result, the LIC can rectify things, try to improve its functioning and live upto the expectations of the community.

Unfortunately, the LIC that published the counter for the study paper in its magazine - 'Yogakshema' refused to publish the rejoinder entitled Raw Deal for Policy Holders prepared by the respondent.[11] It is to be noted that the magazine of the LIC is financed from public funds. It is difficult to understand why the LIC, which is a monopolistic state instrumentality surviving on public funds, should feel shy of publishing rejoinder if it has nothing to fear. By denying information to the consumers as well as other subscribers the LIC cannot be said to be acting in the best interest of the community. Therefore, the Supreme Court in the instant case treated such an attitude on the part of the LIC as both unfair and unreasonable. The respondent's fundamental right of speech and expression clearly entitled him to insist that his views on the subject should reach those who read the magazine so that they have a complete picture before them and not one sided or distorted one.[12] It is submitted that the LIC is charging still unduly high premium rates by refusing to prune its avoidable expenses and the study paper had little impact on the style of functioning of the LIC.

The Supreme Court in its momentous decision LIC of India v. Consumer Education and Research Centre[13] has sent shock waves to the LIC by holding the view that the rates of premium must be reasonable and accessible. The court without any hesitation held that while prescribing terms and eligibility conditions in issuing a general life insurance policy of any type, public element is inherent. The LIC owes a public duty to evolve policies subject to such reasonable, just and fair terms and conditions accessible to all the segments of the society for insuring the lives of eligible persons.[14] Generally those terms and conditions are contained in an insurance contract in a standard form. It is entered into between parties who are unequal in bargaining power. Normally the inequality of bargaining power is the result of great disparity in the economic strength of the contracting parties. In such a case where is the freedom of contract? The validity of those terms and conditions remain untested. Therefore, the eligibility conditions must be conformable to the preamble, fundamental rights and directive principles of the Constitution.[15]

The Sezhivan Committee Report also after its elaborate study of the working of the LIC on insurance recommended in the year 1980 for improvement on several factors of the working system. Particularly, it had recommended making available policies to wider sectors of the society.

It concluded that the cost of providing life insurance policies is high and beyond the means of a large section of the population both in urban and rural areas.[16] It is submitted that the report clearly reflects the study of paper published in 1978 by Prof. Shaw. Further, it appears that the Supreme Court has fully endorsed the study paper and the recommendations of the Sezhivan Report.

Sezhivan Committee itself had recommended that the Table 58 Term Policy is the cheapest and accessible policy to the people living in rural areas and in the unorganised sectors. Unfortunately, the LIC confined the policy under Table 58 to already covered salaried sections and commercial firms who by and large insured either under the whole life policy or endowment policy thereby excluding the benefit to other people who can afford to take the policy so as to ensure their social security.[17] If the term policy is extended to others, it would percolate not only to the people in private, unorganised sector and people in self-employed sector but also larger segments in urban and rural areas would be reaping the benefit. Therefore, the Supreme Court categorically said that such a classification based on employment in government, semi-government and reputed commercial firms has the insidious and inevitable effect of depriving lives in vast rural and urban areas to have life insurance. Hence, the above said classification was held to be offending Art. 14[18] and socio-economic justice envisaged under the Constitution.

Upon the study of these two landmark judgments one can witness the social consciousness and concern of the Supreme Court and its activist role in upholding and safeguarding the preambulary message of socio-economic justice. Certainly this trend would go a long way in promoting socio-economic justice which is very essential in strengthening the roots of political democracy of the country. It is to be noted here as to how the Supreme Court as the watch-dog of the Constitution is constantly watching and managing the risk against which the lives of many common men are insured.

IV. CONCLUSIONS AND SUGGESTIONS

From the above, the following conclusions are drawn:

The Constitution was enacted to secure to all the citizens of this country social and economic justice. Life Insurance is essential to make the life meaningful and worth living. It is to make livelihood a means for sustenance. It is therefore, a measure of social security covering risk at all levels. Social security is a facet of socio-economic justice to the people particularly to the rural masses. In the long run, socio-economic democracy is sine-qua-non to make political democracy truly participatory democracy.

The following suggestions are mooted to rectify and remedy the situation:

1. Life Insurance policy should be easily accessible to all the segments of the society and within the means of a common man as adumbrated under the Constitution. It is because the LIC is charged with the duty of securing and developing life insurance business to the best advantage of the community.
2. While issuing a general life insurance policy of any type, the LIC should keep in mind the inherent public interest considerations. It owes a public duty to evolve policies subject to certain terms and eligibility conditions. However, those terms and conditions must be just, fair, reasonable and inconsonance with the Constitution. The rates of premium must also be reasonable and accessible. They should be viable and easily available to the general public. It is understandable that the rates of premium charged under the Rural Postal Life Insurance (RPLI) are lesser and cheaper than the rates of premium chargeable by the LIC. Therefore, the LIC should rise to the occasion and revise the premium in the light of the Supreme Court's pronouncements in the above said two cases, study paper prepared by Prof.Shaw and the Sezhivan Committee Report.
3. The citizens of this country have right to know and freedom of access to any information about the working of the LIC. Instead of denial of this freedom of the citizens by the LIC, it should ensure free flow of information to the public. So that, the public will come to know whether or not the LIC is functioning in the best interest of the community.
4. Instead of health insurance[19] and pollution insurance[20] which are insufficient to a poor workman, we can have a social insurance scheme covering every citizen of the country. Unfortunately, we don't have either the old comprehensive National Insurance system or the New

Social Insurance programme as existing in the U.K.[21] Therefore, it is suggested that there is a need for rebuilding the social security system in the country upon a modernised social insurance scheme protecting fairly the people against unemployment and sickness etc., than any other scheme of private insurance. The modern social insurance scheme is to be taken up by the government itself by enacting an appropriate legislation to mitigate the sufferings of the dependants/ victims of natural calamities, starvation deaths and the debt driven farmers' suicide cases etc.

REFERENCES

1. See the Directive Principles laid down in Part IV, of the Indian Constitution.
2. See the Preamble of the Constitution.
3. Norman Turmiss and Timorthy Tilton, The Case for the Welfare State: From Social Security to Social Equality, Bloomington, Indian University Press at 15 (1977).
4. See Social Justice: Strategies for National Renewal, The Report of the Commission on Social Justice (1994).
5. See Olga Tellis v. Bombay Municipal Corporation, AIR 1986 SC 180.
6. Muralidhar Dayandeo Kesekar v. Viswanath Pandu (C.A.No.952/77) on Feb.22, 1995.
7. See LIC of India v. Consumer Education and Research Centre, AIR 1995 SC 1811 at 1826.
8. Sukhdev Singh v. Bhagatram Sardar Singh AIR 1975 SC 1331.
9. See Section-6 (1) of the LIC Act, 1956.
10. See LIC of India v. Manubhai D.Shaw AIR 1993 SC 171 at 180.
11. Id. at 179.
12. Id. at 180.
13. See Supra Note 7.
14. Id. at 1827.

15. Ibid.

16. Id. at 1814.

17. Id. at 1823.

18. Id. At 1822. Art.14 of the Constitution provides for right to equality.

19. Kirloskar Brothers Ltd. v. E.S.I.Corporation AIR 1996 SC 3261 at 3264.

20. See M.K.Sharma v. Bharat Electronics Ltd. AIR 1987 SC 1792.

21. William Bevridge inspired the British people with his vision of a comprehensive National Insurance System. For details see supra Note 4 at 226.

* * *

26

RISK MANAGEMENT FOR SUSTAINABLE DEVELOPMENT

Dr. K. Ramakrishna Reddy

Associate Professor, Sri Krishnadevaraya Institute of Management, S.K.University, Anantapur.

Man has always been a risk bearing person. One may even go to the extent of saying that human history would have been monotonous and dull had there been no risk element at all. As long as we live in the flow of time, we are confronted with an unknown tomorrow. What it brings and what it fails to bring has challenged man to reach a higher and higher potential of his being. Man is in eternal quest of the unknown. The cost of this journey may be regarded as one of risk bearing and uncertainty.

This cost, predetermined or otherwise has always been a legitimate item of our accounting. Whosoever was successful in identifying before hand this cost - its nature and dimension, its occurrence and its recurrence, and the flow of its consequence - stole a march over others not only in earning profits but also in adding to the fund of our knowledge, theoretical as well as technical, encouraging a whole stream of new entrepreneurs into this formerly unforeseen area of activity and events.

We thus learnt to insure ourselves against unforeseen events and their consequences. Today the theory and practice of insurance is ready to enter into new areas of activity. If we are to believe them, they say there is no area where they cannot march and consolidate their activities.

Man is not only a risk bearer but also a risk promoter and a cause of risk. It looks as though as traditional and historical risks either vanish into insurable costs and hedging operations, or become normally manageable, new ones seem to raise their head assuming all the properties of a so called risk. As our social consciousness becomes ever awake we tend to discover newer and more varied types of risk involved in our day to day activity.

The drought, the flood, the so called risks due to natural forces, remain today as a private concern of the individual incumbent or group. The advancement in technology in issuing forewarnings seen to be unmatched with our willingness to profit by that information. The usual complaints relate to one of 'poor will' than of poverty of resources.

We have also a new kind of risk blowing across not only our country but also the entire world. I refer to the risk of unevaluated adoption of technology and ways of living generated in different cultures. A prominent illustration is in the field of environment. It should also include the risk of knowledge piracy in assuming to myself, patent rights, global policeman rights and so on and so forth.

It is here this study's purpose is significantly discovered and located. Can we group broadly risks, the cost of which is a not a mere matter of individual concern, but which demands group collective, social , corporate, Government action. How to define a risk whose overall incidence is social in character; when small farmers witness a crop failure without a debt abrogation or redemption, is that a matter to be considered as private and personal to the farmer, or should it be viewed as a public risk, if unmet would deplete the supply and skills of our farming community?

In this given framework, the need for understanding risk and risk management is very significant to maintain economic stability in the modern society. Risk exists wherever the future is unknown. Risk may be defined as the variation in possible future outcomes. The greater is the risk, the less predictable this future outcome, becomes. Because the adverse effects of risk have plagued mankind since the beginning of time, individuals, groups, and societies have developed various methods for managing risk. Since no one knows the future exactly, everyone is a risk manager not by chance but by sheer necessity. Risk is not the problem of past. Risk is the problem of future. Risk in insurance terminology refers to insurable perils. For an economist or a statistician risk represents the number of possible outcomes from an event. A risk may be pure or speculative. A pure risk is one that offers only the prospect of loss if it occurs. The non-occurrence of the risk allows the planned activity to proceed as normal. A speculative risk can result in a gain or loss depending on its occurrence. Moreover in a general sense, pure risk is the pessimist's risk while the speculative risk is the optimist's risk.

Risk exists not only in the real world of production but also in financial world. Market liberalisation, introduction of sophisticated technologies and processes, emergence of new and different forms of business and a larger play in the field of global trade and finance are making financial and trade transactions riskier. It is also a fact that as the economic system transforms itself, market imperfections and speculative actions of some of the participants could generate uncertainties, increase volatility and create substantial economic risks. Even though, systematic risks can be prevented by putting appropriate macro-economic and structural policies in place, the risks at the micro-level would persist requiring proper understanding quantification and management. A risk management would be " The identification, analysis and economic control of those risks which can threaten the assets or earning capacity of an enterprise". Risk management viewed as a positive help to operational managers in assisting them to achieve their objectives. It will definitely cost but this cost is against the greater benefits which are derived.

Today, Risk Management stands in contrast to the intuitive and traditional methods of managing uncertainty. Theory of risk management does have its limitations but its value lies in the fact, that by measuring what could go wrong and estimating its likelihood, firms and institutions have a better chance of making sensible decisions. Today many of the financial institutions particularly the large global banks are operating more as risk managers rather than as a traditional banking institutions. The study of risk management is very vital for many reasons. First, more persons become risk managers at some stage in their professional careers than ever expected to do so. We must all manage the exposures we face in our personal lives. Second, even if you do not become a professional risk manager your activities will affect your organization's risk manager. You will in turn be affected by his or her activities. Third, risk management and insurance touch our lives in other highly significant ways through the organisations and families they save or stabilize through loss indemnification, the accidents they either prevent or reduce in severity, the long term projects in which they invest and the security they provide by reducing the uncertainty in our lives.

Insurance is a key tool of risk management. Insurance pricniple has variety of applications in economic affairs of the country in general and in particular in family, business, and corporate situations leading to conservation and preservation of the economic values ultimately leading to long term capital formation. By adopting in a correct way, insurance produces important benefits for both the organisation or family and for society. Both private and public insurance institutions have to be restructured from time to time to increase their role in risk management and in the economic, social and political life of a democratic nation. Especially, in the context of privatization, the risk management through various systems and programmes of insurance has acquired all more attention. Here it is not correct to assume that government is trying to limit its responsibility in executing programmes for the welfare of the people. The importance of the insurance business to all of us is demonstrated by the fact that the United States Supreme Court over 70 years ago labeled the private insurance business "a business affected with a public interest", thus subjecting it to much closer government regulation than most businesses.

It is realized that most of the modern strategies are aimed at, not only for socio-economic development but also for sustainable development of a nation. Insurance is one of the important strategy to reduce the element of risk and make it possible for economic agents to maximize their portfolios. Infact, insurance and re insurance market is essential for sustainable economic growth and development. It complements economic activities, stabilizes trade and commerce and help mitigate uncertainties affecting economic agents. In a broad sense, insurance enables active risk management. For better risk management techniques, derivative products are being developed helping the financial institutions and corporates to prepare for a riskier world. There is a need for study about more refined hedging mechanisms to insure against currency., interest rate and credit risks as well as risks relating to capital market instruments. The vast experience and skills of American market economy in the field of insurance, as a strategy for sustainable development at micro and macro levels may act as fundamental lesson for underdeveloped market economies. The present study is a humble attempt to create more awareness among Indians. It is also an humble attempt to provide valuable information for American global traders in insurance industry.

The objectives and hypothesis of the study

The present study is proposed to inquire the following objectives:

1. To study the risk due to unevaluated adoption of technology and ways of living generated in different cultures.
2. To study the emerging issues in risk management in Agriculture, Industry and financial Institutions of United States of America.
3. To understand the role of Insurance as a strategy for sustainable development.

The proposed study will try to test the following Hypothesis:

Insurance as a strategy is more effective than other strategies in the context of risk management for sustainable development.

By associating myself with experts in the field of risk management in United States I could appreciate, understand and analyse different dimensions of risk management. The sources of experience and information in US are highly useful for my study which makes my visit to US more meaningful. More over, US experience in the field of insurance and risk management is a classical direction to the rest of the world. Hence, my visit to US is more relevent and meaningful to undertake the proposed study.

REFERENCES

1. Ahearn J.L. and Pritchott S.T. : Risk and Insurance, 5th ed., St.Paul, West Publishing Company, 1984.

2. Allen T.C. and R.M. Duvall, A Theoretical and Practical Approach to Risk Management, New York, The American Society of Risk Management Inc., 1971.

3. Berliner Baruch : Limits of Insurability of Risks, Englewood Cliffs NJ, Prentice-Hall Inc., 1982.

4. Boglini, Norman A, Global Risk Management, New York, Risk Management Society Publishing Inc., 1983.

5. Business India, Of Risk and Reward, Bombay, 1995.

6. Business Review, The Hindu, Madras, India.

7. Gordon C.A. Dickson, Risk Management - Study Course 655, Distance Learning Division, Cambridge, 1991.

8. Green MR and Serbein O.N, Risk Management: Text and Cases, 2nd edn., Reston, Va, Reston Publishing Co., 1983.

9. Hallman G.V. and Rosenbloom J.S., Personal Financial Planning, 3rd ed., New York McGraw-Hill Book Company, 1983.

10. Hammond J.D. (ed), Essays in the Theory of Risk and Insurance, Glen View Ill: Scott, Foresman and Company, 1968.

11. Hardy C.O. :Risk and Risk-Bearing, Chicago, The University of Chicago Press, 1923.

12. Insurance Times, Dec. 1998, Calcutta, India.

13. Jeanne Subramaniam, Business India, An Area of Darkness, Bombay, 1995.

14. Life Insurance Corporation of India - Annual Report, 1993-94.

15. Pfeffer, Irving, Insurance and Economic Theory, Home Wood Ill, Richard D, Irwin Inc., 1956.

16. Rangarajan C, Reserve Bank of India Bulletin, Insurance and Risk Management in a Liberalized Economy, 1993.

17. Schoemaker, Paul JH, Edperiments on Decisions under risk : The expected utility Hypothesis, Kluwer-Nijhoff Publishing Co., Boston, 1980.

18. Snider H Wayne (ed), Employee Benefits Management, New York, The Risk and Insurance Management Inc., 1980.

19. Stevanson DK, American Life and Institutions, Ernest Klett Verlog GMBH & Co., K.G. Stuttgart, Germany, 1990.

* * *

27

INSURANCE (RISK MANAGEMENT) AS A WELFARE MEASURE OF THE STATE

Dr. K. Venugopal Rao
Assistant Professor
Dr. C.N.Krishna Naik,
Associate Professor, Sri Krishnadevaraya Institute of Management, S.K.University, Anantapur.

In every walk of life one is exposed to some risk or other. Risk is the uncertainity underlying any business. Risk is the deviation of the actual form the expected. Holding a portfolio of investments, foreign currencies involve risks. These are all called financial risks. Wherever there is uncertainity, there is risk. Risk is something which is now taken up upfront rather than be left to circumstances or fate to decide. The risk is unavoidable and unpreventable. However, the ill-effects of risk can be minimised by risk control and riks management. The field of risk management is just opening up in India. There are certain instruments and techniques of risk management.

Insurance indeed is the mechanism to reduce the element of risk. The main function of insurance is to provide protection against the possible chances of generating loses. It eliminates worries and miseries of losses at destructin of property and death. Further, it provides capital to the society as the accumulated funds are invested in the productive areas. The industry, the business, an individual and a group of persons' are benefited by insurance. The objective of the paper is to identify and examine insurance as the welfare measure of the state.

The pace of development of a growing economy like India, depends on the saving-income ratio which determines the level of investment. Generating domestic savings, particularly from an expanding national income, holds the key to economic prosperity. Changing economic panorama, pragmatic fiscal and monetary policies, rationalisation of tax structure, strengthening of agricultural base, liveral industrial development policies, liberal attitude of the government towards welfare activities, generation of important infrastructural facilities are some of the key developments which indicate that life insurance business has emerged as the best mode of community savings and a shield against the uncertainities of modern life.

The LIC has been promoting social welfare in a big way through social oriented schemes. In order to extend insurance cover at the lowest cost or by charging the minimum possible premium, the corporation has made special efforts through group insurance schemes to cover the economically backward sections.

The LIC has a network of 1,900 branches, 18,000 development officers, and around half a million full-time and part-time agents. GIC and its subsidiaries have more than 4,000 branches spread all over the country. Group insurance schemes, social security schemes, those covering landless labourers and other IRDP schemes with government assistance, form around half of LIC's entire volume of business.

LIC today services 6.5 crore individual policies with 2,54,572 crore as the sum assured. LIC covers nearly 30 per cent of the insurable public in the country, world-wide, LIfe Insurance companies do much more than merely provide covers against death risk. The focus particularly is on pension-related products. General insurance business is dominated by GIC and its 4 subsidiaries:

1. New India Assurance
2. Oriental Insurance
3. National Insurance
4. United India Insurance.

Non-life insurance touches less than one per cent of the population. The Insurance Act of 1938 governs the insurance business. When the life and general insurance businesses were nationalised in 1956 and 1973, the LIC and the GIC and its subsidiaries were given special dispensions.

The products of LIC & GIC : The following are the products offered by insurance companies.

- Life Insurance
- Fire Insurance
- Marine Insurance
- Medicual Insurance
- Catastrophe Insurance
- Project Insurance
- Motor Insurance
- Industrial Insurance
- Rural Insurance

The Need Levels

The insurance producs are offered in accordance with the needs of people.

Level one	:	Family
Products	:	Whole life plan, Bima Sandesh, Bima Kiran, Jeevan Surabhi.
Level Two	:	Children
Products	:	Children deferred, anticipated, jeevan Balya, Jeevan Kishore, Jeevan Sukanya (female child) Jeevan chaya
Level Three	:	Post-Retirement
Productts	:	Jeevan Dhara, Jeevan Akshy, Old Pension Plan
Level Four	:	Special needs
Products	:	Jeevan Griha, Bhavishya Jeevan, Asha Deep, Jeevan Shree

Thus, risk in every phase of life is covered as a welfare measure.

Health Insurance

Only around 5 per cent of India's population is covered by health insurance schemes. Contributory social security schemes and employees state insurance schemes are operated by the Central and State Governemtns for workers, their families and other beneficiaries. The schemes reimburse medical expenses upto specified limits.

India's best-known and most comprehensive scheme is Medi-claim marketed by the GIC and its four subsidiaries. Set up in 1913, Medi-claim provides reimbursement of expenses incurred for the treatment of illness. In 1984, to help travellers meet the costs of treatment abroad, Overseas Medi-Claim was introduced. Subsequently, it was extended to students going abroad for study and employment.

LIC has no separate health insurance policy but offers coverage, for 4 specified diseases within one of its life insurance plans.

Asha Deep - Cancer, paralytic stroke, renal failure involving both kidneys and coronary artery disease where by-pass surgery has been done are covered for a minimum benefit of Rs.50,000 and a maximum benefit of Rs.3 lakhs.

Insurance Education

People awareness about welfare schemes is low. For instance, New India Assurance's Janata Personal Accident Policy designed for the poor, with a death benefit of Rs.25,000 and a yearly premium of just Rs.15, has managed to cover not even one per cent of the population, though it has been in operation since 1976. Target clientele often cannot muster up Rs.15 for thepremium. Hence, thee is a need to educate the people about the availability of various welfare schemes initiated by the State for the betterment of the people.

Over the years, the nationalised insurance companies have considerably expanded their business and established an extensive presence throughout the country. However, the lack of competition has caused complacency in the insurance industry which is reflected in insufficient responsiveness to customer needs, high costs, excessive lapsation of life policies, overstaffing and serious lags in technology. Despite overall growth of insurance, several lines of business have not been sufficiently developed and there is a vast untapped potential.

Currently, GIC is reformulating its 160 policies to meet customer requirements. Though foreign and private companies are allowed, LIC & GIC are confident that they well be still leading int he area because of reach and distribution network. Once the foreign majors enter the insurance scene, the domestic sector will see a host of new services on the lines of those available abroad.

In conclusion, risks in life and in business can be managed through insurance. Insurance is playing substantial role in minimising the ill-effects of risks. It is acting as a shock absorber. LIC and GIC with its subsidiaries offering such risks as health insurance, life insurance, fire insurance motor insurance, marine insurance etc. Insurance policies, undoubtedly are a serving as welfare measures of the state.

REFERENCES

1. S.M.Jha, Services Marketing, Himalaya Publishing House, Bombay, 1964.
2. Business World, 22 June, 1997.
3. Business World, 21, October, 1995.
4. Business World, 22, May, 1997
5. The Hindu, Survey of Indian Industry, 1994, 1996.

* * *